MODI DOCTRINE

MODI DOCTRINE

The Foreign Policy of India's Prime Minister

Sreeram Chaulia

BLOOMSBURY
NEW DELHI • LONDON • OXFORD • NEW YORK • SYDNEY

First published in India 2016

ISBN 978 93 86141 15 6

10 9 8 7 6 5 4 3 2 1

Bloomsbury Publishing India Pvt. Ltd
Second Floor, LSC Building No.4
DDA Complex, Pocket C – 6 & 7, Vasant Kunj
New Delhi 110070
www.bloomsbury.com

Typeset by Manipal Digital Systems
Printed and bound in India by Thomson Press India Ltd

To 'Team India', which has to
play a long innings in the global arena

Foreword

Under the leadership of Prime Minister Narendra Modi, India's foreign policy has grown more dynamic and proactive. During his two years in office, there are many landmark achievements and developments which have transformed India's global positioning. His outreach efforts in every corner of the globe have laid a strong foundation for furthering India's economic, strategic and cultural interests. The clarity of his vision, the resoluteness of his determination, the amicableness of his style and the speed of his actions on the global stage have been exceptional in both content and form. A new lease of life has been enthused in India's foreign policy.

It is not an exaggeration to say that the 'Modi effect' is also being felt in multilateral forums such as the United Nations, the G20, the Climate Change regime, and the global trade system, where India is today seen as an important actor with a potential to be a major power and a problem-solver. On all the big crises facing the international community, such as terrorism, armed conflicts, environmental degradation and economic shocks, Mr. Modi has been visible in trying to unite fellow world leaders and forge a common front. By expanding India's friendships and partnerships with key countries in different regions of the world, he has offered new hope of peace, stability and economic prosperity.

India is a vast nation with a young, talented population that has high aspirations and dreams. Mr. Modi considers himself the repository of these hopes and has adopted the central agenda of economic development and empowerment of his people. He is purposefully pursuing a foreign policy that serves India's domestic transformation. According to a report by the New York-based Moody's Investors Service in April 2016, net Foreign Direct Investment (FDI) inflows into India hit an "all-time high" under Mr. Modi's able stewardship, "reflecting India's relatively strong growth prospects and government efforts to liberalise foreign investment regulation."

This milestone has been attained largely due to the new energy shown by Mr. Modi in his foreign policy and his stress on improved governance within India. His personal touch and amazing ability to persuade and convince foreign investors and government leaders to "come and Make in India" are the main reasons why India is continuing to have high GDP growth even as many other emerging economies are struggling. The contrast in economic prospects between India and other members of the BRICS grouping shows that any nation can rise to the top provided it has the right political leadership and direction.

Mr. Modi is viewed as a man who is singlehandedly improving India's image and profile through a combination of commercial diplomacy, diaspora connectivity and strategic relationship-building with regional powers. The humungous commitments of FDI that have emanated from sovereign wealth funds based in the Gulf is a vote of confidence in Mr. Modi's abilities to convert the potential of India into a reality. The fact that Gulf nations are now cooperating closely with India to counter radicalization and terrorism shows a new degree of confidence that the region has in Mr Modi as an indispensable partner.

One of the specialties which sets apart Mr. Modi's foreign policy is his incredible popularity among the millions of Indians across the world. Be it the IT professionals in Silicon Valley, the Indian students in Australia, the migrant workers in Dubai or the large Indian community in London— across the Indian diaspora he has unleashed a new sense of pride in being Indian. These migrant Indians are the human bonds that intimately tie India to the world. Mr. Modi has been a wonderful champion of his diaspora. His policies towards enhancing their welfare and tapping into their talent have been both imaginative and long overdue.

In a short time, he has built a new constituency for India, in every corner of the world, wherever an Indian is settled.

As a global investor with a base in the Middle East and Singapore, I feel proud of the way Mr. Modi has galvanised the diaspora to give back to India and to reconnect with our homeland with a sense of mission and purpose. His trademark domestic and foreign policy initiatives are profoundly impacting on NRIs and Overseas Citizens of India (OCI). No previous Indian leader has done so much for the diaspora and I feel that Mr. Modi is a trailblazer whose efforts in mobilising NRIs and OCIs will go down in history as a milestone.

In the sphere of international security, Mr. Modi has also shown a willingness to move beyond traditional Indian reluctance and engage in defence diplomacy and cooperation with partner nations. The contribution of India in evacuating stranded citizens of several countries from Yemen in close coordination with the Government of Saudi Arabia has been one of Mr. Modi's accomplishments. The capacity of India to engage in 'rescue diplomacy' is a big asset for the world. As the head of the nationalistic think tank, India Foundation, which advocates for a robust foreign policy to take India to its designated place in the world, I am vindicated by Mr. Modi's overseas successes.

It is therefore a delight to be writing the Foreword to this book, which captures all the major facets of Mr. Modi's foreign policy. This is the first full-length book outlining India's international relations in the Modi era. The author, Dr. Sreeram Chaulia, is a talented young scholar who has come to prominence as an astute observer and commentator on India's role in the world. His numerous academic and popular writings and television appearances have educated audiences on finer aspects of foreign policy and statecraft. This book is a testament to his intellectual prowess on a worthy topic that is of massive contemporary relevance. A great civilisation of Asia like India needs positive messaging and action at the helm. Dr. Chaulia's book goes into detail to make the case that Mr. Modi is the need of the hour and the man of the moment that India requires and the world expects.

Today who in the world would not want a deeper understanding of Mr. Modi, his motivations, and the actual conduct of his foreign policy? Seeing Mr. Modi in action during his foreign visits and when he is hosting global dignitaries in India leaves no doubt that he has made India more consequential and impactful. One must read Dr. Chaulia's book thoroughly to gauge what is the larger essence and outcome of Mr. Modi's foreign policy. The former Canadian diplomat David Malone wrote a book in 2012 with a suggestive title: *Does the Elephant Dance?: Contemporary Indian Foreign Policy*. Dr. Chaulia's book argues that Mr. Modi has changed that very metaphor by projecting a new India as a swift-footed lion on the prowl rather than an elephant.

I commend this work for its original scholarship and am certain that it will be cited and translated into other languages as a standard book on the exciting international odyssey that India has taken since 2014.

*by **Shaurya Doval***
Director, India Foundation & Managing Director, Zeus Caps

Acknowledgements

In October 2012, my editors at the *Times of India* requested a column on why the United Kingdom dropped its policy of ostracising the then chief minister of Gujarat, Narendra Modi. It was the first trigger for me to probe this remarkable politician's international importance. I argued in that piece that Britain had realised Modi was 'prime minister material of the future'.[1] Since then, thanks to other prescient editors at *The Economic Times* and *The Asian Age*, who also commissioned periodic essays related to this theme, I had followed the foreign angle of Modi's career closely.

While many fence-sitters were unsure whether Modi would win India's general elections in May 2014, I had taken it as a *fait accompli* and begun thinking of how he could transform India's foreign policy much before his triumph in the polls. I wrote a column in April 2014 for *Russia Today* in Moscow that there was a prospect of a 'Modi Doctrine' to totally overhaul India's dealings with the world. I would like to thank each and every editor of Indian and international news media outlets who boldly indulged in my futuristic prognoses.

This book is the outcome of almost daily observation and interpretation of Prime Minister Modi's utterances, gestures, actions and press releases on external affairs. In this task, I was assisted by a bevy of talented Bachelors and Masters students at the Jindal School of International Affairs: Hima Bindu, Atharva Deshmukh, Maryada

---

[1] Chaulia, Sreeram. 2012. 'UK has a Change of Heart, Hits 'Like' Button for Modi', *The Times of India*, October 14th

Ganeshgarhia, Rajesh Ghosh, Kamal Madishetty, Achyut Mishra, Tanuja Raghunath, Abizer Shaikhmahmud, Aman Singhal, Tahhira Somal and Srilaxmi Sriram. The timely tracking, translation and collation of data about Modi's international policy-making that they did were crucial for writing this book. My faculty colleague Tridivesh Maini also offered useful background.

The institutional backing I get at Jindal School of International Affairs from my administrative assistants, Lalit Kumar and Swarnima Singh, has been top notch. They handle so many small chores so that I could focus on big matters like Modi and India's rise in the world. I thank them profusely for being such dedicated helpers. The photography of our university's audiovisual department's Sunit Pandit deserves applause. The cartographic maps produced by Pratap Narayan of Vertex Designs exude excellence.

The leadership and intellectual freedom given by my close friend and Vice Chancellor of O.P. Jindal Global University, Professor C. Raj Kumar, were constant sources of strength that enabled me to write this book. It reflects admirably on the world-class university he heads that I have published three singly authored books in the last seven years while being employed here in a hectic academic and administrative position.

The writer of the Foreword to this book, Shaurya Doval, is an exceptional and influential thought leader with a patriotic mission to ensure India's rise in the world. I consider it my good fortune that he has lent his weight and credibility to this project. I am also specially indebted to Jitendra Singh, Minister of State in the Prime Minister's Office, who heard me patiently on new, out-of-the-box ideas for India's foreign policy metamorphosis under Modi, and encouraged this book.

In assessing Modi's true impact on India's global standing, I benefited from numerous discussions with the head of the Foreign Affairs Department of the Bharatiya Janata Party (BJP), Vijay Chauthaiwale, and the Director of the Syama Prasad Mookerjee Research Foundation, Anirban Ganguly. Their simplicity and openness are incredible assets for the BJP and India.

Many accomplished policymakers and scholars read this manuscript and gave me feedback and uplifting blurb endorsements. I am eternally grateful to them. In this regard, the favours extended by my faculty colleague Abdulfattah Ammourah, George Kurian (Pappen) and Commander Vijay Krishan Kaushik were invaluable.

Bloomsbury is a superb, professional and friendly publishing house. The managerial and editorial inputs I got from Praveen Tiwari and Nitin Valecha are out of this world. I want to keep writing for them for eternity.

This book would have been impossible without a rock-solid, stable and fulfilling life partner. My best half, the artist and filmmaker Usha Rani Damerla, has shown me new vistas and showered me with so much love that this work had to come out. She is my all-weather anchor and motivator. Her confidence in me exceeds my own self-estimation. I owe everything positive that has come my way in the last two decades to her and cannot express in words how she moulds my destiny.

The quality time I get with my two stress-relieving children, Debarchan and Kranti, is a priceless behind-the-scenes contributor to this book. My father, Prafulla Kumar Chaulia, is my first respondent and also my staunchest critic. The endless chats I have had with him about Modi's revolutionary effect on India and its external relations are reflected at different junctures in this book. My mother, Chandrakala Chaulia, remains my truest believer. Her prayers and faith in my abilities have taken me to wherever I am today.

A book about Modi's innovative and far-reaching foreign policy is ultimately the result of the Indian prime minister's magnetic, compelling and charismatic persona. I would definitely not have written this work if not for Modi's inspiring agenda for change. To him, this book is a humble submission and vindication.

July 22, 2016
Sonipat

Contents

Introduction

> *'Media asked me before the polls — Modi ji what will be your foreign policy? They thought I am not experienced I assured them we will not lower our eyes, nor will we show them eyes. We will meet their eyes and talk with the world.'*[1]

A Foreign Policy Revelation

Narendra Modi is a force of nature. There is infinite energy and boundless enthusiasm in India's fourteenth prime minister who strives relentlessly for taking India forward in economic development and modernisation. To realise what he calls an 'Indian century', he has pledged, 'every moment of my life and every particle in my body' to be devoted 'to the work of my country.'[2] No sphere of policymaking has remained untouched by his alert mind and hands-on style of active leadership, since he assumed India's highest political office in May 2014.

Standing tall amidst the varied realms of policies which have undergone a distinct '*Modi*-fication' is foreign affairs. Matters relating to foreign relations have traditionally been viewed in India as a rarefied field that takes a backseat in discourse when compared to pressing

---

[1] Das, Bijaya. 2015. 'India has the Advantage of Youth Power: PM Modi in Singapore', *India* Today, November 24th. URL: http://indiatoday.intoday.in/story/modi-in-singapore-pm-addresses-indian-diaspora-in-singapore/1/530539.html Last accessed on January 2nd, 2016

[2] IANS. 2015. 'Modi Tells Diaspora 21st Century is India's Century', *Business Standard*, September 28th

domestic issues which have greater political resonance. From the word go, when Modi was sworn into power with the heads of governments of the South Asian countries in attendance, the degree of prime ministerial attention and importance given to international relations has been extraordinary by Indian standards.

As one commentator had put it a few months after he stormed into global consciousness, 'Modi has surprised many by investing considerable political capital in high-powered diplomacy so early in his term, even though he came to office with little foreign-policy experience.'[3] Another argued that despite being a newcomer to international politics, Modi proved to be 'a revelation on the world stage, a complete natural.'[4] To claim that Modi has taken India to the world and brought the world to India is no understatement.

The frenetic pace of his foreign travels, the high-profile powwows he does with his international counterparts, the plethora of agreements across multiple sectors that he signs, and the spellbinding speeches he delivers overseas are all a part and parcel of his trademark style of wooing and sweeping the world off its feet. Equally eye-catching are his innovative means to host visiting foreign dignitaries in different corners of India and the business he does with them. It is a charm offensive and an astute pitch for national interests rolled into one big thrust to position India as a major power whose time to shine on the world stage has finally come after decades of disappointment.

Modi often plays variously on the refrain, 'big change is in the air', to assert how the country is being increasingly perceived as a positive force for good, and that 'the reason why the world looks at India differently today is the willpower of 1.25 billion Indians'.[5] But whenever he poses the question as to what brought about this change, the crowd thronging to

---

[3] Chellaney, Brahma. 2014. 'Modi Reshapes India's Foreign Policy', *Deutsche Welle*, December 30th. URL: http://www.dw.com/en/opinion-modi-reshapes-indias-foreign-policy/a-18159829 Last accessed on January 8th, 2016

[4] Agrawal, Ravi. 2015. 'Narendra Modi's Year One: Did he Live up to Expectations?', *CNN*, May 25th. URL: http://edition.cnn.com/2015/05/25/opinions/agrawal-modi-first-anniversary-in-power/ Last accessed on December 14th, 2015

[5] TNN. 2015. 'PM Modi's Dubai Speech: Key Highlights', *The Times of India*, August 17th

hear him in iconic venues unanimously roars—'Modi, Modi, Modi!' Apart from the political rhetoric imbued in such back-and-forth between a magical orator like Modi and his adoring fans, there is more than a grain of truth in the proposition that India's importance in the world has grown by leaps and bounds, largely due to its prime minister's willful exertions in global arenas.

Just as in the USA, where it is a media ritual to dissect how a new president has fared after his first hundred days in office and then again at the end of a year in the White House, India has witnessed a fair amount of stocktaking of the Modi government's performance on the occasion of key milestone dates. What is remarkable in the reports issued by the opinion makers and an assortment of public sentiment is that foreign policy is the area where Modi scored the highest grades.

According to an opinion poll conducted by *India Today* on the eve of the first anniversary of Modi's government, 22 percent of Indian respondents rated 'foreign policy successes' as his biggest achievement, next only to 'reducing inflation and price rise' (25 percent), and ahead of 'clean India campaign' (17 percent) and 'reducing corruption' (16 percent).[6] Another survey by *Times Now* around that time showed a whopping 71.5 percent of Indians saying that Modi's foreign policy was better than that of his predecessor,[7] the demure and phlegmatic Manmohan Singh who was India's prime minister from 2004 to 2014. Approval of Modi's foreign policy is also reflected in the polls held by the Pew Research Center in Spring 2015, which found that 'roughly nine-in-ten (91 percent) have confidence in Modi's handling of international relations, including more than seven-in-ten (73 percent) of those surveyed who express a lot of confidence.'[8]

Purists would contend that foreign policy is a knowledge-intensive, elite domain whose success or failure cannot be subjected to whimsical contests of mass likes or dislikes, but the statistical affirmation of the foreign policy that Modi desires and receives from the Indian people is itself a sign that he is different from previous Indian prime ministers in taking public diplomacy

---

6 Deka, Kaushik. 2015. 'Good, but can do Better', *India Today*, May 21st

7 TNN. 2015. 'In 1st Year, More Hits than Misses: Times Now Poll', May 26th

8 Stokes, Bruce. 2015. 'The Modi Bounce', Pew Research Center: Washington, D.C., p.5

seriously and making international affairs resound in the domestic theatre. Fostering interest in India's role in world affairs and instilling in the Indian psyche a curiosity and expectation about external matters is one of the intangible gains that Modi's prime ministership has produced in a nation that has been historically inclined to domestic affairs. It is another matter that many experts of international affairs have also issued ringing endorsements of the way Modi has impacted and transformed India's foreign policy,[9] but the fact that he draws so much publicity in the process is a welcome change in India where domestic developments had hitherto dominated the national imagination and discourse.

This book analyses the wellsprings of Modi's high-octane conduct of foreign relations and explains the impact he has made in world affairs through a unique mix of personal charisma, drive and strategic astuteness. It critically evaluates the success of his foreign policy towards different countries and regions of the world since assuming India's most powerful office in 2014, as well as the mark he has made in advancing India's interests in specific thematic-issue domains of strategy, geopolitics and geo-economics.

The key research questions which underpin this book's narrative are: 1) What elements of style and substance set apart Modi's foreign policy from that of his predecessors? 2) What is Modi's worldview, and how does this fit his political and ideological upbringing as a cultural nationalist? 3) How is Modi perceived by his foreign counterparts, in international public opinion and forums, and what does this tell us about the changing image and profile of India? 4) What are the signature achievements in Modi's foreign policy (both in geographical and thematic terms) and how do they amount to a paradigm shift in India's relations with the world? 5) Can Modi propel India to the status of a 'leading power' in global affairs through his innovative diplomacy? 6) What is still missing in Modi's foreign policy arsenal, and how can he fill the gaps for the rest of his tenure as prime minister?

---

[9] See for instance, Mohan, Raja. 2015. *Modi's World: Expanding India's Sphere of Influence*, New Delhi: HarperCollins; Sajjanhar, Ashok. 2016. 'Modi gets an A Plus for his Handling of Foreign Policy in 2015', *The Daily Mail*, January 1st; Pant, Harsh. 2015. 'India in 2015: A Foreign Policy Transformed', *The Diplomat*, December 29th

The central argument of the book is that Modi is globalising and revolutionising India's foreign policy like no other prime minister since Jawaharlal Nehru. This work is driven by observation and belief that Modi is the right person at the right time to raise India's international stature to a great power, and that he has grasped this mantle as the centrepiece of a new doctrine to guide foreign policy. Modi's extraordinary attention to and investment of time and energy into foreign policy, and all that he has accomplished in this field can be interpreted as the elements of a 'Modi Doctrine' with unique characteristics and long-term implications.

A Doctrine to Shepherd India's Ascent

This book provides a critical assessment of how Modi altered India's approach and method towards dealing with the world as a complement to and a subset of his revolutionary shift in governance at home. For lay readers who follow current affairs, students, teachers as well as practitioners of diplomacy, the book pushes the claim that there is a place for individual personalities in bringing about major shifts in foreign policy, and situates Modi within the concept of 'transformative leaders' who execute fundamental changes with inspirational content, as opposed to routine 'transactional leaders' who are content with a modest managerial style.[10] If India is today punching closer to its full potential in the boxing ring of global politics and economics, it is the result of the changes that the prime minister has wrought. Counterfactually, if Modi had not become prime minister, we would be seeing little to no difference in the country's conventional manner of conducting international relations.

The main conceptual difference that Modi has brought about since becoming prime minister is at the level of imbuing Indian foreign policy with doctrinal purpose. His government has articulated a clear and coherent worldview that differs starkly from preceding regimes which ruled India. He has emphasised key principles and beliefs to steer India's interface with the world, and has enunciated a set of defined methods and means to achieve long-term objectives. Such farsightedness, organisational and planning insight was totally lacking

---

[10] Nye, Joseph. 2014. 'Transformational and Transactional Presidents', *Leadership*, Volume 10, Issue 1

before Modi came to power, and this had left a sense of bewilderment among pundits and laity about what India really was and wanted from the international system.

Diplomatic doctrines are defined as 'unilateral declarations of policy designed to elicit domestic public support, to serve as axiomatic policy guidelines for domestic decision-makers and bureaucrats, and to announce basic policy to foreign governments.'[11] They are simple and concise statements of will and purpose and are associated with memorable phrases and slogans of political leaders. Their relevance lies in the frequency with which leaders appeal to the big concepts contained within them to justify day-to-day foreign policy behaviour. National security bureaucracies and the communications paraphernalia of the state devote time, energy and money for formulating particular bilateral and multilateral strategies in accordance with the spirit and letter of the doctrines propagated by their chief political executive. The doctrine spells out how national resources are to be allocated, distributed and deployed.

For the international community, the presence of a foreign policy doctrine is helpful to glean a country's intentions and place it within a certain framework. It is a prism through which national interests can be delineated for the long-term and furthered in the international system. A clear cut foreign policy doctrine defines a nation's personality to the international audience, and establishes it as representing distinct values and forms of action. In short, a doctrine is a lever to advertise a state's preferred national image and exert weight in world affairs. If one studied the rise of any great power in history, there would be a grand strategy akin to a doctrine figuring pivotally in the story. The most recent entrant into the club of great powers or possibly superpowers, China, adopted a grand strategy in the late 1990s of 'increasing the country's international clout without triggering a counterbalancing reaction.'[12] The Chinese proclivity to think ahead and plan for a Sino-centric world order to be realised through a 'hundred-year marathon from 1949 to 2049',[13]

---

[11] Overholt, William &Marylin Chou. 1975. 'Foreign Policy Doctrines', in Merritt, Richard (ed.) *Foreign Policy Analysis*, Lanham: Lexington Books, p.149

[12] Goldstein, Avery. 2005. *Rising to the Challenge: China's Grand Strategy and International Security*, Palo Alto: Stanford University Press, p.12

[13] Pillsbury, Michael. 2015. *The Hundred-Year Marathon: China's Secret Strategy to Replace America as the Global Superpower*, New York: Henry Holt & Co.

involving economic and military accumulation of power, played a crucial role in its spectacular climb to the summit of the international order.

Devoid of a foreign policy doctrine and a long-term strategic gaze, a country muddles through and plods along without reaching the pinnacle in global power configuration. Until Modi's takeover of the reigns of foreign policy-making, one of the nagging problems bedeviling India was the question of identity and self-definition. How did India view itself in world affairs? Was it a wannabe great power or, as Amitabh Mattoo put it, a 'reluctant superpower' which is awkward and hesitant to recognise its own coming of age and to assert itself on the global stage?[14] Was India a leader of the Global South or has it abandoned the causes that win followers among fellow developing countries? Was it satisfied being a hegemon of South Asia or did it have broader ambitions of exerting influence in the rest of Asia and beyond?

Before Modi arrived on the national scene with a bold stride and certitude, ambiguity and confusion were the default answers to such fundamental *raison d'état* queries. The government of Manmohan Singh did not dwell on the lines of 'who are we?' This neglect left a void in defining India's core national interests and imbuing them with a deeper mission. Bharat Karnad has argued that the post-independence Indian elites had misguided priorities due to the absence of strategic foresight. They were obsessed with the violent threat from small states like Pakistan, even though the northern giant China represented the main security challenge to India and should have been the object of India's long-term military and strategic planning.[15] In Karnad's words, 'absence of political vision and will, insensitivity to strategic geography, and unimaginative foreign and military policies have prevented the country from achieving the great power status.'[16] This book contends that Modi is slowly correcting decades-long strategic laziness and putting India's

---

[14] Mattoo, Amitabh (ed.). 2012. *The Reluctant Superpower: Understanding India and its Aspirations*, Melbourne: Melbourne University Press

[15] Karnad, Bharat. 2014. 'An Elephant with a Small Footprint: The Realist Roots of India's Strategic Thought and Policies', in Bajpai, Kanti et al (eds.) *India's Grand Strategy: History, Theory, Cases*, New Delhi: Routledge

[16] Karnad, Bharat. 2015. *Why India is not a Great Power (Yet)*, New Delhi: Oxford University Press

priorities on the right track. Until Modi, thanks to confusion about India's international identity, long-term policy planning and scenarios about the state of the world to formulate a grand strategy for the year 2025 and beyond had been missing altogether in the seat-of-the-pants universe of Indian foreign policy.[17] Since becoming prime minister, Modi has invested his mind and effort into dispelling the anomie and drift, which naturally entails in a foreign policy sans an inborn sense of self and place in the world.

The last time an Indian prime minister was associated with a systematic cluster of ideas, principles and well-honed tools to direct foreign policy was in the 1970s and early 1980s, when the Indira Doctrine, imputed to Indira Gandhi, was in vogue. Simply stated, it was a replica of the nineteenth century American Monroe Doctrine for Latin America, and applied to South Asia, i.e. an unstated but evident intent on New Delhi's part to deter intervention of outside players in its backyard. As one scholar had summarised the Indira Doctrine, 'Indian security policy in South Asia is based on denying external powers a regional foothold, with military force if necessary.'[18] This doctrine was sub-regional, not global in scope, and it was not an all-encompassing roadmap that determined how Indira Gandhi acted in the world at large. Nor was it officially announced or communicated because of its obvious hegemonic contours and its attendant liabilities for India's image in its neighbourhood. Arguably, some aspects of the Indira Doctrine persist to this day when it comes to India's nervousness about American or Chinese penetration of what New Delhi considers to be its natural sphere of influence.

However, this book argues that Modi has transcended the Indira Doctrine and has broken fresh ground in reimagining South Asia through a liberal prism. The Modi Doctrine is also much more comprehensive and far-reaching in its application, surpassing the confines of South Asia, and situating India as a shaper of outcomes beyond its immediate neighbourhood. It is a rulebook for India's coming-out party in international affairs.

---

[17] This point is well illustrated in Malone, David. 2012. *Does the Elephant Dance? Contemporary Indian Foreign Policy*, Oxford: Oxford University Press

[18] Hagerty, Devin. 1991. 'India's Regional Security Doctrine', *Asian Survey*, Volume 31, Issue 4, p.352

In 1997-98, India followed an abortive Gujral Doctrine, named after the short-lived prime ministership of Inder Kumar Gujral. Again, this doctrine was South Asia-centric and implied an attitude of magnanimity on India's part towards its smaller neighbours. In essence, it meant 'India does not ask for reciprocity, but gives and accommodates what it can in good faith and trust'[19] so as to improve the overall political climate in the subcontinent. Shaking off the tag of 'Big Brother' in South Asia has been a constant requirement in Indian foreign policy, even after Gujral exited from the scene, but his doctrine hardly had any lasting impact and was too narrow in time and space to become a landmark.

This book argues that the Modi Doctrine constitutes a superior advancement over the previous two known doctrines in Indian history because it is quintessentially Indian, but is in tune with the globalised zeitgeist of the twenty-first century. It is both, a mirror to and a motor of India's amplified footprint in international affairs. It merits comparisons with other epochal foreign policy doctrines in world history, not in content, intent or method, but in scope, coherence and worldwide significance.

Doctrines propounded by great powers have typically been militaristic and aggressive in nature, asserting bully-like qualities and stretching out an iron fist against perceived foes. The Truman Doctrine of 1947 heralded the Cold War by laying out a global agenda for the USA to roll back communism by 'supporting free peoples who are resisting attempted subjugation by armed minorities or by outside pressures'.[20] The Brezhnev Doctrine of 1968 announced the right of the Soviet Union to intervene militarily and by other means in the entire Eastern Bloc to defend communism against Western threats.[21] The Reagan Doctrine of the 1980s shifted from classic American containment of communism to more blatant direct assistance and proxy wars to favour

---

[19] Sabur, A.K.M. 2001. 'The Challenge of CBMs in South Asia: A Bangladeshi Perspective', in Ahmar, Moonis (ed.) *The Challenge of Confidence Building in South Asia*, New Delhi: Har-Anand Publications, p.143

[20] Bostdorff, Denise. 2008. *Proclaiming the Truman Doctrine: The Cold War Call to Arms*, College Station: Texas A&M University Press, p.5

[21] Ouimet, Matthew. 2003. *The Rise and Fall of the Brezhnev Doctrine in Soviet Foreign Policy*, Chapel Hill: The University of North Carolina Press

those fighting against it across the world. It is credited for winning the Cold War for the USA by militarily overwhelming its Soviet adversary and ushering in a unipolar world in 1991.[22]

The Bush Doctrine of the 2000s embarked on a planetary war of preemption and unilateral interventions after the September 11 attacks in the name of countering terrorism, and left no corner of the world unscathed.[23] Lesser recognised American foreign policy roadmaps like the Nixon Doctrine (1969) and the Carter Doctrine (1980) also revolved around military strategy, but lacked the same heft and impact as the aforementioned others. Owing to the brazen resort to military force and controversial interventions violating international laws, as well as misapplications and policy setbacks, American foreign policy doctrines have been panned by sceptics as wasteful and counterproductive.[24] Nonetheless, superpowers relied on doctrines to carve out their desired zones of influence and it would be folly to counter-factually imagine the USA or the USSR being behemoths without doctrines underpinning their might.

When one looks at some of the seminal doctrines engendered by leaders who headed middle powers, they tend to be non-militaristic and more liberal in their outlooks. This difference is understandable because materially weaker states lack the military capabilities to have their way in the world by dint of force. The Yoshida Doctrine of post-World War II Japan is a noteworthy grand strategy that deliberately maintained a low profile in international political and security issues, devolved defence of the mainland to American security guarantees, and instead prioritised a diplomatic posture of fostering economic ties abroad to promote breathtaking GDP growth at home. It 'worked brilliantly for the Cold War years'[25] and is widely credited for paving Japan's path to the top echelons of global economic power and prosperity.

---

[22] Scott, James (ed.) 1996. *Deciding to Intervene: The Reagan Doctrine and American Foreign Policy*, Durham: Duke University Press

[23] Dolan, Chris. 2005. *In War we Trust: The Bush Doctrine and the Pursuit of Just War*, London: Ashgate

[24] Danforth, Nick. 2016. 'Thank Goodness there's no Obama Doctrine', *Foreign Policy*, January 12th

[25] Pyle, Kenneth. 2014. 'The Sea Change in Japanese Foreign Policy', Washington, D.C.: The National Bureau of Asian Research, p.1

The Davutoğlu Doctrine of the 2000s is another fascinating foreign policy strategy evolved by Turkey's then foreign minister and former professor of International Relations, Ahmet Davutoğlu, to increase the Turkish influence in the Middle East by means of peaceful diplomacy and commercial exchanges. Its core goal of forging new friendships in the region through trade and non-ideological partnerships served Turkey well for a while and raised its salience as an emerging power with something to give to the world.[26] Phrases bequeathed by this doctrine like 'zero problems neighbourhood' and 'central power' entered the vocabulary of international diplomacy, even though Turkey lost its attractiveness as a hub for peacemaking and economic dynamism after the Arab Spring uprisings in 2011, and the subsequent grinding wars in Syria and Iraq.

On the surface, the Modi Doctrine appears to have ideas similar to those enshrined in the Yoshida and Davutoğlu doctrines. With a pronounced stress on 'neighbourhood first policy'[27] as well as on trade and FDI for economic development, Modi does echo the Japanese and Turkish cases. But the fire in his belly is to engineer India to 'position itself in a leading role, rather than just a balancing force, globally.'[28] This means that the Modi Doctrine inevitably includes a military dimension, as well as other facets of geopolitical and security responsibilities which have to be shouldered by great powers. In a later part of this book, we will see how Modi revved up India's 'defence diplomacy', a hitherto neglected phenomenon in Indian foreign policy.

Modi has paid greater attention to the military in shaping India's national security. The abysmal allocation of an average of less than 2 percent of GDP to defence spending was a retrograde policy which India has jettisoned under Modi to send a signal of its will to raise its material capabilities. Military diplomacy is also becoming more integral to India's historically civilian-dominated foreign policy matrix. Modi knows that all great powers past and present have done so without

---

[26] Grigoriadis, Ioannis. 2010. 'The Davutoğlu Doctrine and Turkish Foreign Policy', Athens: Hellenic Foundation for European and Foreign Policy

[27] Ramachandran, Rajesh. 2014. 'Narendra Modi's Push for Strong Relations with Neighbours', *The Economic Times*, July 3rd

[28] IANS. 2015. 'India Should Emerge in a Leading Role Globally: PM', *Business Standard*, February 7th

exception and is unabashed about the betterment that the Indian military can generate for the planet.

The Modi Doctrine is by no stretch of imagination a defence-heavy strategy, but the military gets its long-due place as a prime purveyor of India's 'hard power' and a provider of stability across continents. Modi's advice to his ambassadors that 'new actors and new threats to global peace and prosperity' have arisen, and that India 'had a great responsibility in helping the world counter these challenges to peace'[29], signify that his doctrine is more holistic than the parochial, piecemeal and unidimensional ones that preceded him.

Given the paucity of doctrines, Indian foreign policy before Modi's advent was a saga of ad hocism, improvisation and unpredictability that did not behoove a nation that aspired to great power status. Writing during the Manmohan Singh era, professor Harsh Pant made the following critique of India's aimlessness:

'A major power's foreign policy cannot be effective in the absence of a guiding framework of underlying principles that is a function of both the nation's geopolitical requirements and its values. Indian foreign-policy elite remains mired in the exigencies of day-to-day pressures emanating from the immediate challenges at hand rather than evolving a grand strategy that integrates the nation's multiple policy strands into a cohesive whole that can preserve and enhance Indian interests in a rapidly changing global environment.'[30]

To fully appreciate the monumental contribution of the Modi Doctrine, we must examine why Indian leaders before him failed to develop a culture of doctrines despite their numerous advantages. The first and foremost reason was the lack of profound personal interest in foreign policy, shown by most Indian prime ministers with the notable exception of Nehru. Having attained the post of the head of government through trials and tribulations of an extremely competitive electoral process and intra- as well as inter-party competition, and saddled with people's overwhelming expectations for domestic governance, they hardly

---

29 Ibid.

30 Pant, Harsh. 2008. 'India's Search for a Foreign Policy', *YaleGlobal*, June 26th. URL: http://yaleglobal.yale.edu/content/india%E2%80%99s-search-foreign-policy Last accesses on January 14th, 2016

had time or ken for arcana of diplomacy. Therefore, the political bosses delegated most of the formulations on India's external relations to the career bureaucracy, which by its very nature has been overcautious, non-committal and insistent on ad hoc decision-making in the name of retaining flexibility of choices. The insular mindset of the Indian Foreign Service cadre and the absence of world class scholarly work in India to feed practitioners of diplomacy with fresh ideas exacerbated the glaring lack of doctrines and grand strategies.[31] The result of the political abdication and bureaucratic monopolisation has been a foreign policy that is short in horizons and low in long-term strategy. This book explains how Modi entered the frame like a Julius Caesar and transformed this myopic system through a '*veni, vidi, vici*' (I came, I saw, I conquered) operation.

Before Modi, Indian foreign policy suffered from shortage of diplomatic capacity and political will and direction from the top. Modi is yet to reverse the pathetic trend of understaffing and under-equipping of India's career in foreign service corps, but under him, the Prime Minister's Office (PMO) has invested its own prestige and power to push for a more expansive and global foreign policy. It has been open to new ideas on foreign policy from outside the bureaucratic environs and has overcome the legacy of parochial navel-gazing and complacency. Although India cannot match the fat checkbook diplomacy of China around the world, there are more creative means for the former to be involved in solving global security and economic crises. Circumspect and reactive thinking, which were the hallmarks of India's foreign policy in recent decades, are being replaced with a more proactive and engaged 'big picture' diplomacy that aims to situate India as a power centre or pole in the international system which is reordering global institutions and solving global problems.

In distant parts of the world, India before Modi had primarily hewed to economic interests without displaying any stake in resolving regional conflicts and security dilemmas. This book reveals how the Modi Doctrine is gradually making India step up to the plate in regions and themes where New Delhi has previously been missing in action. Much

---

31 For a scathing attack on the slow-moving and ill-adapting Indian foreign policy bureaucracy, see Tharoor, Shashi. 2012. *Pax Indica: India and the World in the Twenty-First Century*, New Delhi: Penguin, Chapter 9

of this paradigm shift owes to Modi himself as a globally perceptive and prescient leader. Modi's Bharatiya Janata Party (BJP) projected him as a strongman who is the answer to the anxieties and rising expectations of India's people. What many did not anticipate was the way he would play a forceful hand in diplomacy as well as in internal affairs. Veteran journalist Dileep Padgaonkar likened Modi to President Vladimir Putin of Russia, Prime Minister Shinzo Abe of Japan and President Recep Tayyip Erdogan of Turkey as conservatives and nationalists who have eerie similarities.[32] Interestingly, all these three international figures patented a hard-nosed foreign policy style and substance that has forced the world to sit up and pay serious attention to their respective claims and interests.

Having gained the keys to the nation from a huge mandate of India's electorate, Modi's overarching goal in foreign policy has been to ensure that the coming decade does not go down as a lost phase when the country could not grasp its historic international opportunity to claim its place as a leading power. The wishy-washy hemming and hawing about obtaining power in the world and wielding it for global good, which characterised the old India, is now gone because Modi is convinced that he cannot wait for the 'Indian century', but has to will it into reality through concerted policies.

Among Modi's personality traits that augur well for a revolution in Indian foreign policy is his ability to smash impossible systemic hurdles and inertia to implement what he envisions. Where ordinary politicians see limits and try to work within inherited boundaries, Modi has dared to break the logjams and used his personal might to ram through modernisation projects during his long tenure as the chief minister of the Western Indian state of Gujarat. His leadership could willfully remake the entrenched 'system' instead of succumbing to it.

As the Modi wave was swamping India in May 2014, when he won a historic landslide election victory, I spoke to the then ambassador of Turkey to India, Burak Akçapar. Like most diplomats in New Delhi, he was upbeat about the new government not only because Modi will be good for bilateral relations between India and his country, but also

---

[32] Padgaonkar, Dileep.2014. 'In the Footsteps of Putin, Abe, Erdogan', *The Times of India*, April 4th

because he packs in a badly needed 'push factor' to shake up a red tape-ridden and somnolent Indian state architecture.

Vested interests and intermediaries who resist and block every reform or shift held back India not only in the domestic arena, but also in foreign policy. Complacency, smugness, quotidian management of issues, and an attitude of 'satisficing' (aiming low to obtain an adequate outcome rather than the optimal or maximum one) have been the markers of Indian foreign policy, which was not known for boldness or unconventional forward planning in a dynamic global environment until Modi arrived with loads of ambition and 'can-do' spirit.

Interestingly, similar inertia was pointed out to be hurting the USA at the turn of the millennium by the former American National Security Adviser and Secretary of State, Henry Kissinger. He argued that 'satisfaction with the status quo causes policy to be viewed as a projection of the familiar into the future'. He presciently warned the then USA's ruling elites against 'the temptation of acting as if the United States needed no long-range foreign policy at all and could confine itself to a case-by-case response to challenges as they arise.'[33]

Transposed to the Indian foreign policy context, nothing short of a well-defined Modi Doctrine was required to effect fundamental change. The central tenet of this doctrine is the overriding goal that India must become an acknowledged great power or what Modi's Foreign Secretary S. Jaishankar has labelled as 'transition to a leading power' rather than just a balancing power between two preeminent poles, viz. China and the USA.[34]

A Grand Strategy for Our Times

Before Modi, many troubling unknowns in grand strategy persisted as to the prospect of India counterbalancing either the USA or China, the number one and two powers in the world. No precise answer existed

---

33 Kissinger, Henry. 2002. *Does America Need a Foreign Policy? Toward a Diplomacy for the 21st Century*, New York: Simon & Schuster, p.19

34 MEA. 2015. 'Remarks by Foreign Secretary at the Release of Dr. C. Raja Mohan's Book', Ministry of External Affairs. URL: http://mea.gov.in/Speeches-Statements.htm?dtl/25491/Remarks_by_Foreign_Secretary_at_the_release_of_DrC_Raja_Mohans_book_Modis_WorldExpanding_Indias_Sphere_of_InfuencequotJuly_17_2015 URL last accessed on January 16th, 2016

for the riddle of whether India should bandwagon with the USA in order to ward off the immediate strategic threat posed by China or if India should remake the wider global order by checking American hegemony through forums like BRICS and the Shanghai Cooperation Organization (SCO).

Unofficial doctrines enunciated by former diplomats and commentators such as the 'Nonalignment 2.0' strategy advocate equidistance from both China and the US.[35] But the Modi Doctrine has rendered such tracts irrelevant by positing that India has the wherewithal to build itself up as an independent third power centre in world politics, with its own group of adherent nations and its own brand of, say a 'Mumbai Consensus', that is distinct from the Western Washington consensus or the so-called 'Beijing Consensus'. While prioritising speeding up of economic growth as the ultimate guarantor of a more powerful India, the Modi government has pursued a multipolar world in which India is a pole in its own right rather than a mere pendulum swinging in an à la carte basis from issue to issue between China and the US.

Too often in the past, India's foreign policy targets have been decided in a fashion where it missed the forest for the trees. Restoring and maintaining high GDP growth, countering terrorism or securing the territorial integrity of the country were counted as ultimate objectives in themselves. But in the Modi Doctrine, they are crucial ingredients and means in a march to great power status that accrues privileges and influence to the Indian state and Indian people across the world.

Some career bureaucrats in New Delhi's corridors of power deliberately underplay India's rise and even castigate this notion as a 'Western construct'. But Modi's electoral mandate and periodic expressions of public confidence in his foreign policy reflect a tremendous aspiration for upward mobility of Indians of all hues. India's people are not happy being at a subsistence level or content with incremental improvements. Modi has taken this message and applied it to foreign policy by conferring on his team a turbocharged mission of aiming for the top in the global power configuration. The people have given Modi

---

35 Khilnani, Sunil et al. 2012. *Non-Alignment 2.0: A Foreign and Strategic Policy for India in the Twenty First Century*, New Delhi: Centre for Policy Research

a blank cheque to redirect the ship of India's international odyssey and surge ahead. He has heeded the call.

When envisaging India as a leading power and planning towards that end, Modi has consciously situated it within a larger universe of nation states and a global structure. By orienting foreign policy solely towards producing economic benefits for India's people or preventing transnational terrorist attacks on Indian soil, India was not operating in a zone that appealed to the wider world. The Modi Doctrine has basically rewritten the fuzzy concept of 'national interest' in a way that the international community now finds a buy-in and enables Indian interests to be realised instead of resisting and stymieing them.

Modi's brainchildren like the International Solar Alliance (ISA) and a global social movement against extremism and terrorism, reify a unique trait that he brings to Indian diplomacy of making the world cheer for India as it rises. In the present Indian prime minister's own words, he feels 'proud to have been communicating what we can do for the world, which is so different to what happened many times (in the past) when our leaders have communicated what India wants.'[36]

The effective communication and outreach aspects of the Modi Doctrine will be elaborated in the first chapter of this book. Here, it suffices to mention that Modi is an experienced innovator open to fresh ideas and has delivered an imaginative and creative foreign policy that not only doggedly pursues materialistic interests, but also enhances India's soft power. He has enhanced India's desirability in the global public eye by launching and supporting good causes that demonstrate India as acting as a responsible emerging power, thereby winning plaudits as an indispensable actor for supplying global public goods.

Under Modi, India is visible internationally because it has finally found a grand strategy infused with a hunger to be big and important in the world. As subsequent chapters of this book will demonstrate, Modi's stances towards individual countries like Pakistan, China, Russia and the US evolved with the flow of time and events, but they comported with a grand strategy. Systemic foreign policy overhaul was necessary for India to leap forward in the international system and Modi provided this vital input.

---

36 Price, Lance. 2015. *The Modi Effect: Inside Narendra Modi's Campaign to Transform India*, London: Hodder & Stoughton, p.255

Buoyed by a broad vision of refashioning the world order, Modi's India is doing better and is emerging stronger in the eyes of the international community. Predictions by some retired Indian civil servants that Modi would simply continue what the Manmohan Singh government had done in foreign policy, because the bureaucracy stays on while political rulers come and go, were aimed at undermining Modi's promise and potential in foreign affairs. Thankfully, such voices did not find primacy and Modi went ahead and steered Indian foreign policy in new directions.

Revamping the ship of the state

Opinions are divided on whether or not Modi is inherently anti-bureaucratic and has the gumption to consistently overrule the counsel of career civil servants in either domestic or foreign affairs. For example, on his 'Act East' policy revamp, he is said to have run into resistance from 'insular' bureaucrats programmed with old-fashioned 'default impulses' of opposing trilateral or plurilateral security partnerships. The outcome was that he ended up not signing on to 'trilateral security cooperation with Australia and Japan'.[37]

But at other times, Modi has bulldozed his path across the objections of India's Teflon-coated and narrowly preoccupied bureaucracy. At his inauguration speech as India's prime minister in 2014, he promised to 'actively engage with the global community to strengthen the cause of world peace and development'[38] and walked this talk from day one by ensuring that heads of the governments of all South Asian neighbours of India (except Bangladesh's Prime Minister Sheikh Hasina, who was touring Japan) were present at his swearing-in ceremony. It was an unprecedented diplomatic coup and an early indicator that Modi would not let foreign policy languish in the glacial routines of unimaginative bureaucracy.

In January 2015, just one day after hosting the US President Barack Obama in India, Modi sacked India's highest-ranking diplomat, Sujatha Singh, six months before the end of her tenure. This relatively rare development opened a window into the foreign-policy reforms Modi

---

[37] Mohan, Raja. 2014. 'Not so Easy to Act East', *The Indian Express*, November 22nd

[38] Kazmin, Amy. 2014. 'Narendra Modi Sworn in as Indian prime minister in Lavish Ceremony', *Financial Times*, May 26th

planned to undertake and raised questions about the appropriate role of the bureaucracy in shaping India's international outlook. By most observers' reckoning, Singh was ordered to remit office on grounds of under performance and failure to keep up with the foreign policy changes under a hyperactive Modi, who is a hands-on manager, a hard taskmaster and demanding political boss to bureaucrats. Though Singh refuted speculation that Modi was unhappy with her leadership of the Ministry of External Affairs (MEA), word spread that she could not satisfy his desire to maximise India's strategic partnerships with Japan and Israel and was found wanting in revving up India's economic diplomacy.

Until Modi's advent, India's career diplomats were hardly subjected to performance-based scrutiny or criticism on specific policy stances, either by India's Parliamentary Committee on External Affairs or by the head of government. The only debates on India's international positions and strategies occurred in the news media, evoking contemptuous yawns in the MEA, whose career diplomats pooh-pooh commentary by outsiders for their supposed ignorance about what really happens behind the scenes in the conduct of foreign policy. For a result-oriented prime minister such as Modi, unaccountable and uninspiring bureaucrats in India's foreign-policy establishment are liabilities. In his mind, their heads have to roll for the country's global standing to rise as per the blueprint he has scripted. This determination is exemplified by his blunt admonition to his diplomatic corps to 'shed old mindsets'.[39]

At the same time, like an experienced corporate human resource manager, Modi wants to reward and promote meritorious and skilled diplomats who notch up notable successes, such as Singh's replacement, S. Jaishankar, who served with distinction as India's Ambassador to China and the USA, and who is credited with ensuring that Obama returned to India for a historic second time. The Indian Foreign Service (IFS) has both outstanding individual officers as well as mediocre ones who are unable to adjust their lenses and adapt to fast-morphing geopolitical and geo-economic developments. Modi has tried to separate the wheat from the chaff.

---

[39] PTI. 2015. 'PM Modi asks Indian Diplomats to Shed Old Mindsets', *The Economic Times*, February 7th

After her shock dismissal, Singh's parting shot insinuated that the prime minister is running an individualistic show and undermining the institutional strengths of the MEA.[40] Criticism of Modi for operating a personalised form of rule is not new. This book uncovers many examples of how he acted on his own on crucial foreign policy junctures. In fact, many prime ministers before him have arrogated to themselves the ultimate foreign-policymaking levers at the expense of the MEA. The Prime Minister's Office, particularly the National Security Adviser (NSA) who works within this prestigious office, has been a nerve centre of India's foreign-policy framing since 1998 and will remain so under strong-willed prime ministers like Modi.

The functional straddling has left some MEA mandarins crying out against 'usurpation' of their turf, producing an ambience of internal institutional tussles. Such internecine clashes are natural and they occur even in the USA, which has a far longer history of evolved diplomatic processes than India. Yet, it would be uncharitable to interpret the handover of the baton from Singh to Jaishankar as a morale-killing blow to an already emasculated MEA. Rather, the move was an affirmation of the Modi mantra to his top bureaucrats: perform or perish. It was a personnel overhaul done within the macro guidelines of the Modi Doctrine.

Novelties and lacunae

The Modi Doctrine is a story of not just raising the bar of what India hopes to achieve in global politics and economics and chasing down the goals with chosen instruments and single-minded focus. It is also a universe of new thematic emphases and additions to the lexicon of Indian diplomacy. Modi has issued a pithy formulation of 'three Cs', viz. connectivity, commercial ties and cultural bonds, as the foundations for India's deepening engagement in Asia.[41] Across the world, he has proclaimed 'three Ds', namely democracy, demography and demand, as India's USPs and tickets to great power status.[42]

---

[40] IndiaToday. 2015. 'Sujatha Singh Hits Back at Modi Government for Sacking her, Asks was this Necessary', *India Today*, January 30th

[41] PTI. 2014. 'PM Modi Meets Myanmar President U Thein Sein', *The Times of India*, November 11th

[42] PTI. 2014. 'Narendra Modi Gives 3-D Formula for India to Become a Global Leader', *Daily News and Analysis*, September 28th

Some of these evocative business school textbook-style formulations overlap with and build upon the BJP's *panchaamrit* or 'five pillars' foreign policy strategy.[43] While the Modi government's foreign policy does not meticulously implement each and every precept of the BJP's vision, the current Indian prime minister has not deviated from his party's 'pillars' outline. The Modi Doctrine has never failed to invoke *Sammaan* (national honour and dignity before the international community), indulge in *Samvaad* (intense diplomatic engagement and dialogue in far corners of the globe), seek *Samriddhi* (shared economic prosperity and mutually beneficial exchanges with nations on a planetary scale), provide *Suraksha* (national, regional and global security through military diplomacy and modernisation) and revive *Sanskriti evam Sabhyata* (cultural and civilisational linkages between India and the entire world). As the first chapter of this book will show, the legacy of the BJP and its parent body, the cultural nationalist organisation Rashtriya Swayamsevak Sangh (RSS), does percolate into the Modi Doctrine.

To sum up, the Modi Doctrine is a breath of fresh air to execute a paradigm shift in Indian foreign policy. It rests on the fulcrums of India aiming broader and higher, thinking long-term, deploying more human and material resources, restructuring its policymaking stable, forming new coalitions, forging novel ideas and institutions, and stepping up to assume greater international responsibilities. It is a package and talisman to navigate India in a globalised world. It is the answer to a dilemma that Modi described with repetitive emphasis after becoming prime minister, 'the whole world is looking at India with expectations. But we are not ready. The world is ready but we are not ready.'[44]

The scholar Ian Hall claims that while Modi has suffused Indian foreign policy with 'new energy' and speed of delivering on promises, 'his approach is essentially pragmatic, and his objectives are similar to those pursued by his two immediate predecessors—Atal Bihari Vajpayee and Manmohan Singh.'[45] But this book rejects such superficial readings of continuity and

---

43 Tiwari, Ravish. 2015. 'BJP Calls for a Muscular Foreign Policy: Panchamrit to Replace Panchsheel', *India Today*, April 4th

44 PTI. 2014. 'World Looking at India with Expectations: Narendra Modi', *Daily News and Analysis*, December 25th

45 Hall, Ian. 2015. 'Is a 'Modi Doctrine' Emerging in Indian Foreign Policy?', *Australian Journal of International Affairs*, Volume 69, Issue 3, p.247

proposes that the Modi Doctrine is undertaking a paradigm shift both in India's mental makeup and modus operandi in world politics and the global economy. It seconds C. Raja Mohan's more sanguine evaluation that 'the reorientation of India's international role might well have acquired an irreversible momentum under Narendra Modi.'[46]

While basically supportive of the Modi Doctrine, this book also recommends course corrections and rejigging in specific issue areas where Modi's foreign policy has been found wanting or is less successful. The prescriptive portions of the book are meant to fuel debate within India and abroad as to what will be required in the near to medium terms for India to leap forward and take its due place in the comity of nations. My motto is to comprehensively sketch out Modi and his international trysts as they exist, but while doing so, I also offer normative and practical suggestions on what else Modi ought to incorporate into his foreign policy matrix to maximise his dreams of a mighty and secure India.

The next decade will be seminal for the global power transition that is underway between West and East and between Global North and Global South. India is poised to be a beneficiary because the tailwinds of this transition are with rising Asian powers. Modi is acutely aware of this window. He remarked to his diplomats that 'the present global environment represents a rare opportunity, when the world is keen to embrace India, and India is moving forward with confidence.'[47] It takes extraordinary leadership in foreign policy and a master plan for India to ride the crest and take its due place as a great power. The vehicle of the state has an accelerator which needs a firm foot to be pressed at the correct moments and a strategically astute driver behind the steering wheel. Modi can justify the tag of a foreign policy statesman if he satisfies these criteria in the years to come.

Schema of the book

Chapter 1 of this book traces Modi's panache in foreign affairs and distinctive style of 'retail diplomacy' to his early political training and

[46] Mohan, Raja. 2015. *Modi's World*, Op cit, p.214

[47] DHNS. 2015. 'Modi Urges Envoys to help India take Global Leadership Role', *Deccan Herald*, February 7th

experience as a *prachaarak* (organiser or preacher) for the Rashtriya Swayamsevak Sangh (RSS), the cultural fountainhead of the BJP, and then subsequently as an international spokesman-cum-salesman for the Western Indian state of Gujarat, where he was the chief minister for a decade before becoming India's prime minister. It argues that Modi's outreach and popularity overseas are well-honed techniques from his foreign travels during the RSS and Gujarat days, and that he revels in contact diplomacy and personal diplomacy unlike previous prime ministers because of his early successes in building a mass appeal abroad and securing concrete material benefits for Gujarat from 'sub-unit diplomacy'.

The chapter analyses Modi government's claims that 'personal chemistry' has become a central asset in its diplomatic toolkit and evaluates the advantages for India to have a prime minister who has 'bromances' and personal friendships with world leaders such as the US President Barack Obama and the Japanese Prime Minister Shinzo Abe. The chapter ends by raising broader questions about body language and emotions in the conduct of foreign policy and how Modi's personality-centred foreign relations have benefited India's image globally.

The chapter also shows how Modi kindled the curiosity of the Indian public about world affairs through unprecedented adoption of social media and publicity about his foreign policy, in keeping with his *prachaarak* schooling. In the process, he has raised the global consciousness of Indians and has also donned the role of a teacher to the nation about the relevance of international engagement.

Chapter 2 takes up Modi's lovefest with Non-Resident Indians (NRIs) and Overseas Citizens of India (OCIs), which is not only a legacy of his RSS and Overseas Friends of BJP (OFBJP) thinking, but also a re-imagination of the notion of 'Mother India' as both a territorial and a civilisational entity that exists wherever the diaspora is settled. The chapter threshes out details about why Modi is such a rock star with NRIs, how he has brought back a sense of pride and connection among India's 25-million-strong diaspora to the homeland, and the series of policy measures he has taken to integrate the diaspora with India's economic growth story.

The chapter concludes by looking at the advantages of mobilising the Indian diaspora as a lobby and a force multiplier for India's foreign policy and proposes some new ideas for Modi to further leverage the amazing asset of India's diaspora.

Chapter 3 elaborates how Modi has elevated trade and commerce to take centrestage in India's foreign relations, and connects it to his sharp mercantile sense, his proverbial 'Gujarati business genius' and the rediscovery of India's identity as a commercial, seafaring nation. It assesses big leaps in attracting Foreign Direct Investment (FDI) into India since Modi took over as prime minister and the importance he has given to wooing centres of world finance. It gives examples from his foreign visits of CEO forums and interactions and reveals why he as a 'CEO Prime Minister' is so much at ease in the company of business titans.

The chapter also looks at Modi's strenuous efforts to rebrand India as modern and open to business, his efforts to connect Indian states directly with foreign counterparts for FDI and trade, and how this has been received globally. It ends by looking at domestic impediments which hobble the full potential of realising Modi's dream of maximising inward FDI and doubling India's goods and services exports.

Chapter 4 critically explores Modi's strategy of dealing with existing great powers, viz. the USA and China, and how he is trying to position India as more than a mere 'swing state' or a balancer between these two power centres. It analyses the current state of triangular relations among the USA, China and India and where Modi has departed from earlier Indian leaders in his diplomacy with Washington and Beijing.

The chapter also discusses the key prerequisites for India to build its comprehensive national strength (hard and soft power) to one day reach the same level of recognition in the world as the USA and China, and asks whether Modi is pressing all the right buttons to rev up India's overall national power. Lastly, the chapter evaluates Modi's performance in multilateral forums like BRICS, G-20 and the United Nations and shows how this is geared at positioning India as a 'leading power' that can redress the world's problems.

Chapter 5 looks at Modi's outreach to specific regions of the world like South Asia ('First Concentric Circle'), Indo-Pacific ('Act East'), the Indian Ocean ('India's Ocean'), Africa and Latin America ('South-South'), the Middle East ('Look West'), Europe and North America and argues that his theories of 'big picture' and 'smallest one matters' have constructively changed India's attitude toward faraway places.

The focus of the chapter is on Modi's departures from previous Indian governments such as an unapologetic embrace of Israel and Japan. It also discusses specific gains for India in energy security, counter-terrorism, economic modernisation, urbanisation and industrialisation from Modi's frantic deals and agreements signed with crucial partners and sub-regions. This chapter touches upon on how the Modi Doctrine, while treading new terrain, must push for preferential trading agreements, economic corridors and defence linkages with strategically vital regions of the world.

The ***Epilogue*** dwells on what else Modi needs to do in foreign policy in the years ahead to realise his vision of the twenty-first century being not just an Asian century but an Indian century. It prescribes a concrete set of policy measures, bureaucratic reforms and course corrections to make the Modi Doctrine more robust and trailblazing. It recapitulates the dialectic between domestic reforms and changes in India, and the degree of success Modi can sustain overseas. It signs off by rounding up the main point of the book that Modi has decisively transformed India's foreign policy for the better and globalised what used to be a parochial national identity and outlook.

Chapter I
The *Prachaarak* as Diplomat-in-Chief

Whose is the responsibility of building Motherland, for progress of Motherland, for development of Motherland, for revolutionizing Motherland, that our Mother India once again occupies the high seat of world leadership? This responsibility lies with the Swayamsevaks.[1]

Khaki shorts, global dreams

This book is neither an account of Indian foreign policy in general, nor a biography of Narendra Modi. It is rather a work on Modi's foreign policy, auguring a balance between biographical inputs about his personality traits and an analysis of how these have been refracted on to his vision and strategy in international affairs.

The Modi that we see today in world forums as a complete natural who enjoys every bit of being a rock star and a brand ambassador who carries India's pride and self-confidence on his shoulders is not a sudden avatar that was confected once he swept the general elections in 2014. Instead, it is a composite of over three decades of incremental training in public affairs and relations, wherein he developed a trademark style and philosophy about the way the world works and how he fits in it.

There was a budding diplomat in Modi prior to his assumption of the seat of India's prime minister, and even before he rose to the post of

---

[1] Modi, Narendra. 2008. *Jyotipunj*, New Delhi: Prabhat Prakashan, p.58

chief minister of his home state of Gujarat. The earliest signs of what can now be labelled as the Modi Doctrine, especially its penchant for personal diplomacy, derive from the travels, impressions, learnings and work experiences from the period of his youth and middle age. The eras when Modi was first a political unknown and then a promising regional satrap of the BJP hold clues to the diplomatic evolution and maturation of a leader who connects local and global phenomena and interests better than any Indian politician in recent memory.

In 1978, when Narendra Modi was twenty-eight, he was appointed as a *Vibhaag Prachaarak* (regional organiser in charge of six districts of the state of Gujarat) of the Hindu nationalist body, Rashtriya Swayamsevak Sangh (RSS). The distinction was bestowed upon him by the RSS' leadership after observing certain qualities and personality traits that Modi had honed since 1958, when he joined this cultural institution as a child, donned its khaki shorts uniform, and grew in it as family.

Chief among the reasons for Modi's promotions in the RSS were his oratory, mobilisation of large groups of people, spirit of resisting oppressive political authorities which were antithetical to Hindu nationalism, cultivation of one-on-one friendships, planning and execution of projects, and a marked ability to promote the RSS' image as a social service entity that selflessly rescues the afflicted during calamities and serves the downtrodden on a continuous basis.[2]

By the early 1980s, these assets propelled him to the status of *Praant Pramukh* (deputy head of the RSS for the state of Gujarat), where he continued to display leadership talents that set him apart from his contemporaries. In 1987, the national head of RSS nominated him to be 'sent' to the BJP for direct political work. Modi described why he was picked for this transition,'the BJP was in need of a young man, who could work hard and run about, and dedicate himself to the cause.'[3] And true to this billing, he made his way up the BJP ranks due to his workaholic nature and a skill for mass contact. Developing networks of followers, spreading the Hindu nationalistic ideology and building branches and sub-branches of the RSS and BJP were intrinsic to his rising career graph.

---

[2] Makwana, Kishor. 2015. *Modi: Common Man's PM*, New Delhi: Prabhat Prakashan

[3] Ibid. p.114

Years later, as India's prime minister and the architect of a hyperactive foreign policy, Modi was asked during a marathon visit to New York as to how he beats tiredness and stays alert to keep meeting hundreds upon hundreds of Indian-American visitors into the wee hours of the night despite a punishing official diplomatic schedule. He smiled and is reported to have replied, 'this is part of my job.'[4] Communicating and contacting peers and followers is a central component of the Modi Doctrine, which corresponds to the BJP's foreign policy pillar of *Samvaad*. Unlike earlier Indian prime ministers, including Atal Bihari Vajpayee who was an RSS *vistaarak* (full-time worker, less experienced than a *prachaarak*) in the 1940s, the *prachaarak* in Modi is a gregarious and extroverted individual who revels in social company.

The most visible manifestations of the Modi Doctrine are the Indian prime minister's record number of foreign visits and his showpiece hosting of dozens of foreign heads of governments in India. By the end of his first year in office, Modi had globetrotted to a whopping eighteen countries—an all-time high in the history of independent India. As of July 2016, he had covered forty-two countries in total, six of which hosted him twice and one of which received him four times. A roving prime minister who prioritises international engagement through ever-multiplying personal footfalls, Modi has done ample justice to the BJP's *Samvaad* concept. Through an omnipresent diplomacy of continuous, frequent and sustained interactions with the world, he has deployed the full political will of the nation's highest office at the service of India's interests abroad. Harking back to his modest *prachaarak* background, he says in his folksy words,'we are hardcore Ahmedabadis (reference to his hometown in the state of Gujarat). We believe in single fare, double journey.'[5] In fact, the Indian prime minister often takes quadruple or quintuple journeys, such as his breathtaking visits to five nations spread across Asia, Europe and North America within a span of 140 hours in June 2016.[6]

---

[4] PTI. 2015. 'PM Modi Meets Several Hundred Indian-Americans in New York', *The Times of India*, September 26th

[5] Narayan, Sanjoy & Shishir Gupta. 2015. 'Single Fare, Double Journey: PM Modi's Mantra for Tours Abroad', *Hindustan Times*, April 9th

[6] Sharma, Aman. 2016. 'PM Narendra Modi's Tour Covers Five Nations in 140 Hours', *The Economic Times*, June 6th

Touring, travelling and contacting as many interlocutors as possible through a kinetic diplomacy are visceral to the Modi Doctrine. One need not look beyond Modi's RSS background to understand why so much weightage is accorded to contact diplomacy. Professor Pralay Kanungo, in his book *RSS' Tryst With Politics*, writes:

'...*prachaaraks* are the links between the various levels of the RSS, whom the constitution defines as unpaid, full-time workers of high integrity whose mission is to serve the society through the *Sangh*, and who, of their own free will, dedicate themselves to the cause. Most *prachaaraks* are recruited in their early twenties. They are usually college-educated and have been associated with the RSS activities since their early adolescence. They usually know Hindi, English and the language of the area in which they work. They also have flair for travelling.'[7]

Endowed with quintessential Gujarati streaks of entrepreneurship, seafaring psyche and an outgoing personality, Modi is at home in international settings and presents a picture of a nationalistic yet a globalised Indian. For foreign policy aficionados, he has been a dream prime minister who is consistently and innovatively universal in vision and action. Enjoying an absolute majority in India's parliament, and free from the pressure of any national-level opposition party worth its salt at home, he has been able to devote much time and energy to strengthening India's position overseas than any other Indian prime minister since Nehru.

During the 1990s, when Modi was carving out a place in Indian politics as a *prachaarak* and promoter of the *Sangh Parivaar*, (the extended family of Hindu nationalist organisations like RSS, BJP et al), he had opportunities to undertake numerous foreign journeys and offered glimpses of what would turn out to be the Modi Doctrine. Old timers who remember the Modi of those days say that whenever he visited the USA, 'he had India on his mind' and would wonder at epic landmarks like the Statue of Liberty, 'why something like that could not be done in India.' Everywhere he went from Chicago and

---

7 Kanungo, Pralay. 2002. *RSS' Tryst with Politics: From Hedgewar to Sudarshan*, New Delhi: Manohar Publishers, pp.79-80

Boston to Texas and California, 'he was interested in governance and infrastructure—roads and rivers and urban regeneration; how Americans were approaching problems and what India can learn from it.'[8]

As a confidante of the BJP's first Indian prime minister, Vajpayee, Modi was also deputed to travel abroad to countries like Malaysia and Australia for diplomatic and party work. This international baptism had a profound impact on him and seeded ideas in him which would go on to form the Modi Doctrine. In Modi's recollection, 'I was lucky to visit more than forty countries, and because of that I got very good exposure. I understood how the world is moving, what type of things are developing and where my country stood. I had to think about it: why is my country like this? Why are others improving? Israel doesn't have any rain, but Israel is improving. Why are we not?'[9]

After becoming the prime minister, he has kept up with this habit of travelling overseas with an open mind and communicating incessantly to learn best practices to implement them as per the local Indian context. One of the highlights of the Modi Doctrine is that he does not treat *Samvaad* as dialogue only with elites in foreign nations. Mixing with ordinary citizens of these countries, glad-handing them, pressing the flesh etc., are intrinsic to his incredibly photogenic and choreographed public diplomacy.

Retail diplomacy with personal touch

Now in his sixties, Modi the global traveler still believes in meeting school and college students, employees of private-sector firms, monks, artists, scholars and others from a cross-section of the society he is contacting, constantly 'looking for takeaways for India, as he did in his earlier visits years ago.'[10] In the Modi Doctrine, foreign policy is not just a government-to-government, business-to-business or even

---

[8] Rajghatta, Chidanand. 2014. 'Narendra Modi Returns to his Stomping Ground as Prime Minister after a 14-Year Exile', *The Times of India*, September 25th

[9] Marino, Andy. 2014. *Narendra Modi: A Political Biography*, New Delhi: HarperCollins, p.95

[10] Variyar, Mugdha. 2014. 'Modi's Tryst with America: From SanghParivaarPrachaarak in 1990s to Indian PM', *International Business Times*, September 26th

people-to-people affairs. It is also a leader-to-people channel that must create social goodwill in foreign lands for India's dynamic diplomat-in-chief.

In the USA, there is a term for the fervent direct contact that some politicians make with voters in order to win their abiding trust—'retail politics'. Political communication experts Judith Trent and Robert Friedenberg define it as 'meeting voters, talking to voters, and shaking as many hands as possible.' They add that retail politics carries invaluable benefits such as making the public more committed to the leader, giving the people a feeling that they are important, humanising the candidate seeking the public's attention, and developing an interpersonal relationship that lasts.[11] The Modi Doctrine has reinvented what used to be a coy and elitist Indian foreign policy by transposing the hustle and bustle of retail politics on to diplomacy. Modi is the type of world leader who leaves a lingering impression on the VIPs as well as on the everyman.

Later in this book, I will explain how the Modi Doctrine has proved to be a moonshot for India's soft power. Here, we must delve deeper into the wellsprings of Modi's retail diplomacy and his reliance on personal chemistry, which has been painted as a 'powerful tool in enhancing India's diplomatic engagement' and 'a different approach' from 'diplomacy as usual.'[12] As India's prime minister, Modi is famed as a 'tactile man' and a 'hugger of global proportions' who displays plenty of affection and wears his heart on his sleeve during diplomatic trips.[13] He strikes easy personal bonds with interlocutors of different wavelengths. Effusive socialisation, which is his forte in world politics, happens with a definite purpose and outcome in mind. But it is done in a completely unpretentious and human manner to endear and disarm his counterparts. The demonstrativeness is part showmanship, but is also a

---

[11] Trent, Judith & Robert Friedenberg. 2011. *Political Campaign Communication: Principles and Practices*, Lanham: Rowman & Littlefield, p.297

[12] PTI. 2015. 'PM Modi's Personal Chemistry has Enhanced India's Diplomatic Engagement, says Foreign Secretary S. Jaishankar', *Daily News and Analysis*, July 17th

[13] Taylor, Adam. 2016. 'Narendra Modi Won't Stop Hugging World Leaders no Matter how Awkward it is', *The Washington Post*, January 25th

strategic method to promote goodwill for India. Once a *prachaarak* and always one in his heart, Modi 'believes that hugs fetch more dividends; they are not about cuddly politics alone.'[14]

Friendship is a recurring facet in the Modi Doctrine, and it can be traced back to his cultural and political baptism in the RSS and the BJP. Right from the word go when he began to be noticed in these organisations, Modi had a knack to befriend rank-and-file, equals and superiors alike. Maintaining friendly vibes with those who matter is an art that Modi has mastered from his *prachaarak* days and has sustained it as a mantra of success throughout his life. Himanshu Shekhar has underlined that Modi sees 'open arms for friendship' with other nations as a 'good fortune', and that the Indian prime minister knows well the cardinal lesson that 'most of the successful nations across the globe have maintained amicable relationship with their neighbouring countries' in particular.[15]

In a subsequent chapter, I will explain why such a reading of history is relevant and how it enabled Modi to try and remake South Asia. Here is one example enough to illustrate the value of friendship in the Modi Doctrine. The US President Franklin Delano Roosevelt's progressive 'Good Neighbour Policy' of the 1930s attempted to reassert Washington's slipping influence in Latin America by eschewing arm-twisting tactics of the past. It turned around the whole region for a while to be supportive of American foreign policy. In Greg Grandin's view, it 'institutionalized Washington's authority, drawing Latin American republics tighter into its political, economic and cultural orbit through a series of multilateral treaties and regional organizations.'[16] Although US presidents after Roosevelt reverted to form during the Cold War and destabilised Latin America again, his 'Good Neighbour Policy' with its overtones of friendship between large nations and their small

---

[14] Biswas, Soutik. 2015. 'Why Narendra Modi Hugs the Headlines', BBC News, September 29th. URL: http://www.bbc.com/news/world-asia-india-34389044 Last accessed on January 13th, 2016

[15] Shekhar, Himanshu. 2014. *Management Guru Narendra Modi*, New Delhi: Diamond Books, p.114

[16] Grandin, Greg. 2007. *Empire's Workshop: Latin America, the United States and the Rise of the New Imperialism*, New York: Henry Holt & Co, p.4

surrounding countries remains a model for how a great power can secure its backyard and then go out to lead the world.

Commitment to amiable and friendly relations with the rest of the world is, of course, a clichéd and ritualistic tenet of Indian foreign policy since inception. But Modi has taken bold diplomatic initiatives based on a reading of the strategic stakes, personal trust and a fraternal spirit with countries including those that have historically been seen as inimical to Indian interests, thereby creating an example to the world, and unspooling an alternative paradigm for the conduct of foreign relations. The symbolic personal rapport through which Modi has rewritten the stoic and impersonal style of Indian diplomacy generates leverage for him to utilise these relations for amassing India's soft power, and as a backup when there is trouble. As the former Indian Foreign Secretary Lalit Mansingh says, Modi's 'break from the traditional ways of diplomacy' gives him 'a personal connect to use that to manoeuvre during tense situations.'[17]

During the interregnums when Modi is not boarding and descending Air India One planes from foreign visits, he is frequently seen embracing the US President Barack Obama, French President Francois Hollande, Pakistani Prime Minister Nawaz Sharif, Facebook CEO Mark Zuckerberg and other notables for camera flashlights. He sways Chinese President Xi Jinping on a traditional swing in his native Gujarat, clasps hands for eternity with the Arab sheikhs, runs a no-holds-barred 'bromance' with Japanese Prime Minister Shinzo Abe, and shows off selfies on Twitter with the Who's Who of the world.

Among the multiple friendships that he carefully nurtures, the one with Obama is obviously the most consequential one due to the global strategic implications of an Indian and American leader standing shoulder to shoulder. Obama's second visit to India in January 2015, which Modi assiduously engendered through diplomatic leg work, set tongues wagging about his rare personal chemistry with Prime Minister Modi. From the moment President Obama stepped down Air Force One, the public display of affection with Prime Minister Modi was the subject of media gossip and scholarly introspection. Holding hands,

---

[17] Khanna, Pretika. 2015. 'Narendra Modi Rewriting Diplomatic Lexicon', *Mint*, December 28th

bear hugs, appreciative taps on the shoulder, sharing of jokes, a joint radio show and frequent huddles between the two leaders to talk not just business, but even how much sleep each of them gets on the job revealed them to be intimate on a one-to-one basis.

The human angle of friendship between Messrs Obama and Modi added a special meaning to the India-US 'Delhi Declaration of Friendship' released on 25 January, 2015. So compelling was the mutual attraction that Modi even delivered a sermon on diplomacy to the press corps by asserting that 'relations between countries depend less on full stops and commas and more on the relationship between leaders, the chemistry between them.'[18] By this he implied that even as bureaucrats engage in pragmatic bilateral negotiations with their counterparts, friendship and warmth at the summit level are more decisive drivers. Indeed, political will and pressure from heads of government are confidence-boosters to iron out wrinkles in the minutiae of diplomatic give-and-take.

What exactly is the secret formula behind the chemistry of what journalists dubbed as 'Mobama'?[19] There is no room for vain sentimentalism in the Modi Doctrine. Bonding and warmhearted links are designed for a greater cause than simply feel-good signals at the interpersonal level. In the words of Harvard Professor Joseph Nye, 'friendship (between world leaders) helps, but it's icing on the cake. The cake is national interest.'[20] Two world leaders can hit it off only when there is an underlying convergence of material interests. Modi said as much,'this chemistry has not just brought me and Barack closer but also brought Washington and Delhi—and the people of our countries—closer together.'[21]

The prospects of US-India policy coordination to shape the strategic balance in Asia, and US-India trade and investment zooming into the stratosphere are basically Nye's 'cakes'. For the cake to be adorned with

---

18 PTI. 2015. Barack Obama-Narendra Modi Chemistry on Display', *The Indian Express*, January 25th

19 Kumar, Anita. 2015. 'India Loves 'Mobama', the Budding Friendship of Modi, Obama', *McClatchy*, January 26th

20 Nicholas, Peter & Brian Bennett. 2011. 'For Obama, it's Business before Friendship with World Leaders', *Los Angeles Times*, April 5th

21 AFP. 2015. 'Obama, Modi break Nuclear Impasse, Hail New Friendship', *The Express Tribune*, January 25th

a captivating topping like the body language of 'Mobama' is a huge bonus. In September 2014, Modi hosted Chinese President Xi Jinping in his home city of Ahmedabad in Gujarat and strolled alongside him on the banks of the cleaned-up Sabarmati River. The sight of the two Asian supremos rocking in a traditional Gujarati swing was a photo-op, but it could not convey a picture of genuine friendship between Messrs Modi and Xi. The reason was obvious, China and India have a trust deficit and strategic competition between each other, facets which are relatively muted in case of the US-India equation. Notwithstanding the personal touch that Modi gave to Xi's visit, real chumminess was missing due to the structural problem of clashing interests.

Apart from common interests, ideology is another binding factor in determining friendships among international personalities. Some of the most famous 'buddies' in world history have been forged in the crucible of shared worldviews. Former US President Ronald Reagan and former British Prime Minister Margaret Thatcher were 'closest political and dearest personal friends.'[22] Their conservative, pro-business mindsets engendered a natural bond and sustained it through the final years of the Cold War. Likewise, the personal camaraderie between Modi and Japanese Prime Minister Shinzo Abe is predicated on identical cultural nationalism, conservatism and passion to reform their respective economic systems.

On the Left, the most outstanding personal friendship of the twenty-first century was between Cuba's ageing communist legend Fidel Castro and his anointed successor, the late Hugo Chavez of Venezuela. Labelled as a 'father-son' connection, Castro and Chavez spearheaded the socialist charge in Latin America through an extended series of embraces that had no daylight between them. Their endearment was 'unprecedented in Latin American history', with plans at one stage in 2004 to formally merge the two countries and rename the consolidated territory as 'Cubazuela'.[23]

Since ideological affinity is the cement for fraternising, the Modi-Obama fondness is somewhat anomalous. In contrast to a decidedly

---

[22] Russell, Alec & Andrew Sparrow. 2004. 'Thatcher's Taped Eulogy at Reagan Funeral', *The Telegraph*, June 7th

[23] Córdoba, José. 2013. 'The Future of Cubazuela', *The Wall Street Journal*, March 1st

business-friendly and characteristically extroverted Modi, Obama is a Left liberal and typically aloof politician harping about inequality and admonishing 'fat cat' capitalists. Ideologically, 'Mobama' seems to be an oxymoron. But as the two leaders' addresses to the CEOs Forum in January 2016 in New Delhi demonstrated, both believe from their guts in the intrinsic value of expanding US-India business ties. The American liberal and the Indian conservative are on the same page when it comes to promoting financial gains for their respective corporate sectors. Later in this chapter, I will demonstrate that pragmatism and open-mindedness to different ideological perspectives are inbuilt into Modi's personality, and that this is in spite of the widespread assumption that the RSS and BJP are narrow, rigid and bigoted organisations.

Modi and Obama are also leaders who excel in using 'Town Hall' venue oratory as part and parcel of their foreign policies. The heart-tugging address that Obama delivered in Siri Fort Auditorium in New Delhi in January 2015 was comparable to the touching speech Modi gave at Madison Square Garden in New York in September 2014. However, political style, ideology and national interests are not the only motors of special friendships in international relations. Circumstances also contribute.

The American president during World War II, Franklin Delano Roosevelt, was a dyed-in-the-wool Leftist who allied with the Rightist British Prime Minister Winston Churchill to ward off the systemic threat posed by the fascism of Adolf Hitler. Hailed as an 'epic friendship', Messrs Roosevelt and Churchill were so comfortable in each other's company that, in 1941, the former apparently barged into the White House bathroom and found the latter wearing 'nothing to hide'.[24] The extraordinary threat posed by Nazi peril was instrumental in this unlikely friendship.

All this is not to claim that emotions do not matter at all between individuals representing their nations. Sentiments do intrude into the rational, coldhearted processes of diplomacy. Feelings-based proximity of leaders acts as a talisman to channelise hard bargaining between states because diplomatic interlocutors lower down the hierarchy get the drift that their big bosses desire a deal. The intangible, but substantial

[24] Wilson, James. 2015. *Churchill and Roosevelt: The Big Sleepover at the White House*, Columbus: Gatekeeper Press, p.119

outcome of Modi's chatty equation with Obama is that it can act as a balm to soothe divergences on concrete issues. In later chapters of this book, I reveal how Modi acted as a remover of obstacles and sticky problems in India's bilateral relations with major partners. Some of these breakthroughs were eased by virtue of his indefatigable pursuit of personal friendships with heads of governments.

Sangh Ideologue, India's Flagbearer

Since the RSS is a cadre-based ideologically firm institution with a recognisable line on social, economic, political and foreign policy questions, it is worth asking how much of this baggage Modi has internalised, and which bits of these crept into the Modi Doctrine. As a *prachaarak*, Modi has an unalloyed faith in the primacy of culture and spirituality as defining elements of India as a nation and its calling cards in international affairs. Like American exceptionalism about a 'shining city on a hill', which guided generations of US presidents in their foreign policy rhetoric and substance,[25] the Modi Doctrine has devised an Indian exceptionalism revolving around its civilisational greatness and cultural gifts to humanity.

Modi has written about this dimension in glowing terms as,'India is not identified by its political system, form of government or power of the state. India is identified on the basis of its cultural heritage…(with) thousands of years…of sacred continuity.'[26] Taking inspiration from the nineteenth century Indian mystic and revivalist, Swami Vivekananda, who spread Indian spiritualism as its strongest virtue around the world, Modi has taken upon himself a millennial burden of propagating and preaching the positive sides of Indian culture to mould international public opinion. As prime minister, he remarked that 'we are the people whom the world has probably not understood in the manner in which we should have been. India has given the world neither community nor communalism. Our saints and sages (rishis and munis) and traditions have given the world spiritualism and not communalism.'[27] Earlier, as the chief minister of Gujarat, he had said

---

[25] Restad, Hilde. 2014. *American Exceptionalism: An Idea that made a Nation and Remade the World*, London: Routledge

[26] Modi, Narendra. *Jyotipunj*, Op cit. p.21

[27] PTI. 2016. 'India has given Spiritualism, not Communalism to World: PM Narendra Modi', *The Times of India*, January 10th

that,'God has determined India's duty to do good of the world. Its divine and internal power shall inspire it to work for the world's well-being.'[28]

The cultural refrain in the Modi Doctrine mirrors the BJP's foreign policy pillar of *Sammaan* or national dignity and honour. Modi's 'cultural and civilisational diplomacy' has been praised by his party as 'the distinguishing core of the PM's international engagements, be it his visit to the Buddhist temples in Sri Lanka or to religio-cultural sites in Japan.' Further, it says,

'Our foreign policy today reflects Bharat's age-old cherished cultural and civilisational values in a more significant and profound manner than ever before. While our approach is determined by the imperatives of the globalised world, it is also rooted in our inheritance of a timeless tradition of intellectual and economic engagement through peaceful co-existence. The Prime Minister has restored pride in Bharat's civilisational identity and cultural traditions and drawn global attention to it in a manner that befits this oldest civilisation of the world.'[29]

Pride and nationalism have been motivating states in determining their national image and interests in foreign policy forever, but the Modi Doctrine's push for promoting Indian culture abroad and highlighting intercultural similarities and oneness between Indians and people of friendly countries is noticeable. Later in this book, while discussing how the Modi Doctrine gave a huge fillip to India's soft power, I will return to the Indian prime minister's successes in touching the national psyches of other countries. But here, we must acknowledge that the *prachaarak* tendencies of extolling India's ancient culture are formative blocks of the Modi Doctrine. One need not be a psychoanalyst to discern this continuity between Modi's RSS and BJP schooling and his conduct as India's prime minister.

From the moment Modi rose to the national high office of India's prime minister in 2014, comparisons have proliferated between him and other historical and contemporary politicians in order to place and contextualise the man who heads the world's largest democracy. Is he a hardliner or a soft liner? Is he a hawk or a dove? The temptation to liken

---

[28] Makwana, Kishor. Op cit. p.311

[29] HBL. 2015. 'Party all Praise for Modi's Civilisational Diplomacy', *The Hindu Business Line*, April 3rd

him to some remarkable figure or the other grew because of heightened global expectations that he would be in the league of history-making individuals with a solid impact.

Parallels between personalities across space and time are often expressions of visceral emotions, likes and dislikes felt by observers. Most of the Hitler-Modi likenesses have been dished out by social liberals, secularists and those on the Left in India because they detest his nostrums and basic worldview with its Hindu nationalist tones. As the next section of this chapter shows, the episode of anti-Muslim violence when Modi was leading the state Gujarat, has never skipped his critics and their estimation of what kind of person he is. Painting any hated politician as a modern-day Hitler is the easiest and most natural technique to make one's case in an oversimplified and hard-hitting fashion.

If liberals impute a Nazi gene in Modi, what about the conservatives? Sadanand Dhume, a columnist for *The Wall Street Journal*, wrote after Modi's electoral triumph in 2014 that he would be India's Ronald Reagan or Margaret Thatcher. These two Right wing icons of the 1980s were also revolutionaries in their own right who completely altered the socioeconomic structures of the USA and the UK through business-friendly deregulation and wholesale privatisation. The fact that Modi always had a soft corner for entrepreneurs, received universal backing of private sector big guns, and had laid out the red carpet for investors by slaying red tape in Gujarat had fed a frenzy of speculation comparing him to the neo-liberal Reagan and Thatcher.

Modi's comment that the 'government has no business to do business' and should remain small, efficient, less intrusive and facilitative of entrepreneurship[30] does bear an eerie resemblance to Reagan's famous libertarian maxim,'government is not the solution to our problem; government is the problem.' The neoliberal angle finds reaffirmation in Modi's victory in the general election of 2014, which was deciphered by many as a sign that the majority of people in India aspired for rapid upward mobility rather than entitlements to welfare handouts and tidbits from the government. Modi appears closer to

---

[30] Shekhar, Himanshu. *Management Guru,* Op cit. p.40

Reagan and Thatcher and far from the ideals of an interventionist, care-giving state espoused by leaders like Franklin D Roosevelt or Clement Attlee. His deregulatory economic stance is also at variance with the 'integral humanism' of the RSS, which proposes a third way between free markets and socialist command state.

Modi's choice of conservative economists such as Arvind Subramanian and Arvind Panagariya as his advisers leave little to doubt that the Indian prime minister aims to steer India towards greater economic freedom. The extensive concentration of the Modi Doctrine on commercial diplomacy or what the BJP calls *Samriddhi*, comes out of this ingrained mercantilist thought which Modi finessed at the state level as the chief minister of Gujarat during the years 2001 to 2014.

Apart from dyed-in-the-wool liberals and conservatives who wish to project their deepest fears and hopes on to Modi on economic policy, a bevy of opinion makers and commentators have dished out their own theories as to which world personality he reminds them of in his foreign policy. The Chinese state-owned media's pin on Modi has hailed him as 'India's Nixon' who will pragmatically overcome contradictions and sidle up to China, just as the US President Richard Nixon had achieved a diplomatic masterstroke by opening up to America's hitherto mortal enemy, Mao Zedong, in 1972.[31] While Chinese elites are strategically wary of Modi's tough-minded take on India's national security and defence preparedness vis-a-vis hostile neighbours, they take heart from his admiration for the Chinese model of urbanisation and infrastructure modernisation, which he studied from close quarters during his chief ministership.

Modi's economic agenda of overcoming India's unemployment crisis through the China-styled FDI-premised heavy industrialisation and developing the manufacturing sector via his flagship 'Make in India' campaign dovetail well with the view of Greg Sheridan of *The Australian* that he 'could be India's Deng Xiaoping and may turn out to be as big an influence on global history as the legendary Chinese leader.'[32] In the same vein, John Cassidy of *The New Yorker* has reminded us that as the

---

[31] Zongyi, Liu. 2015. 'Modi's Nixonian Pragmatism Refreshes Ties', *Global Times*, May 14th

[32] Sheridan, Greg. 2014. 'India's Game Changer', *The Australian*, May 19th

chief minister of Gujarat, Modi's 'role models were Asian strongmen, such as Singapore's Lee Kuan Yew.'[33] How can Modi simultaneously be both a free market neoliberal and a state-guided capitalist like Deng or Lee? In a later chapter, I will argue that the economic thinking behind the Modi Doctrine is more complex and compound than these simplistic labels of bygone periods of history.

The veteran Indian journalist Dileep Padgaonkar credits Modi and peers like the leaders of Russia, Japan and Turkey, who are all social conservatives and hyper-nationalists, for offering their respective publics a 'sense of self-esteem and a moral and cultural compass to navigate through the choppy seas of globalization.'[34] Indeed, the *Samriddhi* and the *Sammaan* pillars of the BJP intermesh in a kind of culturally nationalistic yet market-based logic that best conveys Modi's foreign policy.

Since there are only a finite number of policy options and prescriptions on social, economic or diplomatic questions, it is always possible to see what Modi says or does from the angle of another world leader of the past or present. To compare is to classify a politician, and create a coherent narrative about what she or he is doing in the real world of policy. We also compare with an awareness that phenomena which have occurred or are occurring in India may also have happened in other parts of the world, along roughly the same lines and patterns. But Modi is, of course, Modi with his own inimitable characteristics, style and personality. He is no one's clone, but actually governs on domestic and foreign affairs with a bit of Reagan and a pinch of Deng. He rules with a combination of ideas from Left and Right, attesting to the fact that he transcended the RSS and the BJP in some aspects.

The German pioneer of *realpolitik*, Otto von Bismarck, once quipped that 'politics is the art of the possible.' Even for a man like Modi, whose political career is a saga of leaping over hurdles that circumscribe lesser mortals, there are constraints shaping how he manages and changes India and the world. He may be averse to welfare economics, but has not discontinued some developmental schemes for underprivileged Indians that retain votes. He may be a champion of commercial diplomacy,

---

[33] Cassidy, John. 2014. 'Modi's Role Model: Margaret Thatcher or Lee Kuan Yew?', *The New Yorker*, May 19th

[34] Padgaonkar, Dileep. Op cit.

but did not hesitate to use calibrated military force and tough postures against hostile forces abroad, even if that came at the cost of bilateral trade or investment. The only certainty when Modi became India's prime minister was that he would not be a fence sitter or a prevaricator on foreign affairs. As a strongman with a hardscrabble upbringing in the RSS, he has stamped his own personality and authority that make the Modi Doctrine one of its kind in the annals of Indian foreign policy.

Globalising Gujarat, Priming India

If the *Sangh Parivaar* was the school ground for sowing the seeds of the Modi Doctrine, the thirteen years, when Modi was virtually an elected sovereign of Gujarat, were the finishing ground on which the Modi Doctrine got rounded. Admittedly, the concept of 'sub-unit diplomacy' or 'paradiplomacy', i.e. foreign relations carried out by subnational, provincial or regional governments on their own to promote their respective local interests, was not Modi's invention. But he furthered it to an extent and duration that neither of his contemporaries and pioneers of this phenomenon—Chief Minister Chandrababu Naidu of Andhra Pradesh and Chief Minister S M Krishna of Karnataka—could.

Chief Minister Modi's foreign policy was transformative for Gujarat, whose GDP rose at an annual average rate of more than 10 percent continuously for a decade and surpassed India's national average. Domestic reforms and structural policy changes did account for the miracle of Gujarat turning into 'the growth engine of India', but this outcome could not materialise without a healthy advent of FDI into the state. Thanks to Modi's strategic marketing of the image of Gujarat as secure and different from the rest of India in welcoming investors seeking high returns, FDI equity inflows into Gujarat from 2002 to 2013 were to the tune of $9095 million. This meant Modi's state alone comprised a stupendous twenty-two percent of the total FDI that entered India.[35] And contrary to cases where FDI-fuelled influxes did not translate into poverty reduction, the overall poverty rate in

---

[35] Kochhar, Sameer. 2014. *ModiNomics: Inclusive Economics, Inclusive Governance*, Gurgaon: Skoch Media, p.51

Gujarat fell by 15.2 percent points when Modi held the reins there with his outward looking international pitch.[36]

The diplomacy Modi conducted from Gandhinagar, the capital of Gujarat, generated investments from global multinational giants such as Shell Gas, ABB, Siemens, Ingersoll Rand, General Electric, Hitachi, Novino, McCain, Heubach, Maersk, General Motors, P&O and DuPont, besides a beeline of Indian capitalists. One vehicle through which he could pull these foreign corporations to set up shops in Gujarat, even as other corners of India were warily seen as bureaucratic and politically risky for them, was the biennial Vibrant Gujarat Business Summit. In this jamboree of trade and culture, presaging the national commercial diplomacy strategy of the Modi Doctrine, the dynamic chief minister would personally hobnob with foreign honchos and diplomats, offering assurances which would be fulfilled to a large extent on the ground across the state where industries and infrastructure projects opened.

In his own words, the goal of these summits was 'to bring recognition to Gujarat. We invited the world to come and see Gujarat, and invest here. Confidence and trust are the greatest wealths of Gujarat, and I feel very contented on this achievement.'[37] Even Modi's critics acknowledged that these summits were efficient, innovative and cleverly branded by PR agencies.[38] Modi the *prachaarak* knew the magic formula of getting things done and then propagating about them in the right spin and language. All the razzmatazz that accompanies Modi on his foreign visits today, especially surrounding the copious amounts of FDI that he pulls into India, derive from this initial success of brand-building and selling in Gujarat.

As social media and Web 2.0 technologies were getting mainstreamed around 2004, Modi deployed technological tools and digital platforms to promote Gujarat to investors. Multimedia presentations, information technology (IT) based interfaces and a computerised environment greeted awestruck foreign CEOs and diplomats, creating a futuristic

---

[36] Panagariya, Arvind. 2014, 'Here's Proof that Gujarat has Flourished Under Modi', *Tehelka*, March 29th

[37] Makwana, Kishor. Op cit. p.317

[38] Mukhopadhyay, Nilanjan. 2013. *Narendra Modi: The Man, The Times*, New Delhi: Tranquebar Press, pp.352-355

appeal for Gujarat as a globalised avant-garde state. The perfection in event management and technology-suffused 'wow' factors, which are hallmarks of Modi's international outreach today, were already time-tested in Gujarat. In adopting technology for both domestic governance and his well-packaged sub-unit diplomacy, Modi was ahead of his peers and had set a trend.

A vintage video of Modi in the pre-chief ministership era of the 1990s shows that even at that nascent stage of the internet, he had become an ardent exponent of technology as an opener of new vistas. Introduced as 'very different' from typical old-fashioned RSS *prachaaraks* in his love of technology, and shown to be jabbing at a laptop keyboard in frames, he says that he has a hobby to 'learn about new things' via computers. When the internet arrived, he adds, 'I understood its potential and got lost in it, surfing the web until late into the night and informing myself about various developments around the world.'[39] Today, as prime minister, Modi has not changed much even as web-based platforms have greatly morphed. He wakes up every morning to reach out for his iPad and tries 'to keep up with the latest online applications ever…so much so that it is often Modi who introduces his younger staff to new technology.'[40]

In the context of Indian politics and diplomacy, such a technically open leader and communicator is rare. Speaking in 2013 at a Google Big Tent Activate Summit via Google+ hangout, Gujarat Chief Minister Modi proffered timely advice to fellow Indian politicos who were stuck in a pre-digital sepia-tinted universe,'The time has come for the political class to adapt to technology and reinvent itself. It needs to embrace the internet's many powerful facets. The political class needs to stop seeing technology as a problem creator, and start harnessing it in the right spirit.'[41] In 2015, during a Town Hall-style interaction from the headquarters of Facebook, with its CEO Mark Zuckerberg

---

[39] FTV. 2013. 'Later 1990s Rare Narendra Modi Interview when he was just a Party Worker', Falcon Tvision, September 1st. URL: https://www.youtube.com/watch?v=QbZkWT_hoXI Last accessed on Feburary 8th, 2016

[40] Price, Lance. 2015. 'India's prime minister is Addicted to his iPad too', *The Atlantic*, April 14th

[41] Bhattacharya, D.P. 2013. 'Tech-Savvy Modi says Politics must Embrace the Internet', *The Daily Mail*, March 21st

in tow, Modi expanded his counsel to his foreign counterparts,'To leaders all over the world, you are not going to gain by running away from social media.'[42]

As India's prime minister, Modi has communicated his foreign policy through e-books, websites, dedicated online portals for marquee multilateral events, Twitter feeds, Facebook posts and even emails and SMS messages sent to citizens of India about his tête-à-têtes with world leaders and IT wizards. The Modi Doctrine's *Samvaad* leg has given a complete makeover to Indian diplomacy due to these techniques of mass connectivity, which pushed India's hitherto stovepiped international messaging and image-building into a trendy, cyber mode.

For a Modi who was eager to 'wash off' the negative image circulated worldwide by the horrific anti-Muslim riots of 2002, which he termed as a 'blot during my tenure', all-out commercial diplomacy was a redemptive move. The stigma of being blamed for inaction or complicity in the religious violence and the related setback of visa denials from the USA and some European nations had to be answered with a comprehensive economic developmental agenda as well as outreach to those nations still open to courting him. Modi's economic diplomacy missions in those years took him to China, Hong Kong, Taiwan, Singapore, Israel, Japan, Uganda, Kenya, Japan, Switzerland, Mauritius, Trinidad & Tobago, Guyana, Jamaica etc.

One of the RSS friendships that was crucial for Modi to make headway in Asia and Africa when he was persona non grata in the West was with Ram Madhav, a former *prachaarak* and spokesperson with a wide network of diplomatic contacts around the world. Madhav was a key functionary serving in the backdrop for Gujarat Chief Minister Modi's global engagement activities and was, like Modi, seen to be suave, modern and acceptable for international audience. After Modi became India's prime minister, Madhav was made virtually 'ambassador at large' and had a distinct hand in organising landmark diplomatic events and in smoothing out the rough edges of the Modi Doctrine.[43] For the

---

[42] Warrier, Anu. 2015. 'Modi Sells Digital India to Silicon Valley Giants', *Khaleej Times*, September 28th

[43] Mohan, Archis. 2014. 'Ram Madhav: Modi's Ambassador at Large', *Business Standard*, November 29th

kind of mega roadshows that Modi put up as chief minister, vital tasks of coordination and networking were, thus, performed by his trusted RSS insiders and operatives, albeit those who were deemed to be more sophisticated and globally integrated.

One gets a flavour of the leapfrogging ambition Modi entertained in this sub-unit diplomacy from a quotable quote he issued in 2006,'Gujarat is not competing with other states like Maharashtra, Karnataka and Andhra Pradesh. We may surpass them. I want Gujarat to compete with China, Germany and Japan.'[44] The familiar sight of Prime Minister Modi travelling with a retinue of Indian business titans to ink deals with foreign counterparts was first tried out in the company of top Gujarati industrialists and technocrats who would fly along with him to global destinations in search of agreements and partnerships.

Just as Modi the Indian prime minister trumpets the authenticity of his hypermodern-yet-timeless Indian identity and projects the infinite muscle of India's human resource potential in his foreign travels, Modi the Gujarat Chief Minister had an agenda of promoting Gujarat's regional genius in international forums. There is a telltale video of him taking a ride on Japan's bullet train in 2012 and being asked by a journalist as to what is his 'magnet power' which makes hundreds of Japanese investors and CEOs queue up to meet him. Modi had responded,

'I am a representative of Gujarat. If Japan is attracted towards Gujarat, it is not due to Modi the individual, but sixty millions Gujarati people. Because sixty millions Gujaratis have shown commercial and industrial prowess, it becomes easy for me to explain Gujarat's worth to the world. The whole world, and especially a developed nation like Japan, is now attracted to Gujarat, and this makes all Gujaratis proud.'[45]

In the next chapter, we will see how this same messaging metastasized to encompass all of India in the diaspora diplomacy of the Modi Doctrine.

---

[44] Bhatt, Sheela. 2006. 'I Want Gujarat to Compete with China: Modi', *Rediff*, November 1st. URL: http://www.rediff.com/money/2006/nov/01modi.htm Last accessed on January 22nd, 2016

[45] TV9. 2012. 'Narendra Modi Travels in Bullet Train of Japan', TV9 Gujarati, July 29th. URL: https://www.youtube.com/watch?v=gJXdU3AVd9o&app=desktop Last accessed on February 2nd, 2016

As Modi's political heft grew within the BJP in his third and fourth terms, he began making more noticeable linkages between his sub-unit diplomacy on behalf of Gujarat and the national interests of India as a whole. In 2011, Modi left a positive impression in China as a go-getting chief minister who walks and talks the language of profit and business opportunity. But even then, with Modi not yet certain of emerging as a prime ministerial candidate, one observer had written,

'The invitation, the feting and extensive coverage of Modi's visit is China's way of engaging with what they see as a potential new establishment that may soon occupy the seats of power in New Delhi. If and when Modi succeeds the Chinese would be well prepared to engage the new establishment. The amount of coverage in Chinese media and the level of importance being given to the visit by the Chinese government are signs that they do seem to take Modi's chances rather seriously.'[46]

In June 2012, Modi dispatched a second delegation to China to lure manufacturing firms looking to relocate from their Pearl River Delta hub due to rising costs of production and cramped space. One of Modi's envoys from the Gujarat government paraphrased Modi's purpose of this targeting of China as spurred by a 'grouse that that in 2011, Chinese industries invested more than $60 billion in countries other than India, including Brazil and Russia. Why must India be left out?'[47] Just as Modi the prime minister manages to mix a globalist cosmopolitanism with an 'India first' ideology in his foreign policy, as a *prachaarak* and chief minister, he was able to leverage his Gujarati and Indian identities seamlessly in his sub-unit diplomacy to maximise mutual financial gains and wriggle out of the spell of Western isolation owing to the religious violence which rocked Gujarat after he took over.

Although Modi denied any political motives behind his peripatetic sub-unit diplomacy, executing it to the hilt for a decade earned him handsome personal rewards on his march to the zenith of Indian

---

46 Govindarajan, Amar. 2011. 'Modi Goes to China', *Centre Right India*, November 11th. URL: http://centreright.in/2011/11/modi-goes-to-china/#.VrhBZbduljo Last accessed on February 8th, 2016

47 Rameshan. Radhika. 2012. 'Shunned by US, Modi Courts Israel, Japan', *The Telegraph*, August 13th

politics. In 2012, the UK government terminated a nearly ten-year-long no-contact policy with him, citing pragmatic and legal considerations. That decision was a vindication of Modi's faith in pursuing a determined sub-unit foreign policy. It demonstrated how much he had contributed to the surge of India's states shaping the country's overall foreign policy.

Despite London's boycott of Modi on human rights grounds after the 2002 communal violence in Gujarat, British companies like Cairn Energy and Shell had been doing business in the state's oil and gas sector all along. But this was a trickle compared to foreign investments pouring into Gujarat from other parts of the world. As chief minister, Modi's strongman brand of capitalism enchanted not only India's corporate titans but also multinational corporations from continental Europe, Australia and the US. His aggressive salesmanship in Japan and China about Gujarat as an oasis quite apart from the rest of India in offering efficient governance, relatively lesser corruption and predictable business climate kicked off a beeline of foreign governments and companies to get a slice of Gujarat.

Modi's hyper-charged economic diplomacy hoisted Gujarat into the ranks of the top five states receiving FDI in India. The UK, which was coping with a serious economic crisis and absence of business confidence at home, could not have timed its rehabilitation of Modi better. Convictions of many perpetrators of the religious pogroms of 2002 by India's judicial system and the absence of legal guilt affixed to Modi himself eased Britain's choice to enter into 'active engagement' with him. The USA, which refused a visa to Modi in the past, fell next in line to normalise relations with an Indian politician who was seen as prime minister material of the future.

A crucial force in Modi's conversion from international pariah into an acceptable gatekeeper of a thriving Indian state was the intense lobbying machine of the Gujarati non-resident Indians (NRIs). One British diplomat informed me in 2012 that it was 'awkward' for Whitehall to handle nearly eight hundred thousand people of Gujarati origin on the UK soil, many of whom hero-worshipped Modi, by shunning high-level political communications with their patron in Gandhinagar. The fact that some advanced science and management institutions were also located in Gujarat due to Modi's exertions, and London's interests in forging research ties with them also fed into the rapprochement.

Since the liberalisation of India's economy in the 1990s and the almost simultaneous advent of coalition politics, the incentives for states to venture into the outside world and develop their own mini-foreign policies multiplied. From the pioneering days of competitive bids to usher in foreign investment by Chief Ministers Naidu and Krishna, the decentralisation of Indian foreign policy took on a life of its own. Modi rode the crest of what the American scholar John Kincaid labels as 'constituent diplomacy',[48] where market liberalisation and federalism combined to create incentives for provincial or sub-national governments to engage in independent international exchanges aimed at winning welfare objectives for their peoples.

Modi's remark after the UK's volte-face in 2012 that 'Gujarat and Europe will work together and prosper'[49] was startling because there was no mention of the word 'India' in it, even though the British viewed their opening of channels to him as part and parcel of oiling the broader UK-India relationship. Indian foreign policy at that time was manned by Manmohan Singh's central government which was politically opposed to the BJP. In hindsight, both in terms of trade and commerce and in raising awareness, Chief Minister Modi's foreign outreach was a net addition to India's diplomacy. Some actions of Indian states had unfortunately had an adverse impact on India's national-level foreign policy goals vis-a-vis neighbouring countries like Bangladesh and Sri Lanka. Modi's sub-unit diplomacy had the obverse impact—it gave the world a peek into the dynamism in some pockets of India.

Even after Modi's BJP formed India's first central government in three decades without needing a coalition party's crutches in 2014, the trend of more autonomy devolving into the hands of state governments to carve out foreign policies that have a bearing on themselves has gone on irreversibly. The era of a monolithic nation-

---

[48] Kincaid, John. 2003. 'Foreign Relations of Sub-National Units: Constituent Diplomacy in Federal Systems', in Blindenbacher, Raoul & Arnold Koller (eds.) *Federalism in a Changing World*, Montreal: McGill Queen's University Press

[49] Mitra, Devirupa. 2012. 'Gujarat, Europe will Work Together: Modi', *The New Indian Express*, October 12th

state with a centralised foreign policy is passé and Prime Minister Modi himself is alert to this dynamic. Since he thrived in sub-unit diplomacy from 2001 to 2014, he now empathises with chief ministers who want to emulate him and has in fact consulted and involved many of them in his signature foreign visits and agreements. Later in this book, I will show how under the Modi Doctrine, India's regions are roaring and affecting New Delhi's foreign relations more constructively than in earlier eras.

Around the world for success

The saga of Gujarat Chief Minister Modi fighting back international ostracism and gaining credulity in foreign eyes as India's heir apparent by 2012-13 bolstered his passion for diplomacy that is writ large in the Modi Doctrine. It also taught him unforgettable insights into the way the world is. The phoenix which rose from the ashes of international outcaste could plainly see that foreign policies of most so-called Western liberal democracies were at their root calculative and cunning, even though they were dressed up in moral values. When Modi was an upstart in Gujarat and was blamed for stoking majoritarian Hindu fundamentalism, Western nations could adopt a holier-than-thou attitude and shun him on grounds of threatening religious freedom of minorities. When Modi turned this foreign rejection around, diversified his international partners and used the language of 'log on to Gujarat. If you sow a rupee here, you will reap a dollar',[50] the same foreign powers which had originally rendered him untouchable came trooping in to scoop up profits and to deal with a would-be arbiter of India's destiny.

Shrewdness and cynicism are not part of the public expression of the Modi Doctrine, but as we will see later in this book, the Indian prime minister adroitly exploits the weaknesses of the international system for India's advantage. Indian statecraft goes back millennia to Kautilya or Chanakya, and Modi as India's prime minister has acquired the art of manoeuvring and dodging in the maelstrom of world politics. Given his full-blooded affinity for economic diplomacy, Prime Minister Modi

---

[50] Sharon, Meghdoot. 2004. 'The Architect of Modern Gujarat', *Business Standard*, January 2nd

might have initially seemed to be ignoring what the BJP labels as the crucial pillar of *Suraksha* or regional and global security.

We will see later in this book that these lacunae are slowly being filled as the Modi government's foreign policy matures. A geostrategic direction on what kind of world order India should be shaping, and the grand strategic questions of whether or not India is content to see China rising as a new hegemon or letting the US still dominate some regions of the world, are also by now ensconced within the Modi Doctrine. So, it is reductionist to see Modi's foreign policy as nothing else but an endless iteration of commercial salesmanship and business meets.

Apart from peddling business, the policy learning aspect of the Modi Doctrine, mooted earlier in this chapter as first manifesting in Modi's personality in the 1990s, was blossoming by the 2000s. Sudesh Verma has described Chief Minister Modi as an eager pupil on his foreign visits as, 'Every country Modi visited, he tried to learn new things and figure out if the same could be implemented in Gujarat. If he was impressed with zero tolerance against corruption in the country of Lee Kuan Yew (Singapore), he was also impressed by the tall buildings that housed business offices. The plan to have tall towers in Gandhinagar was drawn up after his visit to Hong Kong in 2004. He wanted to create an international financial hub on the same pattern. Modi visited the Three Gorges Dam to understand how this worked for China. He tried to translate this while developing the Narmada canal system. Modi visited the famous Masai Mara Wildlife Sanctuary in Kenya (and) tried to learn and observe things that could be implemented in Gujarat's Gir forests.'[51]

The open and globalised, rather than closed and insular nationalism of the Modi Doctrine germinated during the Indian prime minister's Gujarat stint. For Modi, India has much to give to the world in ideas and its ancient wisdom, but there is also plenty that it must absorb in the materialistic sphere. Most fascinating are the non-Western models of modernisation that Modi witnessed and imbibed in the 2000s. When he became India's prime minister, this background prompted some to speculate that he had an animosity towards the USA and Europe, and that he would nudge India to foster closer relations with Asian power

[51] Verma, Sudesh. 2014. *Narendra Modi: The Game Changer*, New Delhi: Vitasta Publishing, p.255

centres. Modi's repeated references to the 'Asian century' and his admiration for Lee Kuan Yew do indicate that he respects the economic strides made by non-Western states.

The awe and personal reverence Modi has for Lee was built over encounters when the former was Gujarat's Chief Minister and the latter was 'Minister Mentor' of Singapore. When the Western world had shut its doors to Modi, he found in Lee's government a gracious host and a facilitator of business linkages with Gujarat. Like most fans of Lee, Modi has asked himself how a man could 'miraculously' convert a divided, post-colonial backwater into a sleek financial powerhouse in one generation. It would be no exaggeration to state that Modi likens himself to Lee with the same focus on achieving India's modernisation through state-guided capitalism backed up by efficient governance, zero corruption and an emphasis on technological solutions.

Just as the founder of Singapore, who perfected the art of conducting foreign policy that would contribute greatly to Singapore's economic benefit, Modi, too, is spearheading India's external relations to make the outside environment as conducive as possible to resolve India's internal bottlenecks. The turnaround in foreign policy that is Modi's mark of distinction from 2001 to 2014 in Gujarat, and since 2014 for India, has the agility and ambition of one of the Asian Tigers and Tiger Cub nations that rose from nondescript to global power status within one generation. The phase of world history when India is surging to be a 'leading power' is quite different from that of Japan or China in the second half of the twentieth century, but Modi has seen enough of Asia's success stories to not want a similar trajectory for India to turn prosperous and powerful.

Yet, we will see in subsequent chapters that the Modi Doctrine is not geographically confined to or biased towards Asia or ill-disposed to the West. It is truly multidimensional, multi-vectoral and global in orientation, while synchronously visualising India as the future fulcrum of international affairs. The *prachaarak*'s mystical confidence in India's destiny is unshakeable, but for it to be realised, he is ever-ready to reach out, connect, communicate, befriend, exchange views, ideas, goods, services and find grounds of strategic convergence which redound to the glory of the motherland.

Chapter 2
Dancing with the Diaspora

If there is an Indian anywhere in the world, we don't look at the colour of passports, the colour of his blood. The relation with the Motherland is enough.[1]

The Fourth D

Narendra Modi often employs the concept of 'three Ds'—democracy, demography and demand—in his spiels about India's rise and inherent strengths. But through his foreign policy prioritisation and actions, he implicitly reifies a fourth 'D' that is turning out to be no less integral to the story of India's growing influence in the world, i.e. diaspora. The Modi Doctrine has notable successes thanks in part to the symbiotic relationship the Indian prime minister has fertilised with the vast panorama of NRIs and OCIs (Overseas Citizens of India, who subsume a diaspora category with fewer privileges that were formerly known as Persons of Indian Origin or PIOs) spread out across the world. Their adoration and fanatic fan following keeps Modi's stature as a highflier on the international stage, and his respect and attention to them lends Indian foreign policy a comparative advantage in those corners of the world where the diaspora has planted deep roots. The diaspora is oxygen

---

[1] NDTV. 2015. 'Thousands of Indians in Dubai Roar Approval through PM Modi's Speech', *NDTV*, August 17th. URL: http://www.ndtv.com/india-news/pm-modi-addresses-50-000-indians-at-dubai-cricket-stadium-highlights-1208230 Last accessed on February 9th, 2016

for Modi as a world leader, and Modi is the lodestar for the multitudes who departed India physically but not emotionally and culturally.

Harnessing the talents and loyalties of India's diaspora for improving the material conditions and international image of India is not Modi's creation per se, but he has walked the talk on this strategy like no other Indian prime minister since independence. From a historical and evolutionary standpoint, Modi represents a very different Indian state and nation than the one which approached the diaspora warily and hesitantly since 1947. The Modi Doctrine's diaspora diplomacy is at once a sign of how much India has changed in light of advancing globalisation of the twenty-first century, and of how much one man with a transformative vision can be a catalyst and accelerator of that change. As the previous chapter demonstrated, Modi the *prachaarak* has an uncanny knack for the pulse of people and the mood of the times. In his revolutionary diaspora policy, one can observe these capabilities functioning in top gear for a makeover of India's self-definition and self-worth.

The depth of Modi's reappraisal of India's role in the world and the corollary place of its 25 million odd diaspora is evident from a phrase he used for the homeland in one of his many electrifying speeches before doting NRIs and OCIs in Silicon Valley, USA, in September 2015, '*Bahuratna Vasundhara*' or a land rich with priceless gems that can keep giving generously for the well-being of the universe. Far from the stereotype of India as a poor developing country that survives on handouts and financial support from rich nations and which must prevent the dreaded "brain drain" to the Global North, he struck a chord by asserting that it has been a net giver of countless benefits, including a productive and intergrated migrant workforce that is also replenishing the homeland through the reverse process of 'brain gain.'[2]

To Modi, India is an unsung hero for the plethora of gifts it has showered in international affairs like the ethos of *Vasudhaiva Kutumbakam* (the world is one family), Vivekananda's gospel of spiritual oneness of humankind, Mahatma Gandhi's nonviolence and ecological conservation and the Indian model of 'live and let live' multicultural coexistence. In addition, he has left no stone unturned to heap praise

---

[2] Rajghatta, Chidananda. 2015. 'Brain Drain can become Brain Gain Anytime, Modi Points in his SAP Centre Address', *The Times of India*, September 28th

on the Indian diaspora as keepers of the flame who have been ideal migrants in their host nations by investing sweat and blood to develop those countries. The effect of this effort has been to remind host countries that people of Indian origin are invaluable assets to them and, by inference, that the bilateral relations with the Indian state are leavened by this incomparable human resource factor.

It is not uncommon today for heads of government and other prominent politicians of the host countries joining Modi on stage during his set piece primetime televised speeches abroad, and paying profuse homage to Indian immigrants and their descendants. In November 2015, with Modi in tow at the Wembley Stadium in London, the UK's prime minister David Cameron unleashed a moving tribute to British Indians,

'Over one and a half million people, you are teaching in our schools, policing our streets, starting up our businesses, serving in our armed forces, and displaying values of family, responsibility, enterprise and hard work. These are the values that our country needs more of. So, Prime Minister Modi, I hope you can see what I see every day, British Indians putting the great into Great Britain.'[3]

In November 2014, with Modi on stage at the Melbourne Cricket Ground, Australian prime minister Tony Abbott had declared,

'The greatest bond between our two countries is the half million Australians of Indian background who have contributed so much to building modern Australia. I want to say to all of you, your hard work, your commitment to family and community, your willingness to "have a go" has made this great country even greater. In any one year, there are about 40,000 Indian students studying here in Australia—many of them here in Melbourne. Our duty is to take care of them as our own and to let all of them become ambassadors for India here and for Australia when they go home. I say to all of my fellow Australians of Indian background: you have come to a magnificent country but you have come from a country that is led by a magnificent man.'[4]

---

[3] TNN. 2015. 'David Cameron Addresses Indian Diaspora at Wembley- Full Speech', *Times Now*, November 13th. URL: https://www.youtube.com/watch?v=zoCSWxfWT8Y Last accessed on February 9th, 2016

[4] IL. 2014. 'PM Tony Abbott's Speech at the Reception in Honour of PM Modi', *Indian Link*, November 19th

Obama, whose sizzling chemistry with Modi was dissected in the previous chapter, has also seized upon Modi's mobilisational talents to affirm the stellar role of the three million Indian Americans in advancing relations between India and the USA. At a gathering of corporate leaders in New Delhi in January 2015, with Modi beside him, Obama spelt out the White House's belief that the Indian community in the US held the key to unlocking greater economic integration of the two countries. The US president had remarked,

'I am proud to announce a new public private partnership to help millions of proud Indian Americans directly invest in India's future. Our new Indian diaspora investment initiative will allow folks back home (in America) to generate a new stream of financing for Indian businesses that are investing in non-traditional and too often over-looking markets. Whether it is providing healthcare to rural communities or improving water and sanitation, this is going to be another spark to India's economic engine.'[5]

The Modi Doctrine's dynamic diaspora policy has been so incredibly fruitful that the Indian prime minister's own language and strategy are being parroted by his foreign peers, offering NRIs and OCIs a psychological morale booster of incalculable value. Having been tacitly and explicitly accused by Indian leaders in the past of forsaking India in search of greener pastures, the Modi Doctrine's pride of place for the diaspora comes as music to the ears of Indians who had been treated like unwanted stepchildren by New Delhi for decades.

From benign neglect to outright disowning of the rights and interests of OCIs and NRIs, the post-independence Indian state was prone to blaming them for jettisoning India due to its poverty, infrastructural deficiencies and low quality of life. Well into the 1990s, it was commonplace conversation in India that the 'brain drain' or exodus of skilled and educated Indians was a cause of the nation's underdevelopment, and that the NRIs are living it up by turning their backs on their less fortunate kinsmen in India.

Nehru's policy of 'active dissociation' from the Indian diaspora owing to concern that connecting and advocating for them would impair the sovereignty of host countries left a bitter taste for generations

---

5 Roberts, Dan. 2015. 'Obama Enlists help of Indian Diaspora in US to Bolster Stronger Economic Ties', *The Guardian*, January 26th

of Indian-origin communities abroad. His cold view of overseas Indians was encapsulated in a comment made in India's Parliament in 1957, 'If they adopt the nationality of that country we have no concern with them. Sentimental concern there is, but politically they cease to be Indian nationals.'[6] Ajay Dubey argues that post-independence India's neglect 'saw the suppression, subjugation and marginalization of the Indian diaspora globally because…rivals and opponents of Indians found the Indian diaspora helpless and unsupported by its mother country.'[7]

One activist of the Indian diaspora from Mauritius, Anand Mulloo, writes that his community which was,

'…once told by Nehru to forget about Old India…can no longer be dismissed as a bad memory that anybody would prefer to forget. New India must lend its ears to the voices of the diaspora. The ever-expanding and strengthening diaspora prides itself of the millionaire NRIs in UK, US, Canada and Australia. And the diaspora cannot but revert from time to time to Mother India in a bid to recharge its emotional and spiritual batteries…after years of neglect and abandon, New India wakes up and decides to remember her forgotten children overseas.'[8]

Thanks to the Modi Doctrine, that 'New India' has materialised, and it is uniting the long-lost flock to the mainland in a two-way process of rediscovery that has raised India's power projection capacity.

From the late 1990s, when Modi was a functionary in the BJP, and Vajpayee was the prime minister of India (1998-2004), there was a sea change in the way the Indian government approached the diaspora. The party declared NRIs and OCIs to be 'a part of the great Indian family' and Vajpayee called for 'a partnership among all children of mother India so that our country can emerge as a major global player.'[9] Having been shut out of patronage-based funding of domestic capitalists that was cornered by the ruling Congress party for decades after independence,

---

[6] Nehru, Jawaharlal. 1961. 'Reply to Debate on Foreign Policy in Lok Sabha. 2 September 1957', in GOI (ed.) *India's Foreign Policy: Selected Speeches, September 1946-April 1961*, New Delhi: Government of India, p.130

[7] Dubey, Ajay. 2011. 'India and the Indian Diaspora', in Scott, David (ed.) *Handbook of India's International Relations*, London: Routledge, p.258

[8] Mulloo, Anand. 2007. *Voices of the Indian Diaspora*, New Delhi: Motilal Banarsidass, p.26

[9] Cited in Dubey, Op cit. p.261

the BJP always looked out of India for succour. It deserves credit for rediscovering and assuaging hurt feelings of the Indian diaspora, a process that sped up when Vajpayee was the prime minister.

Once the floodgates were opened to a proactive diaspora policy, numerous policy measures and programmes were unfurled to bridge the gulf between NRIs and OCIs and the homeland. A diaspora Indian day, a ministry for overseas Indian affairs, investment facilitation centres and improvement in connectivity facilities were progressively implemented by the Vajpayee and Manmohan Singh governments. But what the Modi Doctrine has done is think bolder, go farther and galvanise the diaspora like never before, for comprehensive cultural, political and economic empowerment. The halting steps of previous regimes have now been accelerated to the next level by Modi through spectacular speeches backed up by long-due reforms like merging the PIO card and the Overseas Citizen of India (OCI) card, and melding the Ministry of Overseas Indian Affairs (MOIA) into the Ministry of External Affairs.

Darling of the *desis*

If there were a popularity poll among NRIs and OCIs about Indian prime ministers since independence, Modi would be the undisputed favourite. By some reckonings, he surpasses even celebrity Bollywood icons in pulling power in the eyes of the Indian diaspora, who are otherwise voracious consumers and aficionados of India's motion picture productions.[10] This star status accrues not because he is the present occupier of India's most powerful political office, but due to his unprecedented championing of the diaspora's causes and his linking of India's fate to that of its distant offspring.

Even as the chief minister of Gujarat, Modi had a keen eye on channeling the financial and cultural resources of Non-Resident Gujaratis (NRGs) for his developmental agenda in the state. As early as 2002, he had launched an association of NRGs known as Group of American Businesses in Gujarat (GAB-Gujarat) to create 'brand

---

[10] Kalita, Mitra. 2014. 'It's official: NRIs love Narendra Modi more than Shahrukh Khan', *Quartz*, September 18th. URL: http://qz.com/267689/its-official-nris-love-narendra-modi-more-than-shahrukh-khan/

awareness about Gujarat in US' and correct 'doubts created in foreign countries.'[11] His cutting-edge ideas of e-governance and replacing red tape with red carpet to make the administrative apparatus more efficient were first shared with NRGs during the overseas Indian day events organised by the central government of Vajpayee. The combination of enormous wealth and prevalence of conservative Hindu sects among the NRGs worked ideally for Modi to utilise for generating inward FDI into his state and to lobby against the visa denial regime that was slapped on him in the USA and Europe. At the tenth overseas Indian day in 2012, Gujarat chief minister Modi could boast that 'despite the global financial crisis, Gujarat's economy was boosted by record-breaking investments made by the Indian diaspora and companies.'[12]

Since becoming India's prime minister, Modi has magnified the same strategy to a pan-India level, wooing NRIs and OCIs hailing from different regional, religious and linguistic groups as well as different socioeconomic classes. Bikram Vohra, a prominent voice of the diaspora based in the Persian Gulf, calls the Indian diaspora Modi's 'trump card' and explains why he is so beloved among a cross-section of them,

'A man like Modi is a marketable symbol of the country we have left. Modi comes as a salvation making us feel good about being Indians abroad. We do not have to apologise for him. He hits the right buttons. He is articulate, he is sartorially elegant, he is religiously eclectic, choosing houses of worship with a populist eye, he has a Marcus Antonius inflection in his words and so, in capsule, NRIs have found their pop star poster boy. A better bet than the parade ground sergeant major fierceness of Indira Gandhi or the soggy sandwich blandness of Manmohan Singh, this man knows how to package himself. Modi does not embarrass us. On the contrary he injects NRIs with a shot in the arm and improves the morale.'[13]

---

[11] PTI. 2002. 'Group Floated to Promote US Business in Gujarat', *The Economic Times*, October 10th

[12] Singh, Didar&Irudaya Rajan. 2015. *Politics of Migration: Indian Emigration in a Globalized World*, New Delhi: Routledge, p.142

[13] Vohra, Bikram. 2015. 'Why NRIs Gush Over Modi', *Firstpost*, November 13th. URL: http://www.firstpost.com/world/patriotism-from-a-distance-modi-is-the-perfect-poster-boy-for-nris-in-london-as-they-arent-involved-2504576.html Last accessed on February 10th, 2016

Having interacted and empathised with the wounded psyches of the diaspora, Modi relishes sloganeering about 'good days' having arrived at last under his rule in the homeland, and assures NRIs and OCIs that 'earlier, you felt ashamed of being born Indian, now you feel proud to represent the country.'[14] The array of statistics and anecdotes he narrates about how India under him has modernised, has reduced corruption and has turned into the apple of the world's eye owing to its economic growth and political influence draw endless cheering from the diaspora, who naturally compare the orderly and prosperous conditions of their naturalised countries of residence with the India that used to be chaotic, corrupt and mired in abysmal quality of life.

Modi's sellout speeches to the diaspora in memorable foreign locales have a property of shining light on India from outside the country. Like Vivekananda in *fin de siècle* America and the nationalist independence fighter Subhas Chandra Bose in Germany, Singapore and Burma during World War II, Modi is redefining India from abroad. He thrilled 18,000 Indian-Americans in New York's iconic Madison Square Garden in September 2014 with his artistry and common touch, holding forth on what India and Indians are, and how these concepts have evolved. His virtuoso performance in Sydney's Allphones Arena in November 2014 was carried out in the same vein, wherein a grand overseas setting with excited hero-worshipping audience became the platform for reaffirming the virtues and standout qualities of the global Indian who is at home wherever she or he resides.

Modi the orator has, of course, cannily worked the crowds and inspired them even in India, particularly during national holidays like the Independence Day. But when he is abroad, showy events like those held in Madison Square Garden and Allphones Arena are aimed at rallying OCIs and NRIs, as well as connecting them emotionally to resident Indians with a sense of shared pride. That the Indian prime minister is consciously attempting to revive the umbilical cord between Indians who left and those who reside in India, is obvious from the subject matter of speeches in New York, Sydney, Dubai, London etc.

---

[14] Haidar, Suhasini. 2015. 'In Shanghai, PM Marks One Year in Office', *The Hindu*, May 17th

He moves effortlessly between profusely glorifying the expats for their professional accomplishments and reminding them about their duties towards their motherland, which needs their investments, skills and lobbying potency.

He is at one go acknowledging that the OCIs or NRIs belong to their adopted country, and also reminding them at the same time that they are simultaneously also a part of a globalised family of Indians. For the millions in the diaspora spread across the planet through historic and recent patterns of migration, Modi is demagogically systematising the message that the Indian government and people care for and love them. He always addresses them as 'my dear countrywomen and men' and talks of the 'Indian society that is diffused worldwide', melting hard feelings and arousing the diaspora to their feet. The BJP's *Samvaad* or dialogue pillar of foreign policy is personified when Modi is in the company of the diaspora. For flashbulbs and shutterbugs, diaspora diplomacy is the Modi Doctrine at its rhetorical best.

Take, for instance, Modi's memorable usage of a factoid at the Wembely Stadium in November 2015 to rouse British-Indians to their feet and make a foreign policy point about the umbilical links between India and Britain. He 'holds up his watch. What's the time he asks. He turns his timepiece upside down and says that Indian time and UK time are so close that you only need one watch to tell what time it is in both places. Whatever time your watch shows in the UK, turn it upside down and it will show the time in India. Try it. It works.'[15] For the NRIs and OCIs assembled there, it was part entertainment and part confirmation that fate and magical time bind their land of adoption with their motherland, and a vindication of the path they chose to have both the British pie and the Indian curry.

Shashi Tharoor once wittily rephrased NRI as 'Never Relinquished India'.[16] But as was mentioned earlier, many past Indian governments failed to tap into this ingrained cultural and civilisational connection,

---

[15] WSJ. 2015. 'Narendra Modi's Speech at Wembley Stadium: As it Happened', *The Wall Street Journal*, November 13th

[16] Tharoor, Shashi. 2006. *India: From Midnight to the Millennium and Beyond*, New York: Aracade Publishing

which the Trinidadian Nobel laureate of Indian origin, V.S. Naipaul, described as 'a great tenderness' for India despite all its painful and repulsive facets.[17] Modi has succeeded in shifting the discourse about impressions of India as a so-called Third World country frozen in time where snake charmers cast spells on superstitious people and semi-naked peasants sleep hungry. To show that contemporary India is progressing ideationally and technologically, he quipped memorably in Madison Square Garden that 'our ancestors played with snakes but we now play with the (computer) mouse', and added for effect that 'our youth spin the whole world around with the mouse.'[18] Similarly, at Allphones Arena, Modi convinced his diaspora fans that India has the energy and speed to lead the world and offer solutions to global problems. He thundered in Sydney that 'India alone has as much human resources as the whole world put together', and that India could don the mantle of 'guru of the world'.[19]

At the Shark Tank in San Jose, California, he thanked the diaspora for spearheading India's transformation,'Your fingers created magic on the keyboard and the computer, and this gave India a new identity. Your skill, commitment and innovations are wonderful. Sitting here, you are forcing the world to change.'[20] At a community reception for Indian expatriate workers in Doha in June 2016 he avowed, 'people of India in Qatar are never away from India even for a minute. They are re-living India on the soil of Qatar.'[21] In each of these outings, he catered to aspirations of the NRIs and the OCIs so that they hold their heads high and give back in cash and kind to India's economic and political rise. The *desis*, as the Indian diaspora are nicknamed, have found a catharsis in the Modi Doctrine.

---

[17] Naipaul, V.S. 1984. *Overcrowded Barracoon*, New York: Vintage Books, p.51

[18] AP. 2014. 'Modi Wows Madison Square Garden Saying India won't Look Back', *The Telegraph*, September 28th

[19] NDTV. 2014. 'PM Narendra Modi's Full Speech at Sydney's Allphones Arena', *NDTV*, November 17th. URL: https://www.youtube.com/watch?v=3l0ZxzTfbJo Last accessed on February 10th, 2016

[20] TNN. 2015. 'PM Narendra Modi to Indian Diaspora: India is Waiting for You', *The Times of India*, September 28th

[21] NM. 2016. 'PM Modi Addresses Indian Community in Doha, Qatar', *Narendra Modi*, June 5th. URL:https://www.youtube.com/watch?v=71IQVrfa3U4Last accessed on June 8th, 2016

Bolstering Mini-Indias

Modi's diasporic support today is broad and adequately representative of India's socioeconomic, ethnic and religious diversity. It is a catch-all constituency that demonstrates his own evolution from the chief minister of Gujarat to India's prime minister, from RSS *prachaarak* to a syncretic Indian nationalist, and from right of the political spectrum to the centre. Addressing British-Indians in the Wembley Stadium in November 2015, he insisted that 'diversity is India's pride and its strength, and despite the country being home to many religions, over 100 languages and 1500 dialects, Indians have proved how to live together.'[22] Television coverage of Modi's mega events for the Indian diaspora often focuses on Muslims, Sikhs and other minorities with visible markers of appearance, roaring in approval from the bleachers, to reinforce the message that he is accepted across the board among NRIs and OCIs.

Since Modi is attacked by political rivals in India and a few baiters within the diaspora as a 'divisive figure' who stood for Hindu chauvinism, the approval of the vast majority of NRIs and OCIs has been critical for his reinvention as India's deliverer and rejuvenator. Simultaneously, it has made the Indian diaspora more harmonious and capable of coming together to lobby for Indian interests in their respective countries of abode. Vijay Chauthaiwale, the BJP's architect for Modi's mobilisation of the Indian diaspora, has dwelt at length on the Modi effect in patching rivalries and divisions among the NRIs and the OCIs,

'The organising committees, which we set up, consist of representatives from all communities—linguistic and professional groups of the diaspora. For example, the Bay Area organising committee (for the PM's visit to the Silicon Valley in September 2015) has people from all linguistic and religious communities as well as techies, businessmen and hoteliers. We have brought these professional groups together, which would otherwise rarely happen. Even in the UAE we had a substantial number of Muslims in our organising committee. The PM's persona goes beyond any community appeal, religious appeal or sectoral appeal. It also goes beyond the BJP's appeal. People are willing to come together in the name of the PM. It

---

[22] PTI. 2015. 'India Full of Diversity, it is our Pride and Strength: PM Narendra Modi', *The Economic Times*, November 14th

can happen only with Modi. When the larger goal is defined, people are willing to forget, at least temporarily, their differences. The PM's visits are becoming a great unifying force for the communities.'[23]

Smart, symbolic choices in Modi's foreign itineraries and references are part of this unifying agenda. As the first Indian prime minister to visit the UAE in thirty-four years in August 2015, he broke the myth of the Hindu nationalist Modi whose base lies in north India by espousing the cause of NRIs—75 percent of whom are Muslims and Christians from the south Indian states of Kerala and Tamil Nadu. To reiterate that he stood at the centre of the ideological spectrum, he stepped into the Sheikh Zayed Grand Mosque in Abu Dhabi, the third largest in the world after the holy mosques of Mecca and Medina, and clicked a selfie with Sheikh Nahyan, the Minister of Culture of the UAE. It was a special moment to lift spirits of the NRIs working in harsh circumstances and to relay back in India that he respects each and every religion.

As we saw in the previous chapter, personal diplomacy is a standout characteristic of the Modi Doctrine that has smoothed India's relations with numerous strategic partners. The UAE has become a yardstick for it thanks to the chemistry between Modi and Abu Dhabi's Crown Prince Sheikh Nahyan, whom the Indian prime minister has referred to as 'my close friend' and 'special friend' whose 'love I can never forget.' The sight of Modi and Nahyan rising above diplomatic protocols and receiving each other in airports, embracing warmly in public, and committing to improve working conditions for the vast Indian diaspora in the UAE is a reassuring one from the interreligious angle.

Especially remarkable is Modi's success in getting the UAE's government to allot land for construction of a Hindu temple in Abu Dhabi to serve the needs of Indian expatriates. This long-sought move burnished the UAE's credentials as a relatively moderate Islamic country and marginalised the few extremist Emirati Islamists who forbid promotion of places of worship for 'infidels.'[24] What is more, Sheikh Nahyan's government has requested Modi to 'send teams of

---

[23] Mohan, Archis. 2015. 'PM's Visits a Unifying Force for the Diaspora: Vijay Chauthaiwale', *Business Standard*, August 22nd

[24] Roy, Shubhajit. 2015. 'TV Cleric Fired after he Slams UAE Grant for Temple During Modi Visit', *The Indian Express*, September 25th

Indian Imams to train its preachers in using moderate Islam to check radicalisation in that country's mosques at a time the ISIS' spread is worrying it.'[25] The prospect of India's liberal Barelvi clerics spreading their message of tolerance and peace in the heart of the Middle East via the Modi Doctrine is a notable cultural export that boosts the confidence of six million NRIs in the Gulf countries, of whom many are Muslims who suffer from various forms of discrimination for belonging to an 'inferior' variant of Islam.

At the Wembley Stadium, Modi deliberately lavished attention on an Indian Muslim math teacher in the state of Rajasthan who developed dozens of Android phone applications for education and distributed them for free among students. The prime minister proclaimed that 'my India is in that Imran Khan from Alwar'[26], in a rejoinder to opposition cries about growing religious intolerance in the country. He also posited Sufism, which has flourished in India for centuries, as an antidote to the ISIS-type Islamist fundamentalism and observed, 'things happening in the name of terrorism in the world today, sometimes I feel that had the Sufi tradition gained strength, had its influence in Islam grown, whoever understood the tradition would never have thought of picking up the gun.'[27] Modi has also congratulated the NRIs and the OCIs for being role models of coexistence, since 'wherever we go, we show people how to live in harmony and how to care for everyone around.'[28] For the heterogeneous Indian diaspora, such utterances are disarming and befitting to be inspired to rally behind Modi and his foreign policy goals and to be assured that India's multicultural heritage is undiminished.

The Modi Doctrine is effectively pressing in cultural diplomacy to make India more desirable in the eyes of the world, breaking down old

---

[25] Kasturi, Charu. 2016. 'UAE Keen on Indian Imams', *The Telegraph*, February 10th

[26] Panicker, Raija. 2015. 'My India is in the Imran Khan from Alwar, says PM Modi at Wembley', *NDTV*, November 14th. URL: http://www.ndtv.com/india-news/my-india-is-in-the-imran-khan-from-alwar-says-pm-modi-at-wembley-1243208 Last accessed on February 11th, 2016

[27] Roy, Amit. 2015. 'PM Holds Aloft India's Diversity but makes Reference to Islam and Gun', *The Telegraph*, November 13th

[28] TNN. 2015. 'As it Happened: PM Narendra Modi in UK', *The Times of India*, November 13th

stereotypes and enabling the NRIs and the OCIs of all hues to keep their chins up. The projection of Modi as an umbrella nationalist icon under whom every ethnic or religious group flourishes has not eroded his earlier base of Hindu nationalists among the diaspora. For Right wing *desis*, Modi remains a *Hindu Hriday Samrat* (or Emperor of Hindu Hearts) and 'presents to the Hindu NRI the possibility of resolving his or her identity crisis. He is the leader who is unabashedly Hindu, who kept the Navratra fast on his trip to the United States…and promises to these dislocated, culturally confused Hindus a new dawn in their land of origin, a reason for them to feel proud of their original home from where they or their ancestors came.'[29]

Modi's unassailable status with observant Hindu *desis* also derives from the pervasive organisational roots of the RSS and the BJP among sections of the diaspora. Voluntary bodies of NRIs and OCIs like the Hindu Swayamsewak Sangh (HSS) have branches across the world and are linked to the Overseas Friends of BJP, a networking hub for the party in the diaspora. Together, these *Sangh Parivaar* institutions are 'as active, if not more, in putting things together for Modi's public appearances (abroad) as the foreign ministry.'[30] As Chuathaiwale stated, 'once the structure is in place, I back off…but I am still in touch… I help in coordination with the PMO (Prime Minister's Office). The (Indian) embassy is there, but we facilitate.'[31] Nimble-footed *prachaarak* support cadres are Modi's unofficial ambassadors in the diaspora, mobilising on a scale that the bureaucratic and understaffed Ministry of External Affairs is incapable of doing. Meghnad Desai, a prominent British-Indian intellectual, has dissected how Modi's Hindu and commercial memes come together to produce an overwhelming effect among *desis*,'There's an inherent conservatism to any diaspora. Add to that, a large chunk of them are businessmen or business professionals who aren't very political. That's the core of PM Modi's support base amongst the diaspora, as his

---

29 Ashraf, Ajaz. 2014. 'What Explains Non-Resident Hindus' Attraction for Modi?', *Scroll*, November 27th. URL: http://scroll.in/article/691653/what-explains-non-resident-hindus-attraction-for-modi Last accessed on February 14th, 2016

30 Ramaseshan, Radhika. 2014. 'Lie-Low Signal to BJP Friends in Australia', *The Telegraph*, October 26th

31 Mishra, Vandita. 2015. 'Meet Vijay Chauthaiwale, the Man Behind Narendra Modi's Madison Square Template', *The Indian Express*, September 15th

twin messages of pushing trade, while retaining religious conservatism and right-wing beliefs perfectly align with theirs.'[32]

Sabka Saath: Plebeians to Aristocrats

Since the Indian diaspora is varied in its occupational and class compositions, Modi has practised full-spectrum diplomacy to encapsulate all their disparate hopes and expectations. His governance mantra of *Sabka Saath, Sabka Vikaas* or take everyone along and work for everyone's welfare is mostly understood in the context of domestic policymaking within India. But it also has a foreign counterpart, especially in the Modi Doctrine's diaspora component. When Modi had visited the UAE in August 2015, he demonstrated a steadfast commitment to the working class diaspora and reiterated that India values them as much as the millionaires and billionaires among the NRIs and the OCIs. He addressed a gigantic crowd at the Dubai Cricket Stadium to buoy the spirits of Indian workers who make up more than 40 percent of the UAE's labour force and roughly 30 percent of the UAE's population, and contribute as much as 20 percent of India's total inward remittances. He reminded the audience that when the West had slapped economic sanctions on India after it conducted nuclear weapons tests in 1998, Indian workers doing menial jobs in the Gulf countries made a huge contribution to fill India's coffers. In return, he announced an array of new government schemes to assist working class NRIs on consular, immigration, workplace and other contingencies, and also promised that Indian diplomatic missions would be more accessible and answerable to grievances.

But apart from new policy initiatives like the Indian Community Welfare Fund, what impressed the downtrodden NRIs in the Gulf the most was Modi's passionate advocacy for them as his main priority. He said, 'This part of the world has Indians from very poor families who have come here to make ends meet. Whether I can do something for America (which has wealthy NRIs and OCIs) or not, if I fail to work for you I become restless.'[33] During his UAE travels, the Indian prime minister took out time to visit a

---

[32] Haidar, Suhasini. 2015. 'Mr. Modi's Diaspower', *The Hindu*, November 14th

[33] TNN. 2015. 'PM Narendra Modi's Full Speech in Dubai', *Times Now*, August 17th. URL: https://www.youtube.com/watch?v=w-AhA-yjeho Last accessed on February 14th, 2016

labour accommodation in the industrial city of Abu Dhabi and surprised everyone by mingling with the *desi* workers, asking them one-on-one about their working conditions and difficulties. One 'visibly moved' and excited labourer, Arshad Khan from Bihar who was employed at Al Dhafra Waste Management Company, commented that 'it was one of the most pleasant moments of his life, as his Prime Minister asked him about the problems the workers are facing.' His co-workers added that it was 'the first time such a leader has visited them' and that Modi's 'interaction with workers was a strong message to them.'[34] Similarly, Modi's sharing of a meal with blue collar NRI labourers in Qatar in June 2016 inspired the diaspora greatly. One elated worker was quoted after the meeting, "PM Modi is the best PM, he sat with us, asked us about our troubles," Another colleague chimed in, 'It was like meeting someone from our family, it got me teary-eyed.'[35]

Modi has also made a mark for himself in responding speedily and unconditionally to SOS calls from Indian expatriates of working class backgrounds who get stranded in war zones. The remarkable alacrity and efficiency with which his government rescued thousands of helpless NRIs from Yemen, Iraq, Syria and Ukraine when they were trapped in armed conflict areas with immediate threat to their lives and liberties have no parallels in independent India's history. The BJP celebrated Modi's timely attention to the underprivileged *desis* in distress by asserting, 'Indians living in foreign countries now have confidence that there is a government in their country, which is concerned about them and is ready to support them when needed.'[36]

Modi himself reflected on the global significance of his coordinated approach to the NRIs and civilians of other nations trapped in Yemen,'Wherever I went abroad recently, I received a lot of praise for one thing—for saving citizens from around 48 countries from Yemen. Be it America, UK, France, Russia or Japan, we helped citizens from all countries...because of this effort, the world admired India's philosophy

---

[34] Haider, Haseeb. 2015. 'Modi Handshake Leaves Workers Speechless', *Khaleej Times*, August 17th

[35] Rajeshwaril, Anikita. 2016. 'PM Modi Meets Indian Workers in Doha, Moves their Hearts', *The Times of India*, June 6th

[36] PTI. 2015. 'BJP Lauds PM Modi on Evacuation of Indians from Yemen', *The Indian Express*, April 5th

of *sevaparmo dharma* (service is the ultimate religion).'[37] It was a *prachaarak* moment and also a symbolic highpoint for a prime minister who likes quoting the RSS' populist philosophy of *Antyodaya* or uplifting the economically weakest sections of society.

Contrary to depictions of Modi as a pro-business conservative, he has retained and rationalised subsidy schemes for the poor in India to 'give them a fair chance to succeed'[38] Some Modi watchers conjecture that he has made a Leftward turn and 'could possibly be moving towards framing a new framework of 'Hindu socialism' to maximise electoral benefits.[39] But since *desis* living abroad are yet to get facilities to cast votes in Indian elections through electronic or postal ballots, there is no discernible direct political calculus behind the Modi government's attentiveness to the blue collar diaspora. Nor is there a narrow Hindu religious onus in Modi's comprehensive coverage of NRI and PIO issues.

Rather, we should treat his ken for the poor Indian emigres as a strategic impetus of the Modi Doctrine to identify all of India's principal assets overseas, and to gather them under an overarching nationalistic agenda to project Indian power globally. The Modi Doctrine's diaspora policy is a diversified strategy of appealing across class distinctions, which have historically presented a fractious community of *desis* that is internally riven with conflicts.

The expat worker model of the UAE's economic development has been carried largely on the shoulders of the NRIs, and Modi's dialogue with the rulers of Abu Dhabi and Dubai perforce includes matters of improving their living conditions and lessening the exploitation of the unskilled category among them. On the eve of his visit to India in February 2016, Nahyan acknowledged that 'the UAE government and its people valued the contributions of the Indian community in the UAE, and the important role they have played in the various phases of the national development process.'[40]

---

37 ENS. 2015. 'India's Work in Yemen was Praised by World Leaders: PM', *The Indian Express*, April 27th

38 PTI. 2016. 'Subsidies will not be Eliminated', *The Statesman*, January 30th

39 Mukhopadhyay, Nilanjan. 2016. 'Enter, the Hindu Socialist', *The Economic Times*, February 13th

40 KT. 2016. 'India UAE Bilateral Relations are Solid, says Mohammed bin Zayed', *Khaleej Times*, February 11th

Likewise, Modi's meetings with the high officials of the Saudi Arabian government have attempted to increase Riyadh's appreciation of the over two million NRIs working in the kingdom. The Indian external affairs minister, Sushma Swaraj, has said that 'Modi is paying special attention to Gulf NRI welfare issues' and that she herself 'is seriously focusing upon issues pertaining to Indian workers in the region.'[41] That this sincere effort to shore up the diaspora is part of a long-term strategy of the Modi Doctrine is evident from the prime minister's decision in early 2016 to wind up the Ministry of Overseas Indian Affairs (MOIA) which was founded in 2004 and merge it with the Ministry of External Affairs (MEA) that Swaraj heads. This institutional reform was undertaken not just as part of a bureaucratic streamlining and downsizing vision, but also in light of unaddressed grievances of the Indian diaspora and its skepticism of the MOIA 'as a platform for rich businessmen and politicians only.'[42] By segregating diaspora matters from the overall foreign policy of India from 2004 to 2016, opportunities arose for patronage-based politicking, emanating from domestic considerations to erode the functional utility of MOIA. The merger of the ministries under the Modi Doctrine has sent an unmistakable signal that diaspora affairs are now treated as a major leg upon which India will march to great power status.

D for development

Not all the NRIs in the Gulf region are engaged in low-paying, backbreaking menial jobs. The UAE has transformed into a 'dualistic economy', where there are traditionally low-skilled profiles like domestic helpers and construction labourers, but also an advanced white collar sector clustered around finance and Information Technology. 28 percent of high-skilled professionals entering the UAE happen to be Indians with technical and managerial backgrounds. Modi is seeking to encourage such trends so that India's image in the Middle East shifts

---

41 Mohammed, Irfan. 2014. 'Indian Govt. sets Focus on NRI Issues', *Arab News*, July 8th

42 Sathish, V.M. 2016. 'Merger of Ministries by Government in India Sparks Debate among NRIs', *Emirates 24/7*, January 11th. URL: http://www.emirates247.com/news/emirates/merger-of-ministries-by-government-in-india-sparks-debate-among-nris-2016-01-11-1.616861 Last accessed on February 14th, 2016

from a cheap labour exporting nation to a provider of knowledge-based manpower that spurs faster economic growth in that region, and ties it closer to India's own booming service sector.

In the USA, Modi has gone to great lengths to woo the hi-tech diaspora in Silicon Valley to motor India's economic march. His quip that India has transcended talk of public and private sectors and moved on to nurturing the 'personal sector', meaning 'individual enterprise and innovation', and his presence at unique events like 'hackathons' in September 2015 connecting India-based and Silicon Valley-based entrepreneurs, have inspired Indian youth. The Indian-origin chief executive of Google, Sundar Pichai, welcomed Modi to Silicon Valley by mooting a linkage between the IT revolution that has already happened in Silicon Valley and the digital revolution that Modi desires to implement in rural and small towns of India. Modi's diaspora diplomacy in the US West Coast aims to build a bridge between the most successful community of NRIs and OCIs, and the hidden creative geniuses who are yet to emerge to limelight from India's nooks and crannies.

Modi's ambitious Startup India initiative to promote a culture of entrepreneurship and product development among Indian youth is tagged to the inbuilt yearning among NRIs and OCIs to transfer capital investment, high-end knowledge, expertise and know-how that will turbocharge the homeland's economic takeoff. During his Silicon Valley visit in 2015, he spoke about the 'possibility of the digital bridge' wherein NRIs and OCIs who account for fifteen percent of all the startups on the USA's West Coast, can team up with India's budding innovators and 'can touch the life of a young child in a remote village (of India).'[43] Memoranda of Understanding (MoUs) between India's software industry association, NASSCOM, and the legendary NRI software networking group, The Indus Entrepreneurs (TiE), 'to support the creation of a vibrant ecosystem to foster technology entrepreneurship in India'[44] are some offshoots of Modi's belief that the diaspora has the key to India's economic development. Umesh Sachdev, an Indian IT innovator and 'technopreneur', has said that the prime

---

[43] PIB. 2015. 'Speech by Prime Minister Narendra Modi at the Startup Event', *Press Information Bureau*, September 27th

[44] PTI. 2015. 'PM Modi's US Visit: 7 MoUs Signed to Boost Startups in India', *The Economic Times*, September 28th

minister's personal involvement in this field is exciting and that the Indian government's strategy 'should revolve around the three Ps—Promotion, Policy and *Pravaasi* (non-resident) Indians.'[45]

Critics who mock Modi's foreign travels as high in theatrics and low in concrete takeaways ignore the extraordinary rise in inward FDI that India has enjoyed since he took office as well as the intangible gains of creating a circle of mutual inspiration between the diaspora and aspirational Indians in the mainland. In Silicon Valley, Modi fused the American dream with the Indian one at the people-to-people level. 'Inderica'—a confluence of talent and originality between India and America—is on the anvil thanks to the prime minister's active encouragement. This convergence is represented through formations like the Indian Investment Initiative (III), a vehicle to channel Indian American funds into small and medium enterprises in India with the support of the government of the USA.

Modi is well aware that calls to patriotism and self-belief whipped up through speeches are not enough to turn around the dismal image of India in the eyes of its own extended family abroad or to extract the most from them for India's nation-building projects. The Modi Doctrine on the diaspora aims *inter alia* at maximising FDI from the Indian diaspora to motor India's economic growth. Modi's adrenalin-pumping and chest-thumping speeches in New York, Sydney, London, Toronto et al are appetisers to translate goodwill into larger volumes of inward FDI from the diaspora. As he told over eighteen thousand *desis* in Singapore in November 2015, 'FDI is not only Foreign Direct Investment but also First Develop India.'[46]

Towards this end, the Modi government has undertaken policy reforms such as treating non-repatriable investments by NRIs and OCIs as equivalent to domestic investment so that they will not be subject to restrictions related to FDI.[47] The PIO and OCI card schemes have been

[45] Srinivasan, V.L. 2016.'Indian PM to Announce Action Plan for Startups', *ZDNet*, January 6th. URL: http://www.zdnet.com/article/indian-pm-to-announce-action-plan-for-startups/ Last accessed on February 14th, 2016

[46] PTI. 2015. 'FDI is First Develop India, Narendra Modi tells Indian Diaspora in Singapore', *Deccan Chronicle*, November 25th

[47] PTI. 2015. 'Government Relaxes FDI Norms for NRIs, OCIs and OCI', *The Economic Times*, May 22nd

merged since January 2015 by amending the Citizenship Act, giving the former enhanced work, residence and property rights in India and ending byzantine reporting rules. This is the closest India has come to granting dual citizenship to the diaspora and has energised NRI and OCI participation in the Indian economy. NRIs have been permitted to invest in India's National Pension Scheme, delivering relief to low-wage emigres who lack social security in their countries of work. Physical connectivity between nodal hubs of Indian diaspora concentration and different cities of India has also been fast forwarded to ease travel. The British-Indian industrialist Swraj Paul, who was prevented from investing in India by protectionist local capitalists in the 1980s, has argued that thanks to Modi's penchant for simplification and easing of bureaucratic hurdles, 'it was for the first time in three decades that the Indian diaspora is feeling that their contribution to the country has been recognised.'[48]

Modi has ridden the wave of diaspora acclaim to invite NRIs and OCIs to woo them to invest substantial sums in productive sectors of the fast-growing Indian economy. At the Overseas Indian Day in January 2015, he outlined a 'host of opportunities' and reiterated his 'conviction that the Indian diaspora is a great capital for us in the global context. The more we nurture it, the stronger will be our presence globally.'[49] Historically, as political scientist Devesh Kapur has pointed out, FDI from the Chinese diaspora into China exceeded FDI from the Indian diaspora into India by a whopping ratio of 25:1. If one examines overall financial inflows (FDI plus remittances and portfolio investments) into China and India by their respective diasporas, the former receives only twice as much as the latter in absolute terms. In other words, remittances and foreign institutional investments (FII) dominate over FDI in the calculi of the Indian diaspora.[50]

The reason why Indians abroad for years preferred not to give back to India through the FDI route was exactly the same as to why

---

[48] PTI. 2014. 'Narendra Modi's New Policies for NRIs a Welcome Step, Indian Diaspora will Respond: Lord Swraj Paul', *The Indian Express*, September 29th

[49] FE. 2015. 'PM Narendra Modi to NRIs: Opportunities Await You, Let's Transform India', *The Financial Express*, January 9th

[50] Kapur, Devesh. 2010. *Diaspora, Development and Democracy: The Domestic Impact of International Migration from India*, Princeton: Princeton University Press, p.105

individuals or companies worldwide hesitated to come to India. India's red tape, corruption, politicisation of land acquisition, industrial protectionism etc. have earned a notoriety captured by the World Bank's 'Ease of Doing Business Index', which ranked India at a sorry 140 out of 189 countries before Modi took over as India's prime minister. For perspective, China stood at 93rd position at that time, ironically making it a more profitable return-on-investment proposition for the Indian diaspora than 'Mother India'.

Heartwarming invocations to the potential of India and the greatness achieved by expat Indians have to be buttressed by continued policy reforms at home for Modi's 'Make in India' to appeal to the Indian diaspora. The BJP pioneered and mastered the art of securing financial contributions from overseas Indians for political campaigns in India, but the bigger challenge is to exponentially raise amounts of FDI from the diaspora's purses by improving India's governance record. Modi is walking the talk as much as possible by presenting a clean and modern state in front of the world and by tying the NRIs and OCIs in a circle of trust. He has also urged the diaspora to invest in other domestic flagship programmes of his government like Digital India, Clean Ganga, Clean India and Skill India. Upon the suggestions from *desi* lobbying outfits, the Modi government has also introduced tax-free infrastructure bonds that are specially custom-made for NRIs and OCIs. The 'Team India' that Modi bandies about as his workhorses for national transformation packs in enough emotional and pragmatic space to include the diaspora.

Yet, observers have cautioned Modi against taking the diaspora for granted. One writer put his finger on the pulse by opining in August 2015 that 'India's infrastructure is still a shambles, bureaucracy still strangles the country and the much promised red carpet for NRI investors is a long way from being rolled out.'[51] The gap between Modi's breathtaking policy pronouncements on easing visa restrictions and their actual enforcement by India's obstructive officialdom remains a troubling one. With real estate and land acquisition policy changes yet to materialise and fructify, many NRIs and OCIs remain optimistic about India as an

---

[51] Dinda, Archisman. 2015. 'Mr. Modi, NRIs are not Just Money Bags', *Gulf News*, August 22nd

investment destination, but are waiting for even better times to come. Most of them realise that Modi's wholesale modernisation of India is not a quick-fix, small-impact plan, but one with medium-to-long-term gestation periods that will eventually bring substantial changes.

As one diasporic editor from Australia, Ramesh Tanna, puts it,'even though the NRIs of America, UK and other parts of the world have prospered, they have not forgotten India and their native country remains in their heart. While enjoying all the riches and amenities in a foreign land, far away from their motherland, they do desire that similar amenities, progress and various avenues of happiness are available in India also. They have full confidence that Modi can deliver this. This is the prime reason why the NRI community looks up to him and has high expectations of him.'[52]

Lobbying for international power

Apart from economic and cultural leverage, the Modi Doctrine is explicit in seeking to reap political advantages for Indian foreign policy via the lobbying energy of a rejuvenated and reconnected diaspora. Ram Madhav, the RSS and BJP functionary who is Modi's right-hand man in diaspora affairs has commented that 'we are changing the contours of diplomacy and looking at new ways of strengthening India's interests abroad. They can be India's voice even while being loyal citizens in those countries. That is the long-term goal behind the diaspora diplomacy. It is like the way the Jewish community looks out for Israel's interests in the United States.'[53] Chauthaiwale has also spelt out how the Indian diaspora can act as cheerleaders for India by reaching out to local media, legislators and citizens in their countries of residence, 'They can tell them about the good changes taking place in India and remove the image of India as an inefficient place to visit and invest in.'[54] The Indian American academic Ronak Desai has likewise argued that Modi is looking to expatriates to 'provide him with powerful

---

[52] Tanna, Ramesh. 2014. 'With Modi, NRIs Think the Time is Now', *The Indian Diaspora*, December 16th

[53] Lakshmi, Rama. 2015. 'India wants to turn 25 Million in the Diaspora into Global Ambassadors', *The Washington Post*, February 18th

[54] Ibid.

constituencies of support abroad, capable of influencing the policies of their adopted countries.'[55]

Politicisation of the diaspora and their involvement in lobbying on behalf of India are not new processes, but they are being revived and reorganised to match India's great power aspirations under the Modi Doctrine. As early as 1994, the House India Caucus was formed on Capitol Hill in the USA through the endeavour of an enterprising and patriotic NRI, Kapil Sharma, who was inspired by the example of the Congressional Black Caucus which had a track record of winning legislative favours to advance the cause of African Americans.[56] NRIs and OCIs were the fuel for recruiting and sensitising American legislators into what became the Congressional Caucus on India and Indian-Americans. They were the force behind diluting the USA's economic sanctions on India after it conducted nuclear weapons tests in 1998, and also in pushing President Bill Clinton to intervene and force Pakistan to withdraw its invading army from Indian Kashmir during the quasi-war of Kargil in 1999. They also campaigned incessantly to prevent appointment of diplomats considered to have 'anti-India'outlooks to key State Department posts.

In 2002, NRIs and OCIs formed the US India Political Action Committee (USINPAC) that was modelled on the American Israel Public Affairs Committee (AIPAC), and the former plunged into endorsing candidates and funding them for local American election contests, strengthening the Congressional Caucus, and influencing debate, legislative voting and foreign policy framing in Washington D.C. on many burning issues pertaining to India. One of the early advocacy issues which the USINPAC took up was the visa revocation of Modi when he was chief minister of Gujarat. It bombarded Congressmen and policymakers to lift the visa ban on grounds that Modi was a democratically elected politician and that censuring him in that fashion was a 'premature', 'misguided' and 'unilateral' move that would impair India-USA relations. For fifteen years, the USINPAC has been a vigilant voice in Washington and in states of the USA with large Indian-American populations against Pakistan-sponsored terrorism and

---

55 Desai, Ronak. 2014. 'Modi's NRI, NRI's Modi', *The Indian Express*, December 2nd

56 Sanchez, Rob. 2004. 'Pledge Allegiance— to India', *The Social Contract*, Volume 14, Issue 4, p.275

American military aid to Pakistan. It also played a stellar role in carving out an exception for India on civil nuclear commerce with the USA, and promoted trade preferences for Indian exports to the USA.[57]

However, during the latter part of the tenure of Manmohan Singh, Indian-American lobbying waned due to the absence of a single galvanising issue like the nuclear deal,[58] as well as a general disenchantment with India's economic slowdown and what the NRIs and OCIs considered to be Singh's lacklustre leadership. Many Indian-Americans contributed to Modi's election victory in 2014 and the USINPAC's Sanjay Puri has expressed 'genuine excitement' among them after he became India's prime minister owing to the impression that he is a 'strong leader.'[59] Within months of Modi's inauguration in New Delhi, NRIs and PIOs in the USA lobbied to get him to address a joint session of the US Congress. The parallel to the Jewish lobby as a template has today increased in the minds of politically active NRIs and OCIs in the USA, thanks to Modi's own inclination to ramp up strategic ties with Israel and his 'aim to be able to enthuse the Indian diaspora to band together like the Jewish groups to speak for India's interests to the US leadership.'[60]

In September 2014, Modi took personal interest in openly meeting Jewish lobbyists in New York and is believed to be curious to understand how they are so organised and powerful in Capitol Hill and the White House. Insiders said at that time one of the Prime Minister's 'biggest efforts' was to 'consolidate, strengthen and improve the profile of the Indian American community to lobby and wield greater influence on US policymaking, just as the powerful Jewish lobby influences state policy.'[61] Modi is reported to have urged the Jewish lobbyists 'to help push for bettering India-US and India-Israel ties', and the Zionist

---

[57] USINPAC. 2016. 'About USINPAC', *USINPAC*, URL: http://www.usinpac.com/index.php/home/aboutusinpac Last accessed on February 15th, 2016

[58] PTI. 2013. 'Indian Americans' Interest in Lobbying for Indo-US Ties Wanes', *The Times of India*, February 7th

[59] Roche, Elizabeth. 2014. 'Narendra Modi Likely to Leverage Rising Clout of Indian Americans in US Visit', *Mint*, September 25th

[60] TNN. 2014. 'Jewish Lobby in US Bats for India', *The Times of India*, December 15th

[61] Chatterjee, Mohua. 2014. 'Push for India Lobby on Jewish Lines?', *The Times of India*, September 25th

Organization of America (ZOA) was involved in working together with NRIs and OCIs to whet public interest during Modi's tour of Silicon Valley.[62] M.R. Rangaswami, a Silicon Valley investor and an Indian diaspora activist, has reflected on the peer exchanges from the Jewish lobby as, 'We're learning a lot from the Jewish diaspora here and what we have noticed from the Jewish diaspora is that they're willing to contribute, invest, and write checks…Because of the size of India, we could become a much larger community (than the Jews) in terms of population and also in terms of diversity.'[63]

Parallel to Modi and the official apparatus of the Government of India that is promoting political activism of the Indian diaspora in the USA, the BJP as a party has also come up with an action plan to reorient its overseas branches from cultural events and professional networking to lobbying and formation of 'pressure groups'. They have been tasked with targeting 'local lawmakers, Parliamentarians, media and other leading figures and create awareness about our country', and to also 'join hands with the Indian Embassies and hold independent programmes to showcase India's contribution to the world.'[64] What drives the current generation of Indian lobbyists is a devotion to Modi's brand of leadership, 'an emerging version of deeply nationalist India; (not) much interested in appearing on the international stage as Nehruvian, Anglophile or Westernized. Instead, they want India to represent itself as a global economic and political power, having long shed its colonial trappings.'[65]

For the Modi Doctrine's central thesis of establishing India as a 'leading power' to pan out, the diaspora's lobbying capabilities have to be lifted outside the USA in parts of the world where it has traditionally not been vocal, strategic and interventionist. Modi's global travels are

---

62 Majumder, Kunal. 2015. 'Why a Powerful American Jewish Group is Supporting Modi's San Jose Gig', *Catch News*, September 23rd, URL: http://www.catchnews.com/world-news/american-jewish-group-modi-san-jose-event-california-america-silicon-valley-netanyahu-israel-1443006125.html Last accessed on February 15th, 2016

63 Lerner, Adam. 2014. 'The New Indian Lobby', *Politico*, December 14th

64 Sharma, Pratul. 2015. 'BJP Bid to Turn NRI Friends into Lobbyists', *The New Indian Express*, January 25th

65 Sathian, Sanjena. 2015. 'Narendra Modi's Secret Weapon', *Ozy*, URL: http://www.ozy.com/provocateurs/narendra-modis-secret-weapon/41339 Last accessed on February 15th, 2016

incomplete without mobilising the Indian diaspora, no matter how big or small in size and influence, to work for India's future. His electrifying speeches in Canada, Singapore, Malaysia et al have a clear undercurrent of wanting to whip into shape the local NRIs and OCIs to be active votaries for the 'new India' that he represents. Even for the minute Indian expatriate communities in countries like Russia, France and Germany, Modi's 'community reception' events when he visits such nations are meant to infuse an organisational verve and political purpose that have been missing amongst India's European diaspora. The lobbying experience of *desis* in Europe, which pales before that of their much more affluent, technically adept and highly educated American kinfolk, is being boosted as Modi projects an India that they can be proud of.

To see the Modi Doctrine at work in shoring up a weak Indian diaspora body, one can study the way he wooed NRIs and OCIs in Moscow at a 'Friends of India' event in December 2015 to promote the currently missing people-to-people ties. He motivated each Indian student enrolled in a Russian university to encourage five Russian friends to visit India for tourism. Encouraging the diaspora to become cultural ambassadors for India, he said, 'Russians are already attracted to India. Your work should be to open the door and take them in, hold their fingers and bring them to India…as tourism grows, Russians will carry memories back home. The seeds of these memories will produce trees of bilateral relations that have the cool shade of friendship and will draw our two nations ever closer.'[66] Similarly, to the few thousand NRIs and OCIs based in China, Modi repeated the message, 'people in China are eager to know about India. You (Indians in China) are the best people to take India to Chinese citizens. Encourage five Chinese nationals to come visit India. India's tourism will grow, but more than that, China's people will have a new perspective of understanding India.'[67]

From the commoners to the VIPs among the diaspora, the Modi Doctrine has charted out captivating tactics for how each can lobby

---

[66] DD. 2015. 'PM Modi Speech at Friends of India Event', *DD News*, December 24th, URL: https://www.youtube.com/watch?v=1_nPv2Dxyiw Last accessed on February 15th, 2016

[67] PMO. 2015. 'PM Modi at the Indian Community Reception in Shanghai', *Prime Minister's Office*, May 16th, URL: https://www.youtube.com/watch?v=OTfopgrTzFs Last accessed on February 15th, 2016

for India's glory as per her or his respective station and capacity. Modi must be credited for also skillfully playing the kinship card in the diaspora that is geographically closer to India's borders in strategically located islands like Seychelles, Mauritius and Sri Lanka. By linking mainland India to 'little Indias' in the Indian Ocean, he has ensured that the *desis* in these countries will make a critical difference in shaping their governments' foreign policies toward India. Neither China nor the USA can tug at the hearts of people in nations such as Mauritius, the Maldives, Seychelles and Sri Lanka the way 'Mother India' can. When Modi invoked the umbilical cords of cultural affinity in Port Louis, Victoria and Colombo in March 2015, it was more than a rhetorical flourish. He was also reminding the world that the Indian Ocean derives its ethos and character from India, which is back with a bang in the water body named after it.

The *desi* as a hero

The diaspora diplomacy of the Modi Doctrine has not only reorganised and raised the salience of NRIs and OCIs in their lands of residence, but has ultimately also transformed the way Indians in the mainland look at the diaspora. All the packaged televised masterpieces of oratory to the diaspora which accompany Modi's foreign visits have two audiences—the *desis* going wild in front of him and the millions of Indians back home who have started seeing NRIs and OCIs in a new, positive light. One of the principal reasons why FDI from the Indian diaspora into India has lagged that from the Chinese diaspora into China has been a cultural block in India against NRIs as 'not required Indians'. The Chinese scholar Zhiqun Zhu argues that Indians in India proper have for a long time viewed their diaspora negatively as betrayers, deserters and opportunists, and FDI from them as skewing India's social iniquities. In contrast, the Chinese in China have been less ideologically biased. They 'warmly received' money and help from their large and wealthy diaspora and subscribed to the positive metaphor of overseas Chinese as 'fallen leaves' who will eventually 'return to their roots' in China.[68]

---

[68] Zhu, Zhiqun. 2007. 'Two Diasporas: Overseas Chinese and Non-Resident Indians in their Homelands' Political Economy', *Journal of Chinese Political Science*, Volume 12, Issue 3, pp.288-289

By the time Modi took over the task of India's global renaissance, attitudes within the country towards *desis* had already been morphing for the better. Modi's notion of 'brain gain' through a give-and-take between the homeland and the diaspora had been circulating for years in India. But by passionately implementing the diaspora portion of the Modi Doctrine in the far corners of the globe, he has essentially put the *desi* on a pedestal as a hero who is India's pride and an extension of the mind and body of the Indian nation. As he told one mass of NRIs and OCIs in Malaysia, while multitudes back in India watched on television, 'India is not confined to its territory. India exists in every Indian in every part of the world.'[69] The re-imagination of who is 'Indian' is happening not just among the diaspora but within India, thanks to the Modi Doctrine's strategy of conjoining all the scattered pieces of Indian-ness and presenting a formidable force before the world.

Although the Modi Doctrine has mobilised the diaspora to act as a strike force for international power projection, out-of-the-box ideas to maximise welfare of NRIs and OCIs remain unimplemented. Despite Modi's strenuous efforts to cater to the protection of labour rights of low-skilled Indian emigrants in the Gulf countries, the abusive environment has not been fully rectified. I have argued elsewhere that bilateral negotiations, consular access and grievance redressal mechanisms are not sufficient to redress chronic abuses of Indian blue-collar workers in the Middle East and that 'a bolder multilateral diplomatic effort has to be devised by New Delhi' wherein the principal migrant-supplying countries to that region (India, Pakistan, Bangladesh, Sri Lanka, Indonesia, Vietnam and the Philippines) can 'coordinate a unified position on minimum wages and decent treatment of their nationals.'[70]

Likewise, a plan to establish an exclusive university for returning children of NRIs and OCIs was given a go-ahead by the Indian government way back in 2007, as a way of protecting the diaspora from extortion by private Indian universities that charged exorbitant fees and had low standards. But this worthy proposal has not yet been

---

[69] IANS. 2015. 'Modi Lauds Malay Indians, Announces $1 Million for Students', *The New Indian Express*, November 22nd

[70] Chaulia, Sreeram. 2008. 'Blue Collar Immigrant Blues', *The International Indian*, April, p.76

acted upon. When Modi himself was chief minister of Gujarat, he had bid for hosting this NRI University and so did the state of Kerala.[71] Ultimately, like many creative suggestions pertaining to thickening the connection between the *desis* and the mainland, this idea remained unconsummated.

Modi is India's first 'ideas Prime Minister' who is open to experimenting and launching new initiatives if they assist his broad vision and single mission to make India a leading power in the world. The Modi Doctrine, which is not set in stone but work in progress, will be immensely more effective if it incorporates or rediscovers ideas that deserve due attention. Modi is loved by the *desis* because he does not harangue them with what he wants from them, but listens to them with empathy and fills them with hope. His 'great capital' of the diaspora is behind him, but wants more in the years to come to realise their dreams.

---

[71] Bhushan, Kul. 2008. 'Hectic Lobbying on for NRI University', *The Tribune*, April 18th

Chapter 3
The Business of India is Business

Being a Gujarati, money is in my blood...commerce is in my blood. I understand these matters. Businesses do not need concessions. They only need the correct environment to flourish in.[1]

Reclaiming the commercial nation

The Modi Doctrine is more than a strategic map for India's quest to great power status. At a deeper level, it is a template to reform Indian identity to suit the ambience of the twenty-first century and to rediscover a national psyche from a golden past when India had a seafaring, outgoing and global character. Modi sees himself both as a moderniser who is open to integrating India into the contemporary world economy as well as a cultural nationalist who yearns to revive the positive aspects of India's ancient and medieval economic glory. His economic diplomacy is driven by a sense of India retaking its position as a leading commercial power that once determined prosperity and business on a planetary scale.

The historian Prakash Charan Prasad has depicted India as 'the master of the foreign trade of Europe, Asia and Africa', and 'an integral part of the ancient commercial world which extended from the Mediterranean Sea to the Indian Ocean.' He adds that 'the Indians built

[1] PMO. 2014. 'PM Narendra Modi Addresses Business Meet in Japan', *Prime Minister's Office*, September 1st. URL: https://www.youtube.com/watch?v=3FokpNlWGsU Last accessed on February 16th, 2016

ships, navigated the sea and monopolised the international trade both by sea route and land route.'[2] Indian merchants were ubiquitous in trading centres and acted as middlemen between the West and Asia by the virtue of their geographic location and skillful navigation of the monsoon winds.

There was no major civilisation where Indian manufactured goods and commodities were not found. So mighty was India's commercial reputation in the ancient times that the Roman writer Pliny lamented that 'not a year passed in which India did not take 50 million sesterces (silver coins) away from Rome' as payment for Indian and East Asian spices, textiles and luxury goods.[3]

For cultural nationalists like Modi, India's fall from this pinnacle as an economic superpower happened due to foreign invasions, colonial rule and misguided inward-looking policies of the post-colonial Indian state. When Modi's followers declaim that his ascent to India's prime ministership was the moment for India's 'real' independence to commence, there is an implicit undercurrent of India regaining its lost commercial prowess and special status in the world. As Gurcharan Das writes,

'With a 5,000-mile coastline, India has historically been a great trading nation and in some periods, commanded as much as 20% share of world trade (compared to 2% today). It always had a positive balance of trade with the world until the Industrial Revolution in 19th-century England when the mills of Lancashire made our handloom textiles technologically obsolete. After Independence we forgot our trading past, closed our borders in the name of a bogus idea called 'import substitution', denying ourselves the prosperity of international trade. We only opened up in 1991. Today, Modi is trying to recover that past.'[4]

In fact, Modi's own birthplace in Gujarat, Vadnagar, was an important centre for international trade in the first millennium and served as a land port to connect to the Silk Route. He is conscious of the trading legacy of his ancestors. As the chief minister of his state, he was attributed to a zinger that offered a glimpse of his natural self, 'Gujarat is all about trade

---

[2] Prasad, Prakash. 1977. *Foreign Trade and Commerce in Ancient India*, New Delhi: Abhinav Publications, pp.31-32

[3] Takacs, Sarolta & Eric Cline. 2007. *The Ancient World*, New York: Routledge, p.398

[4] Das, Gurcharan. 2015. 'Modi is Building on India's Wondrous Trading Past', *The Times of India*, June 14th

with tradition, commerce with culture, enterprise with entertainment and development with disaster management.' Even as prime minister of India, he has at times harked back to the entrepreneurial heritage of Gujarat. Addressing Indian expatriates in Malaysia, he reminisced, 'From the coast of Coromandel and Kalinga, the ocean carried trade, commerce and culture to the Malaya Peninsula. If there is trade, Gujarat cannot be far behind. So, Gujaratis also joined the trade.'[5] No Indian prime minister before Modi has had this inborn knack for commercial matters, and it is therefore unsurprising that economics is a vital element of the Modi Doctrine.

Hard-charging for FDI

Modi comes across as a sharp business brain with an earthy, commonsensical grasp of monetary matters and a clear liking for financial issues. Most of his public utterances are laced with whopping macro-level statistics about thousands of crores of rupees and millions and billions of dollars of production, savings, investment, sales, exports etc. Security analyst Raja Menon's contention that 'Modi is an economic animal, and he will make India's growth the chief factor in his foreign policy'[6] is not off the mark. Economist Amitendu Palit argues that Modi is guided by the logic that 'high rates of economic growth cannot be generated only by domestic policies and initiatives. These need to be matched by external engagement that, apart from serving geo-strategic imperatives, would be economically proactive by enabling greater exchange of goods and services and fostering business collaborations between India and the rest of the world.'[7]

As we noted in an earlier chapter of this book, Modi's pre-prime ministerial exposure to non-Western centres of economic prosperity led him to admire and learn from examples like China and Singapore, which transformed themselves from their so-called 'Third World' status to middle and high-income societies in the span of one generation.

[5] BS. 2015. 'Speech by Prime Minister Shri Narendra Modi to the Indian Community in Malaysia', *Business Standard*, November 22nd

[6] MacAskill, Andrew & Kartikay Mehrotra. 2014. 'Modi to Use Courtship by World Leaders to Aid India's Growth', *Bloomberg*, May 23rd

[7] Palit, Amitendu. 2015. 'Economics in Narendra Modi's Foreign Policy', Paris: Institut Français des Relations Internationales, p.2

As a keen interlocutor with the East Asian Tiger economies, Modi is convinced that the FDI-led manufacturing-based model of growth is what India needs to lift itself out of the throes of poverty and youth unemployment. According to economist Sanjeev Sanyal, Modi has 'a very specific development strategy' of 'moving India away from its current services-driven growth trajectory to an East Asian-style export-led growth model, based on the mass deployment of labour and capital' for manufacturing, and also 'creating a virtuous cycle of savings, investment, exports and employment creation.'[8]

Others opine that Modi's economics is sui generis, and has its own unconventional paradigms and pathways about how India can grow rapidly. Sameer Kochhar in his book *Modi Nomics* argues, 'Modi Nomics eschews "isms". Modi feels that neither the Soviet style socialist path nor the free-market Western capitalist economy is the answer for India. He is of the firm view that India must craft a unique blend of its own that would leverage the nation's unique strengths and catapult it to the centre-stage of the global economy.'[9]

Either way, the model Modi has laid out for India's future is reliant upon FDI, and the expansion of India's trade with the rest of the world. For financing India's late industrialisation and infrastructural metamorphosis, Modi is conscious that he requires oodles of FDI and has striven to attract as much external investment as possible by dangling his oft-cited 'red carpet'. As he told one assembly of financiers in the City of London in November 2015.

'Never before was India so well prepared to absorb talent, technology and investment from outside. I can assure you that it will get better and better in the coming days. We will be open to welcome your ideas, innovations and enterprises. We are open to carry out necessary corrections in our policies and procedures. India is among the most open countries and at this point of time, it is wiser to be in India.'[10]

---

[8] Philip, Joji. 2014. 'Modi Trying to Replicate East Asian Growth Model in India: Sanjeev Sanyal', *Mint*, October 1st

[9] Kochhar. Op cit. p.13

[10] TNS. 2015. 'India most Open to FDI, Modi tells Investors', *The Tribune*, November 13th

In June 2014, barely a month in office as India's prime minister, Modi addressed young officers freshly inducted into the Indian Foreign Service (IFS), and advised them to project India's full trade and commerce potential globally. That economic diplomacy has mattered greatly to him from the onset is obvious from what he told these probationers, 'The focus should be on the expansion of trade and commerce, and technology transfer. Zero-defect manufacturing and packaging and presentation are among the areas to grow India's exports. Indian herbal medicines were among the best in the world, but are lagging behind Chinese products due to poor packaging. Also, Indian handicrafts have not been presented properly to the world.'[11]

Fuelling India's GDP growth was a cardinal objective of Indian foreign policy even before Modi came to the helm, but the onus he has given to FDI and trade is unseen and unheard of. Indrani Bagchi wrote just before Modi became the prime minister that, 'Manmohan Singh has been beating a similar drum for years, but Modi and his policy team promise to set implementation goals with timelines. Economic development, he has promised, will be hard-wired into diplomats' KRA appraisals. It could include incorporating the foreign trade department of the Commerce Ministry into MEA, and use them to create trade missions in key capitals.'[12]

Eventually, some of these institutional shakeups did not occur due to bureaucratic turf battles, but the various arms of the Indian government have looked more coordinated and unified when it comes to promoting FDI and foreign trade. Modi's dogged pursuit of FDI in every foreign engagement, and his push within organs of his government to go on an all-out economic diplomacy drive ensured that India jumped from fifth place to first as the most favoured destination for foreign investment in 2015, surging ahead of the perennial favourites, viz. China and the USA.[13] A series of 'big bang reforms' to ease regulatory overload, GDP growth of over 7.5 percent per annum, and the salivating prospect of industrialisation through the

---

[11] BS. 2014. 'PM Wants IFS to Help Boost Exports', *Business Standard*, June 13th

[12] Bagchi, Indrani. 2014. 'Perestroika for Foreign Office: Modi Promises to Transform how Indian Diplomats do their Job', *The Times of India*, May 4th

[13] HT. 2015. 'India Emerges Top FDI Destination Leaving Behind China, US in 2015', *Hindustan Times*, September 30th

'Make in India' campaign, have produced a reversal of trends under Modi. India, which had under a previous regime witnessed a net outflow of FDI, has become an object of attention for anyone anywhere in the world with investible surpluses. The plodding elephant that was the Indian economy has been redesigned into a roaring lion which is fleet-footed, dynamic and ready to prowl for markets and business opportunities.

At the heart of this giant leap forward sits Modi the helmsman, spearheading a vastly improved and an almost unrecognisable state-to-investor relations paradigm in India that has won international approbation. The Modi Doctrine does pursue traditional diplomatic channels of government-to-government, government-to-people and people-to-people relations, but it has innovated in the 'G2B' or government-to-business sector. G2B refers to the complex of ties between public administrative entities and private corporations, and has been applied in the discipline of management studies largely to domestic relations between the state and the business community. But the Modi Doctrine has taken it to the international arena by forming a special bond of trust between foreign corporations and the Indian government. India may have been famed for customary hospitality to foreigners, but its record of being open and welcoming to foreign investors has been pathetic since independence due to ideological and protectionist impulses. Modi has thrown out this negative baggage and redefined what it means to be 'business-friendly' on a transnational scale.

In 2014, he narrated an anecdote to illustrate G2B in action while addressing Japanese industrialists and financiers in Tokyo.

'As chief minister of Gujarat, I had understood specific requirements of Japanese businesses. We Gujaratis knew nothing about the sport of golf and what golf courses were. But as Japanese investor delegations started puring into our state, I realised their tastes and am proud to say that I established world class golf courses to facilitate Japanese investment in Gujarat. This was proof of the ideal kind of coordination needed between a proactive government and investors.'[14]

[14] BJP. 2014. 'PM Narendra Modi Keynote Address at Business Luncheon in Tokyo, Japan', *Bharatiya Janata Party*, August 31st. URL: https://www.youtube.com/watch?v=n4r-PWpuF2o Last accessed on February 18th, 2016

Modi adumbrated G2B further in another speech to Japanese corporates.

'You will be happy to know that as soon as I took charge as Prime Minister, I invited Japanese consultants to revamp my office to improve efficiency and productivity. This is part of my governance reform that investors want. Ultimately, what investors want are matters of good governance like single window clearance and quick processing of investment applications through online means. Providing the proper environment for investors is the responsibility of the system and the governance apparatus. If we run a policy-driven state, there will be equal and fair treatment of investors without discrimination by bureaucracy at the lower level. I am creating a special team to facilitate Japanese investments in India and create 'ease of Japan' in India.'[15]

On other occasions, Modi has taken salesmanship and retailing of India as a paradise and heaven for foreign investors to dramatic levels. Speaking in the Silicon Valley in 2015, he asserted, 'I do not believe there is dearth of money. Countries have money but do not know where to invest. I am giving them the address. Here is the place (India).'[16] At the launch of the 'Make in India' week in Mumbai in early 2016, he had the global investors transfixed by saying, 'My friendly advice to you is: don't wait, don't relax. Seize the opportunity and invest. If you take one step, my government will take two steps.'[17]

The *prachaarak* in Modi has never ceased to package and present positives about India in a tantalising and captivating fashion. Later in this book, I will examine how Modi's showmanship has earned laurels for India's soft power. Here, one must acknowledge that the Modi Doctrine has delivered concrete results in economic diplomacy thanks to the glitzy picture the current Indian prime minister has showcased to the world while backing his evocative words with deeds. For international

---

[15] NDTV. 2014. 'Working to Inject Japan-Like Efficiency in PMO: PM Narendra Modi', *NDTV*, September 1st. URL: https://www.youtube.com/watch?v=LISxR1RORVM Last accessed on February 18th, 2016

[16] PTI. 2015. 'India is Heaven for Investors; Want to Make it $20 Trillion Economy: PM Modi', *Daily News and Analysis*, September 28th, 2016

[17] Khapre, Shubhangi. 2016. 'Seize the Opportunity, Don't Wait, says PM to India Inc, Global Investors', *The Indian Express*, February 14th

ratings agencies and measurers of a country's economic performance to be convinced about the investment grade of a country, smart-aleck speeches and gimmickry do not carry weight if they are not combined with fundamental transformation. Modi's talking and doing are two sides of the same coin, and hence his sustained pulling power in the global economy.

The classic vocabulary of commercial diplomacy in the Modi Doctrine sounds like it has been extracted from a business school textbook—marketing, rationalising, simplifying, streamlining, downsizing, reforming and modernising. Take, for instance, the assurances Modi gave to German investors at the Hannover Messe trade fair in April 2015.

'We are removing unnecessary regulations and simplifying our procedures. We are using digital technology to eliminate multiple approvals and endless wait. We will guide you and walk with you in your projects. We have set up Invest India and country desks in it that will be networked to the states. We will nurture innovation and protect your intellectual property. There were institutions in India that seemed beyond scrutiny. Well, they no longer are. We are reforming institutions in ways that has not happened in decades. We are building a tax regime that is predictable, stable and competitive. We will now address the remaining uncertainties.'[18]

Modi's prime pitch to foreign investors about improving governance in India was borne out by Transparency International's Corruption Perception Index, where India rose to the 76th rank out of 168 countries in 2015 from the 85th position in 2014. The World Economic Forum's Global Competitiveness Index saw India end five years of secular decline and move up by sixteen places to 55th place out of 140 nations in 2015–2016. The World Bank's Ease of Doing Business Index has also witnessed India jumping from a lowly 142 to 130 out of 189 countries in 2015. Neither the corruption nor competitiveness and business-friendliness figures are enviable from a comparative global perspective, but they indicate that India is progressively looking better in the eyes of foreign investors.

---

[18] NM. 2015. 'PM Modi's Speech at the Inaugural Session of Hannover Messe', *Narendra Modi*, April 12th. URL: https://www.youtube.com/watch?v=JHdZIiKBrCM Last accessed on February 18th, 2016

Modi's 'Make in India' czar, Amitabh Kant, expects more governance reforms at home year after year, 'which will further improve our position (on Ease of Doing Business). We are absolutely confident of being in top 50 in three years as per the target set by PM.'[19] Given Modi's 'three Ds', particularly the size of India as a market, even if it rises to where China has hovered, i.e., around 80th rank in Ease of Doing Business, it would be sufficient to exponentially increase inward FDI. The 48 percent growth in FDI equity inflows in 2014–2015 could look modest as the Modi Doctrine's commercial diplomacy yields long-term dividends in time to come.

FDI is not a silver bullet for India to hit and sustainably stay in the fast lane of GDP growth, and Modi knows it. But his almost obsessive pursuit of FDI and hard selling of India as a 'bright spot' amidst a limping global economy has cemented an image of India as a 'can do' nation led by the current prime minister who has an intuitive pulse for flooring multinational corporations with words and deeds that are music to their ears. The sleek public relations offensives for which Modi is famed have put India on the world map as a happening and upcoming country, especially in economic terms. Modi has aced what the BJP terms as a key pillar of its foreign policy—*Samriddhi*—or shared economic prosperity. His vigorous hunt for FDI during foreign jaunts and the sizeable inward financial commitments he has secured from Japan, China, the US, Canada, Australia and Germany have reversed the investor alienation that had plagued India for decades. As the Europe-based Indian origin billionaire Prakash Hinduja adjudged, 'foreign investors are engaging the Big four audit companies to get information from India and so far the feedback is that the Modi's government has taken the right steps in attracting investment... investors know exactly what's going on in India and they are getting the right signals on India. Modi has created a buzz among foreign investors.'[20]

---

[19] ET. 2015. 'Ease of Doing Business: India Improves Ranking, Singapore Tops the List, says World Bank', *The Economic Times*, October 28th

[20] Chatterjee, Dev. 2015. 'Modi Govt. on the Right Track in Attracting FDI: Hinduja', *Business Standard*, November 3rd

Since India's baseline for inbound FDI flows was at rock bottom when Modi became the prime minister, it will take more than a few years before India can actually reap a China-style foreign investment-driven sustained GDP spurt. But Modi's fervent efforts to convince international state-owned and private investors to 'come and feel the change in India's regulatory environment', an invitation buttressed by radical changes such as permitting 100 percent FDI in defence and civil aviation sectors and across-the-board easing of onerous visa restrictions, have piqued global interest about India. Critics rightly point out that the ground realities in India are still extremely hostile and nearly impossible for foreign investors, but Modi's plea to the world to 'not go by old perceptions' has been taken seriously. A foreign economic policy premised on a huge domestic restructuring agenda, whose acme is the 'Make in India' campaign, will need time to mature. But the consistency of vision and execution demonstrated in the Modi Doctrine has sent a surge of optimism throughout the world about India rising to the occasion to shape the global economy.

India's head honcho

While there is no dearth of world leaders whose personalities permit easygoing relationships with their counterparts, Modi loves to be in the company of CEOs of domestic and foreign corporations as much as of prime ministers or of presidents. If not for his passion for public affairs and politics, he may well have succeeded in an alternative career as a transnational corporate manager. The tag of 'CEO Prime Minister' which he carries with aplomb and the cutting-edge technological and innovative ideas he dabbles in add to the legend of the Indian leader as a very different species from his dour and bureaucratic predecessors. Modi's propensity for new concepts and acronyms like 'three Ds', 'three Cs', 'five Ts' (Tradition, Talent, Tourism, Trade and Technology) and 'three Ss' (Skill, Speed and Scale) are all coinages that stun interlocutors, and reconfirm his status as a hybrid leader who mixes up the public and the private, the government and the corporate, the national and the transnational to a superlative effect.

In 2015, the professional networking website LinkedIn reported that Modi was 'among the most viewed CEOs' and justified the unorthodox classification by arguing that 'CEOs steer a group of people in a direction, and as a leader, Modi is doing that for India. That's why he has been clubbed under CEOs.'[21] No wonder that business leaders around the world have flocked to him and, by extension, to the new India that he vaunts as having hurtled past its old image as a 'backward' and regressive country. Sundar Pichai, the Indian-American CEO of Google has praised Modi for 'accelerating India's effort to become the next global hot bed of innovation and entrepreneurship.' Another corporate biggie of Indian origin, Satya Nadella, the CEO of Microsoft, went on record that his company would not have been able to realise dreams of opening data centres and getting public sector undertakings to use them, if not for Modi's structural reforms. He has said, 'I am optimistic about the rate of change and adoption' under Modi.

Stephen Schwarzman, the CEO of Blackstone, has given his thumbs-up to Modi by averring, 'India has one of the highest levels of growth and has a pro-reform government.'[22] Mark Zuckerberg, the CEO of Facebook, changed his personal online profile to the Indian tricolour to support Modi's Digital India campaign, and has been sighted hugging the Indian prime minister. John Chambers, the CEO of Cisco was so impressed with Modi that he told him he was 'an amazing ambassador of India's growth story' and that he 'will change the world and change India.'[23] Paul Jacobs, the chairman of Qualcomm, confessed to being 'extremely excited and motivated by the Prime Minister's Digital India initiative' and that 'India under PM Modi's leadership is really moving in the right direction.'[24]. The Chinese founder of the e-commerce giant Alibaba, Jack Ma, has described Modi's speeches as, 'passionate and inspiring', and the media mogul Rupert Murdoch has judged Modi as 'best leader with best policies since independence, but massive task to achieve in most complex nation.'

---

[21] Punit, Itika. 2015. 'Narendra Modi is one of the Most Viewed Indian CEOs on LinkedIn', *Quartz*, August 19th

[22] ANI. 2015. 'After Meeting PM Narendra Modi, Please US CEOs Hopeful about Investment Possibilities in India', *The Financial Express*, September 25th

[23] ET. 2015. 'PM Modi will Change how World sees India: John Chambers, Cisco', *The Economic Times*, September 27th

[24] HT. 2015. 'What Top Tech CEOs said about India as they met PM Modi', *Hindustan Times*, September 27th

At a breakfast meeting with American CEOs in New York in September 2014, Modi created quite a stir. The CEO of Caterpillar, Doug Oberhelman, attended it and shared a revealing portrait of the current Indian prime minister, 'He wasn't at all like the politicians we're used to here. He acknowledged that the last five years have been very difficult for the Indian population, the Indian economy and the world in general, and he vowed and promised to change that. I believed him. He was very serious. I was genuinely quite impressed.'[25] As per one interesting compilation of views of corporate executives who met Modi in the Silicon Valley in September 2015, he stands out *inter alia* for these qualities, 'he means business', 'he gives you confidence', 'he is an attentive listener', 'his grasp of issues faced by startups is very good', 'his understanding of nuances in new technologies and their grey area is very solid', 'he is keen to engage in dialogue', 'he is relentless in his pursuit of economic and social impact in India', 'he is respectful and not dismissive', 'he is very crafty in his use of the news and media, which most tech CEOs tend to not have', 'he allows you to create a good sense of visual imagery in his speeches', 'he understands that people like him and I think that's what helps him drive his agenda forward', and 'he is a great ambassador for India. He gives me the desire to want to engage with India.'[26]

Later in this book, I will analyse the soft power USPs that make the Modi Doctrine unrivalled in the recent history of Indian foreign policy. Here, we must note that in the era of economic globalisation, where power is increasingly wielded by large MNCs and states have relatively lesser command over market forces, the endorsements that Modi garners from CEOs is not trivial for India's overall global status as a rising power. According to the London-based asset value consultancy, Brand Finance, India has climbed rapidly to become the 'world's

---

[25] Kelleher, James. 2014. 'India's Modi Promises US CEOs a Return to Market Reforms', *Reuters*, September 29th

[26] Mohan, Mukund. 2015. '27 Impressions from CEOs and Business Leaders– Prime Minister Narendra Modi and his Visit to Silicon Valley', *Best Engaging Communities*, September 30th. URL: http://bestengagingcommunities.com/2015/09/30/27-impressions-from-ceos-and-business-leaders-prime-minister-narendra-modi-and-his-visit-to-silicon-valley/ Last accessed on February 18th, 2016

seventh most valued "nation brand", with an increase of 32 percent in its brand value to USD 2.1 billion.'[27] Visibility and acceptance in the world of global business has begun to redo the way India is perceived. To have allies and partners among nation states has been the conventional currency for gaining influence in world affairs. But in the Modi Doctrine, India's global web of friends and circle of fans has been widened, and it encompasses a bevy of titans of industry and enterprise who in turn determine foreign economic policies of their respective countries or regions. Modi is, thus, strengthening India politically in the world via his daring economic strides.

A superficial reading of Modi's bonhomie with global business elites would conclude that he is a neoliberal politician who stumps for free market capitalism. Most of the CEOs who flock to Modi are, of course, dyed-in-the-wool neoliberals who rant against government interference in their profit-making endeavours. But Modi is first and foremost a globalised Indian nationalist. He does not subscribe to a global economy or an Indian economy devoid of state guidance and strategic navigation or bereft of care and safety nets for the vulnerable and the poor. His reinterpretation of FDI as 'First Develop India' conveys that he is not into promotion of businesses as an end in itself, but as a means to do what Lee Kuan Yew and Deng Xiaoping did for Singapore and China. Modi sees FDI as a win-win proposition whereby foreign corporations make money in India but, in the process, enrich India. The Modi Doctrine's commercial diplomacy is one instrument in a comprehensive toolkit for raising India's power and prosperity. It rests on a supreme self-confidence that inviting foreign capitalists into India will not reproduce neocolonial practices because the governance system and the state under Modi are strong enough to prevent any exploitation of the poor in India by overseas investors.

Inching up in Foreign Trade

As with FDI, the Modi Doctrine holds the keys to resurrecting India's ancient prestige as a global commercial hub and a dynamo that spurs prosperity in South Asia. The incredible story of contemporary

---

[27] PTI. 2015. 'India World's 7th Most Valued 'Nation Brand': US on Top', *The Indian Express*, November 1st

China's growth as a trading superpower contains a lesson not lost upon Modi. It is that prosperity begins by accelerating trade in one's own neighbourhood. After the USA, the top five trading partners of China are all neighbours in East Asia, viz. Hong Kong, Japan, South Korea and Taiwan. Modi's desire to reorganise South Asian economies around a web of economic interdependence with high volumes of multi-directional trade in goods and services is, thus, based on sound comparative knowledge about what it takes to zoom India's economy and take it to the cockpit of the global economy.

For decades, there has been a familiar air of pessimism about prospects of enhanced economic integration among the eight member countries of the South Asian Association for Regional Cooperation (SAARC). As a formal institution, SAARC has completed three decades of existence, but despite a plethora of technical committees, working groups and mechanisms, it has underachieved in its core goal of ushering in a prosperous and harmonious South Asia. Dismissed as a 'magnificent paper tiger' and a perennial 'white elephant', SAARC has a ring of collective disappointment and unfulfilled potential.

There are rational grounds for this disappointing profile. Compared with counterparts across the world, SAARC presides over the least integrated region, with suffocating barriers to free movement of goods and people across borders. According to the United Nations Conference on Trade and Development (UNCTAD), until 2011 intra-SAARC trade comprised a paltry 5.2 percent of the total trade that SAARC members engage with the rest of the world. Valued at merely US$17.5 billion, intra-SAARC trade involves India exporting around US$15 billion to the other seven nations and importing only US$2.5 billion from them in return. On the other hand, the Association of Southeast Asian Nations (ASEAN) does 26.5 percent of its total global trade among its own members. As much as 22.3 percent of the Common Market for Eastern and Southern Africa (Comesa)'s total global trade is intramural. MERCOSUR, or the Southern Common Market in Latin America has 20.3 percent of its overall trade occurring inside its membership zone.[28]

---

[28] Athukorala, Prema-Chandra. 2013. 'Intra-Regional FDI and Economic Integration in South Asia: Trends, Patterns and Prospects', *UNCTAD Background Paper No. RVC7*, p.2

SAARC's hollow performance in opening up trade is all the more glaring because South Asia is home to 42 percent of the planet's poor and undernourished people. In 1993, at the 7th SAARC summit in Dhaka, member countries committed to an action plan for complete eradication of poverty by 2002. A decade and half after, this forgotten goalpost has passed, a subcontinent-wide economic union that can rapidly pitchfork this populous region out of deprivation remains a pipe dream.

Unlike foreign aid or developmental assistance, foreign trade has a proven capacity to expand economies, create jobs with predictable wage income, and raise the size of the middle class. SAARC's unattainable holy grail of a region devoid of penury can only fructify if and when borders of the eight member states are loosened up for intensified movement of goods, services and personnel. The day caravans carrying exponentially enlarged amounts of merchandise and professionals crisscross SAARC borders with fewer restrictions and objections will be the starting point for a war on poverty in South Asia. This is exactly Modi's plan for the Indian subcontinent as a connected entity that benefits economically from closer integration and reduction of malice. He has declared, 'all South Asian countries are partners in our journey towards development. My vision for South Asia is the same as my vision for India —*Sabka Saath, Sabka Vikaas*.' By applying this slogan not only to domestic governance within India, but also as a driver of his neighbourhood policy, Modi is essentially reminding the world about the centrality of commercial diplomacy. His attitude towards India's neighbours can be paraphrased as 'let us focus on economic growth and mutually beneficial trade, investment and connectivity, and keep the political prejudices and difficult psychological baggage aside.'

SAARC has completed more than one decade since the signing of the ambitious South Asian Free Trade Area (SAFTA). For all its high-sounding slogans of forging a single market for 1.8 billion people, the speed and depth of its trade liberalisation road map has been appalling. The thousands of restricted items and sectors which member countries withhold from tariff reduction targets have made a mockery of the promise of easier intra-regional flow of goods that can combat inflation and rev up ancillary economic activities along trade routes. Thanks to an entrenched culture of corruption, narrow nationalism and trade protectionism based on patron-client relationships between politicians and local producers, South Asian countries are saddled with domestic monopolies or oligopolies that deny consumers the best quality of goods and services at affordable prices. It is almost as if globalisation has bypassed South Asia, and its residents are living in a time warp.

This situation is untenable, and Modi has set out to change it. At a CEO forum in Britain in November 2015, he committed to 'confidently, consistently and ceaselessly working to integrate our economy with the world.'[29] He also intends to usher the rest of South Asia into a virtuous cycle of trade and commerce. For clearing the hurdles and overcoming the deplorable economic inertia in SAARC, much depends on Modi. As a champion of commercial diplomacy and an ardent promoter of mutually beneficial business opportunities through foreign policy, Modi has kindled universal hope among all the SAARC countries. Even viscerally anti-India outfits such as the Maoists in Nepal welcomed Modi after his takeover as India's prime minister, as a harbinger of a balanced approach towards smaller neighbours.

The possibility of India's economic growth acting as a rising tide that lifts all boats in South Asia has, thus, not materialised so far, especially as the former runs a huge trade surplus vis-a-vis other member states. Under a politically powerful and commanding leader such as Modi, India has expressed readiness to import a lot more from its neighbours and also encourage Indian capitalists to invest in productive ventures that generate jobs and export revenues in the rest of South Asia. These offers have come in the spirit of 'positive unilateralism' that was mooted by C. Raja Mohan during the Vajpayee administration[30], and which has now taken on a more concrete shape under Modi. Outward FDI from Indian corporations spans several continents, but it is sparse in India's own neighbourhood due to the prevalence of anti-India politics and protectionist lobbies in SAARC countries. Modi has built up sufficient political capital in SAARC to level the economic playing field and project India, the largest player in the region, as more magnanimous and sensitive to fears of smaller nations of being submerged or flooded by a giant.

---

29 PTI. 2015. 'PM Narendra Modi Hard Sells India as Investment Destination to CEOs', *The Economic Times*, November 13th

30 Mohan, Raja. 2003. 'India's Positive Unilateralism', *The Hindu*, October 26th

Modi's mandate to Indian space scientists to build a 'SAARC satellite', and his determination to beef up road and rail connectivity, and border infrastructure among the SAARC members are sending out positive vibes that India is transcending narrow self-interest and is tending to the needs of the rest of the flock in South Asia. The asymmetry of power between India and its smaller neighbours in SAARC, which often ignites suspicions about New Delhi's intentions and impact, is being converted from a problem into an opportunity as Modi has seized the chance.

Shaken by the advancing Chinese dragon, which has made sizeable economic and military inroads into South Asia, India under Modi is exercising leadership by acting in the general interests of all in the region. The Modi effect can transform the oft-derided 'Big Brother' India into a benevolent major power whose economic dynamism has a positive spill-over on the entire South Asian family. Modi has articulated a plan for building a sub-regional trade block called BBIN (Bangladesh, Bhutan, India and Nepal) that would bypass recalcitrant SAARC members like Pakistan, and would go ahead with roads and corridors for free movement of goods and services. It is India's version of China's 'One Belt, One Road' (OBOR) initiative, although on a smaller scale. The BBIN pact was inked in June 2015 by transport ministers of the four South Asian nations in light of 'findings by various research bodies that transforming transport corridors into economic corridors could potentially increase intraregional trade within South Asia by almost 60% and with the rest of the world by over 30%.' The signatories identified '30 priority transport connectivity projects with an estimated total cost of over $8 billion…These corridors and associated routes were determined based on analysis of patterns of regional and international trade.'[31]

Modi is also eager to boost trade routes with Southeast Asia. He wants to deepen India's presence within ASEAN by means of road connectivity to facilitate easy movement of goods, services and people through the 3,200-kilometre-long India-Myanmar-Thailand trilateral highway corridor, which has been delayed, but is expected to be

---

[31] Roche, Elizabeth. 2015. 'India, Neighbours Sign Pact to Boost Road Links, Trade', *Mint*, June 16th

completed in 2018. Modi's tweet in November 2014 before flying to Naypyidaw, Myanmar, that 'ASEAN is central to our dream of an Asian century, where India will play a crucial role'[32] comes in the backdrop of India's quest to enhance land- and sea-based connections with all the countries of this economically vibrant block. India's terrestrial links with ASEAN's poorer member states are underdeveloped and deserve a ramp-up. The land route from Moreh in northeast India to Mae Sot in Thailand via Myanmar can eventually be scaled up to Vietnam via Cambodia and Laos. From Vietnam, maritime caravans can then take Indian products, skilled professionals and services to Malaysia, Singapore, Indonesia, the Philippines and, ultimately, to Australia.

This path, when it materialises, would cut short currently circuitous and costly journeys and reinvigorate medieval-era lanes of communications that commercially bound India to its eastern stretch and gave rise to the hybrid geographical formulation of 'Indo-China', i.e., the land between India and China. Later in this book, I will analyse Modi's 'Act East' policy and its impact on reshaping geostrategy of the Indo-Pacific region. Here, we can note that the Modi Doctrine's proactive commercial diplomacy has enabled India to make economic inroads into fresh terrain. In March 2015, the Indian government announced formation of a project development company 'to catalyse investments from the Indian private sector through separate special purpose vehicles (to) set up manufacturing hubs in CMLV countries, namely, Cambodia, Myanmar, Laos and Vietnam.'[33] Modi has also allocated $1 billion 'to promote projects that support physical and digital connectivity between India and ASEAN' in keeping with his mantra that 'connectivity is the pathway to shared prosperity.'[34] Such measures cumulatively amount to a new beginning for India to regain its historical importance as an inter-regional trade facilitator.

China is far ahead of India in its trade and connectivity diplomacy, which are premised on the idea of reviving the historical Silk Route by

---

[32] Sasi, Anil. 2014. 'In Myanmar, PM Modi Eyes Regional Connectivity Booster Shot for Trade', *The Indian Express*, November 11th

[33] Baliga, Ananth. 2015. 'India to Push CMLV Trade', *The Phnom Penh Post*, March 3rd

[34] PTI. 2015. 'PM Narendra Modi Proposes $1 Billion Line of Credit for Connectivity with ASEAN', *The Economic Times*, November 21st

road, rail and sea. Beijing's ambitious forward planning aims at placing itself as the centre of an expanding economic zone of prosperity that is buttressed by Chinese-financed super express ways, train lines and ports across the Indo-Pacific. As a far larger manufacturing and trading power than India, China has both the moolah and the strategic blueprint to utilise its humungous Silk Road Infrastructure Fund and the Asian Infrastructure Investment Bank (AIIB), and other bilateral channels of aid to remain the economic arbiter of the Indo-Pacific. Modi has tasked his planners with the responsibility of formulating India's answer to the Chinese Silk Road blitz. Codenamed 'Project *Mausam*', it is a transnational initiative to revive ancient monsoon wind-based maritime commerce and cultural linkages with India as the hub that channels trade among eastern Africa, the Middle East, South and Southeast Asia.[35]

Modi has also proposed to speed up ideas of corridors for trade from Central Asia to India. Speaking at Nazarbayev University in Kazakhstan in July 2015, he enjoined governments and people in the region to remember from history that, 'as Central Asia links to the East and the West, it must also connect to the South, for that is how it always was.'[36] His pointed reference to the 'South' was to India and the subcontinent, which offer a way out of the dilemma that Central Asians confront after becoming sandwiched between Russia and China. The palpitation that countries like Kazakhstan and Turkmenistan have been undergoing under the looming Chinese shadow over their energy sectors has generated an opening that Modi has tried to exploit. His push for India to be admitted into the Uzbekistan-Turkmenistan-Oman-Iran transport corridor for natural gas has been welcomed by the nations concerned, which realise how valuable the Indian market is when energy prices are fickle and volatile.

Modi has pressed upon the urgency of realising a transnational connectivity path for India to tap into Russian gas and fortify its energy

---

35 Parashar, Sachin. 2014. 'Narendra Modi's Project Mausam Manoeuvre to Check China's Maritime Might', *The Times of India*, September 16th

36 NM. 2015. 'PM Modi at Nazarbayev University, Kazakhstan', *Narendra Modi*, July 7th. URL: https://www.youtube.com/watch?v=KCNTufeEFmQ Last accessed on February 19th, 2016

security. The International North-South Transport Corridor (INSTC), which purports to transport freight among Russia, Iran, Central Asian countries and India, can be a game changer, if executed on a priority basis, with the potential to ameliorate India's chronic energy shortage. When operational, the corridor could drastically cut transit time and costs, and open an assured supply line for gas to India. In light of the Modi government's interest in diversifying markets for Indian exporters away from the economically crisis-ridden West and towards accessing hitherto untapped emerging centres in Eurasia, Africa and Latin America, New Delhi has been persuading other stakeholders of INSTC to overcome logistical, banking, insurance and other tariff and non-tariff barriers. The Indian Commerce Ministry has taken on the mantle of 'popularising' INSTC and 'involving Indian companies to better the prospects of INSTC.'[37] Despite a cloud of uncertainty regarding security in Afghanistan and Pakistan, Modi has also gone ahead with speedy implementation of the long-delayed Turkmenistan-Afghanistan-Pakistan-India (TAPI) gas pipeline project and proposed a land-sea route via Iran to mitigate the political risks.[38]

Unlike the Manmohan Singh government, which preferred free trade agreements (FTAs) with developed countries and incurred an uncomfortable trade deficit for India, the Modi regime has stressed preferential trading pacts with Latin America, the Middle East, the Commonwealth of Independent States and Africa. India's Commerce Ministry received a mandate from Modi to accentuate export promotion as the main goal, and to negotiate FTAs 'with a lot of strategic understanding' to upkeep 'India's dignity, position and ability to leverage its market potential.'[39] Thanks to Modi's sagacity and the high GDP growth he has maintained in the Indian economy, many foresee India giving China serious competition as a trade partner in Latin America and Africa. Talk about the 'fastest growing major economy', India, toppling an economically declining China in the Global South confirms

---

37 Arun, S. 2015. 'Government Pitches for Global North-South Corridor', *The Hindu*, December 30th

38 PTI. 2015. 'PM Narendra Modi Pitches for Early Implementation of TAPI Gas Pipeline Project', *The Economic Times*, July 11th

39 Mishra, Asit. 2014. 'India to Negotiate FTAs with Emerging Market Nations', *Mint*, September 11th

the Modi Doctrine's shift to emerging market economies (EMEs) as the bedrock of India's foreign trade strategy.

India's pulling power and appeal for Africa have risen under Modi thanks to the former's higher economic growth trajectory and its brand visibility earned by Modi. With China no longer booming, the contrasting glow on India looks more attractive to Africans who are trying to cope with the sharp slowdown in mineral exports to China and nagging doubts about China's ability to keep investing in and aiding Africa. As Modi's 'Make in India' takes off, India could be the next big consumer of the strategic minerals and commodities which Africa has in abundance. India-Africa trade can zoom from the present levels of over $70 billion to match or even surpass China-Africa trade of $200 billion if one keeps an eye on the future. Here, involving India's small and medium enterprises, and exposing them to counterpart business partners in Africa, particularly on its eastern coast, has high potential. The Modi government has encouraged Indian industrialists to intensify engagement with African nations by holding several trade events for market access and market development in Africa, and like in Latin America, has focussed on 'countries more important from export perspective' in Africa.[40]

The strategic dimensions of South-South cooperation in the Modi Doctrine will be covered later in this book, but one must note here that the thrust on ramping up trade with non-Western countries has effected a much-needed correction in India's foreign economic policy. It has long-term benefits of integrating India with those parts of the global economy which are rising and reducing Indian dependence on rich countries which are struggling to return to high growth and dynamism since the financial crisis of 2008. Following the signing of the USA-led Trans-Pacific Partnership (TPP) agreement, which India did not join, the Modi government has used diplomatic levers to quicken negotiations for the Asia-centric Regional Comprehensive Economic Partnership (RCEP) so as 'to avoid being excluded from major trade accords.'[41]

---

[40] Mishra, Asit. 2015. 'India to Host 53 African Trade Ministers', *Mint*, September 29th

[41] Reuters. 2015. 'TPP Adds Urgency for China, India at RCEP Negotiations', *Taipei Times*, October 12th

The Modi Doctrine's trade mavens see India benefiting from nurturing 'regional value chains and production networks' via the RCEP and thereby strengthening its pivotal place in the Indo-Pacific. As one Indian official put it, 'with the TPP becoming a reality, expediting RCEP is in our interest.'[42] Ganeshan Wignaraja of the Asian Development Bank is of the opinion that 'a breakthrough on RCEP would help mitigate the competitive disadvantage of India being absent from the TPP' and that 'concluding an RCEP agreement would mark a key milestone for the Modi government.'[43] Such a clearheaded consideration of alternative mega-regional trade blocs confirms that Modi's foreign economic policy is not beholden to the West or to generic neoliberal principles of free trade or free movement of capital, but is plugging into wherever there is monetary value for Indian exports and a chance to close its vast trade deficit. The East Asian tiger economies did not follow policies of universal free trade while they were on the ascendant. They maintained protectionist regimens in specific sectors through import substitution methods and eventually became world beaters in exports.[44] Modi's 'Make in India' and export-driven blueprints take a leaf out of these proven strategic trade policies, and are the only historically viable ways for India to leap forward in economic power.

At the multilateral table of the World Trade Organisation (WTO), the Modi Doctrine has attempted to maintain India's traditional role as an aggregator and spokesperson for the collective interests of developing countries, while also not wishing to be seen as obstructing or blocking progress in negotiations. In July 2014, the Modi government displayed early combativeness by refusing to ratify a WTO deal reached in Bali in 2013, and arguing that countries of the Global South have a sovereign right to protect their poor by retaining agricultural subsidies. Exasperated at being accused in the Western media and policymaking circles as a spoiler, the Indian prime minister posed the dilemma on

---

[42] Siddiqui, Huma. 2016. 'India to Expedited RCEP Agreement: Govt.', *The Financial Express*, February 18th

[43] Kumar, Manoj. 2016. 'With TPP Advancing, India Pins Hopes on China-Backed Trade Bloc', *Reuters*, February 11th

[44] Amsden, Alice. 1990. 'East Asia's Challenge', *The American Prospect*, Volume 1, Issue 2

eliminating food subsidies as, 'There are efforts to isolate India over WTO. But tell me: do we choose feeding our poor or getting good press worldwide?'[45]

As a politician who enjoys the attention and felicitation of the international community and the Western media, such a populist stance upsetting Western powers and corporations showed that the Modi Doctrine is no neoliberal manifesto, but a calibrated strategy to extract the best possible terms for India's economic interests from international agreements. By November 2014, the same Modi who was vilified in the West as a deal-breaker applied all levers of his special closeness to Obama and ensured a bilateral accord with the USA, which accepted 'India's right to protect its right to food security cannot be denied by the WTO.'[46] Obama lauded Modi's 'personal leadership in finding a path forward.'[47] As we saw earlier in this book, the Modi Doctrine packs chutzpah and an innate self-confidence about India getting its way in the world through a mixture of principles and strategy. Modi has threaded the needle on complex trade policies with clarity of purpose and mission, and his commercial diplomats have also attempted to use India's advantage in services exports and link them to negotiations for agreements for goods trade.

Yet, all is not smooth sailing for India due to structural changes in the world trading system. In 2015, at the WTO Ministerial in Nairobi, India found itself shortchanged by the USA, the European Union, Japan and Brazil on negotiating issues that mattered to New Delhi. More concessions were given to least developed countries (LDCs) and small vulnerable economies (SVE), rather than to growing powerhouses like India or China, deepening intra-Global South divisions, and putting into question New Delhi's traditional mantle of being a leader of the developing nations' bloc. India had been wary of being separated from LDCs by richer nations and then forced to offer greater and faster market access. It warned the USA against sowing 'divisions among the

---

45 Zhong, Raymond. 2014. 'Modi says India Blocked Trade Deal to Serve the Poor', *The Wall Street Journal*, August 11th

46 Mehra, Puja. 2014. 'India-US Deal Paves the Way for Global Trade Pact', *The Hindu*, November 13th

47 PTI. 2014. 'Obama Praises Modi's 'Personal Leadership' in Breaking WTO Deadlock', *The Times of India*, November 14th

developing world'[48] but could not succeed in rallying all of Asia, Africa and Latin America to stick together.

Perceptions that the African countries did not back India's position on agricultural subsidies unanimously in Nairobi showed the challenges ahead for the Modi Doctrine's multilateral strategy. Due to the lure of preferential trading agreements like the TPP, the USA has been able to differentiate interests of developing countries and erode India's support base. Trade economist Manoj Pant argues that the Global South has been split into two sub-blocs and that 'it would be futile now for India to continue to be the leader of the "developing country" bloc as that no longer exists.'[49] While the WTO has often witnessed across-the-table coalitions between countries of the Global North and South, the variegation within developing countries looks likely to grow due to the plethora of preferential trade deals being done outside the WTO framework. If India is to retain its *primus inter pares* status in shaping the global trading system, and avoid further isolation, it has to conclude major new FTAs of its own. The Modi Doctrine's multilateral strategy has to incorporate signing more preferential trade agreements or expanding the nominally existing ones with Africa, Latin America and Asia. How this can happen in spite of Modi's determination to forge ahead with 'Make in India' industrialisation that will increase 'buy local' stipulations, and has an import substitution undercurrent, remains to be seen. If India is bent on cutting its trade deficit by pushing only exports, its persuasion powers in international trade forums would not go far. Piloting India's multilateral trade destiny and forging a new identity as a 'leading power' that nonetheless wants special and differential treatment (SDT) preferences will be the litmus test for the Modi Doctrine.

Preparing the home base

In April 2015, the Modi government announced a five-year foreign trade policy (FTP) aiming to double India's exports of goods and

---

[48] Arun. S. 2015. 'India Rejects Rich World's Attempt to Create Divisions', *The Hindu*, December 14th

[49] Pant, Manoj. 2015. 'What Happened at WTO's Nairobi Ministerial: Did India Win or Lose?', *Catch News*, December 22nd. URL: http://www.catchnews.com/business-economy-news/what-happened-at-wto-s-nairobi-ministerial-did-india-win-or-lose-1450799139.html Last accessed on February 20th, 2016

services to $900 billion and integrate it with the 'Make in India' and 'Digital India' initiatives. The policy's goal of raising India's share of global exports from 2 to 3.5 percent by 2020 has been critiqued as incremental and insufficient to fulfil Modi's ambition for India to 'assume a position of leadership in the international trade discourse.' Economist Rajiv Kumar has argued that even if India reaches the 3.5 percent mark, it 'will not suffice to give us the status of a major export power or a legitimate seat on the global governance high table. We have to do better than achieving an annual export growth rate of 15% as assumed by FTP.'[50] But given that India experienced a 18 percent contraction in exports between April and December 2015 due to a steep slowdown in China and other emerging economies, and a rout in commodity prices, even achieving the doubling of exports by 2020 looks formidable.

Modi's FTP is cognisant of headwinds in the global economy. His Commerce Minister Nirmala Sitharaman accepts that the 'state of the external environment and new features of the global trading landscape (like FTAs) will profoundly affect India's trade' and erode preferences for Indian exports in markets like the USA and the EU. Her solution to these problems is characteristic of the Modi Doctrine's national self-confidence and self-reliance, 'while the external factors are largely outside our control, there is a lot we can do to strengthen our own capabilities and set our house in order.'[51] Towards preparing the ground for India's exports to skyrocket, the Modi government has adopted many policy reforms. Special Economic Zones (SEZs), which had been languishing due to burdensome taxation, are being revived to make them make them 'effective instruments of industrial production, export promotion and employment generation.'[52] In 2016, the Indian Commerce Ministry pushed for removing onerous taxes on SEZ units 'on the ground that giving this tax benefit would revive domestic manufacturing and provide the much-needed boost to exports, declining in each of the last

---

[50] Kumar, Rajiv. 2015. 'Export Pessimism Again: Trade policy of Modi Government Falls Short on Ambition and Ideas', *The Times of India*, April 9th

[51] MCI. 2015. 'Foreign Trade Policy 2015-2020 Announcement on 1.4.2015: Speech of CIM', *Government of India*, p.1

[52] IANS. 2014. 'Government to Revivse SEZs as Instruments of Growth', *Business Standard*, July 10th

13 months.'[53] The issue had been hanging fire for years because the finance ministry was loathe to let go of a large chunk of state revenues. Turf battles between different arms of the government are not new or unique to India, but Modi has tried to present a 'whole-of-government' approach in the FTP and it should be the ideal going forward. Modi has also emphasised the imperative for India to develop its ports alongside SEZs for export expansion. The Indian prime minister has preached 'port-led development with maximum infrastructure-rail and road connectivity, cold storage and warehousing' for 'realising India's aspirations to become a global power.'[54]

In infrastructure modernisation as an aid to foreign trade, the sub-unit diplomacy which is a special feature of the Modi Doctrine has a distinct role to play. Modi has roped in coastal state governments of India to cooperate with the central government under a grand *Sagar Mala* project which envisages 'port-led direct and indirect development and to provide infrastructure to transport goods to and from ports quickly, efficiently and cost-effectively.'[55] With thirteen states and union territories involved in beefing up trade-related infrastructure across India's 7,500 kilometres of coastline, *Sagar Mala* 'seeks to allow the central government to have a say in the development of non-major ports without adopting a confrontationist approach with the state governments.' It has 'the personal stamp of Modi, incorporating the port-led development model that he successfully delivered in Gujarat during his term as Chief Minister. This includes development port-based industrial parks, captive industries and ancillary facilities such as ship repair, shipbuilding, ship-breaking, bunkering, container freight stations, warehousing facilities, industries requiring significant import of raw materials and industries with large export potential.'[56] The haphazard and conflictual manner in which India's maritime

---

[53] BS. 2016. '200 SEZs Likely to be Exempt from 18.5% MAT', *Business Standard*, January 28th

[54] PTI. 2015. 'Need for 'Quick Pace' Development in Ports, Space Technology: Narendra Modi', *The Economic Times*, October 12th

[55] PTI. 2016. 'Government Identifies 150 Critical Infrastructure Projects Under Sagarmala', *The Economic Times*, February 14th

[56] Manoj, P. 2014. 'Sagar Mala Project to Strive for Holistic Development of India's Maritime Sector', *Mint*, November 7th

infrastructure has developed is set for a complete overhaul under the Modi Doctrine, forwarding the cause of setting India's 'house in order' to compete in the global economy.

Sub-unit economic diplomacy is also picking up pace under Modi in the realm of wooing foreign investors. As we saw in an earlier chapter, Indian state governments like that of Modi when he was the chief minister of Gujarat, have been striking out on their own to attract FDI. But under Modi as the prime minister, Indian states are for the first time being actively encouraged to find solutions to bottlenecks and compete among each other for investors' cash. Modi's model of competitive federalism under the umbrella of overall cooperative spirit in foreign economic policy is driven by logic that backward states will catch up with the ones that are ahead in attracting FDI, and also industrialise through peer pressure. In October 2014, Modi spelt out his progressive sub-unit diplomacy method at an investors' summit in the central Indian state of Madhya Pradesh, 'One hundred billion dollars has applied for visa after my foreign visits. States must make a conducive and friendly atmosphere to attract the lion's share of the $100 billion investment. Grab this opportunity and make the best out of it.'[57] Tridivesh Maini finds it 'encouraging to note that it is not just the States that have already attained reasonable success in attracting FDI (such as Gujarat, Maharashtra and Tamil Nadu) that are making concerted efforts for seeking foreign direct investment, but even those that have lagged behind in terms of industrialisation, such as West Bengal, Madhya Pradesh and Rajasthan.'[58]

The Modi Doctrine's 'Team India' concept is a unifying anthem cutting across political party lines, and is empowering state governments to be ready to make the most of the global economic pie. According to *Reuters*, 'state governments have been sidestepping what officials call reform "traffic jams" in New Delhi, making the

[57] Lall, Lemuell. 2014. 'Modi: Foreigners Ready to Invest $100 Billion in India', *India Today*, October 9th

[58] Maini, Tridivesh. 2015. 'India and Foreign Direct Investments: The Need for Strong Internal Synergies', *The Hindu Centre for Politics and Public Policy*, November 27th

most of greater freedoms under the PM to manage everything from budgets to relaxing rigid labour laws for the first time in decades.'[59] Within months of Modi becoming India's prime minister, the state government of Gujarat set up independent international desks in the USA, Singapore, Japan, Canada and China to 'provide effective exchange of information to foreign investors who are willing to do business here', and to maintain Gujarat's presence in capital rich parts of the world on a continuous round-the-clock basis.[60] As the Gujarat chief minister, Modi had proposed such a move earlier but had been stymied by the politically motivated Manmohan Singh regime. The urgency with which the Modi Doctrine tried to remove barriers to states' foreign economic policies derives from past frustrations and a bolder conception of 'Team India' putting its best foot forward in the global economy.

Modi's incentive to state governments to establish their own Export Promotion Councils with respective Export Commissioners has also succeeded, with over twenty states of India deciding to launch them. Until Modi's arrival as the prime minister, the Ministry of Commerce at the central government level assayed the role of facilitator to promote exports. Under the Modi Doctrine, foreign trade is more decentralised and local government units are encouraged to 'not depend solely on the central government interventions.' In Modi's words, 'until we join manufacturers in export promotion, and unless states and centre work together, we cannot achieve new heights in exports[61].' He has also explained the rationale of autonomy to states using liberating language, 'If we adopt the psyche that Delhi is the giver and states the takers, the nation cannot progress. The states and Delhi should try to walk together, shoulder-to-shoulder, in the same direction, at an even pace. The results will come soon enough.'[62]

---

[59] Reuters. 2015. 'States Sidestep Stalled Reform, go it Alone to Woo Investment', *The Times of India*, August 13th

[60] PTI. 2014. 'Gujarat to Set Up International Desks Overseas to Attract FDI', *Business Standard*, July 6th

[61] PTI. 2014. 'Modi for Impetus to Exports, Promotion Councils for States', *The Times of India*, August 16th

[62] Varma, Gyan. 2015. 'Narendra Modi says India can Grow only if Centre, States Work Together', *Mint*, December 4th

Before and during some foreign visits, Prime Minister Modi sends and takes along state chief ministers and ensures that they have targeted interactions with provincial leaders and businesspersons of the host countries. In May 2015, Modi launched a one-of-its-kind 'India-China Forum of State Provincial Leaders' in Beijing in the presence of the chief ministers of Gujarat and Maharashtra, and had remarked, 'a number of decisions can be taken quickly by the State governments. These interactions also make the State governments more sensitive and aware of the international dynamics and requirements.'[63] Globalising every corner of India and connecting it to the mainstream of international consciousness and activity is one of the achievements of the Modi Doctrine. It offers reasons for hope that the whole of India will overcome parochial vision and imagination, and will capitalise on Modi's spade work.

A $20 trillion India

Sceptics have questioned whether Modi's 'Make in India' manufacturing transformation can live up to its billing, and whether he himself has the stomach to take on vested interest groups and party political wrangling that mar India's full economic potential. Some corporates have also soured on Modi's charismatic personal guarantees, which have not been translated in the field across India's vast landmass into a more conducive environment for FDI and manufacturing to soar. Then there are warnings about extraneous economic conditions in the global economy like currency exchange rates, interest rates in the USA, and China's 'new normal' of average GDP growth, which can all combine to dampen 'Make in India'.[64] We have noted earlier in this chapter that the onslaught of TPP and other preferential trading zones will also hamper Modi's ambitious economic dreams.

But having noted these hurdles, what is undeniable is that the Modi Doctrine has given India the means to strive and excel in the world of business. It has been a shot in the arm for India's lost self-confidence

---

63 Aneja, Atul. 2015. 'States Free to Scale the Great Wall: Modi', *The Hindu*, May 16th

64 Mohan, Deepanshu. 2016. 'India, a Manufacturing Hub?', *South Asian Voices*, February 10th

as a mercantile and maritime nation. In his acceptance speech after being elected as the parliamentary leader of the BJP in May 2014, just before being appointed as India's prime minister, Modi had remarked, 'I am a very optimistic man and only an optimistic man can bring optimism in the country. Let's forget the negativity. Whatever the past may be, there is no need to be sad.'[65] The general confidence levels of Indian corporations and foreign businesses dealing in India have risen dramatically under the Modi Doctrine and remained high.

The ultimate yields of the momentum that Modi has generated in FDI and foreign trade may take time to arrive on everyone's plate. In September 2015, Modi urged patience at a Silicon Valley event by observing that India is a vast country with a tremendous backlog of naysaying baggage and misgovernance, and that it would take time for change to become entrenched. Using colourful metaphors, he said India 'is not a scooter whose direction you can see changing easily. A forty-compartment train takes time. India is such a huge country.'[66] It bore an unwittingly startling resemblance to Modi's dear friend, President Barack Obama, whose response in 2009 to concerns about the slow pace of reform in the USA was, 'Moving the ship of state is a slow process. States are like big tankers. They're not like speedboats. You can't just whip them around and go in a new direction. Instead, you've got to slowly move it, and then eventually you end up in a very different place.'[67]

Even as Indians and India's well-wishers around the world have piled up dizzying expectations for Modi's 'forty-compartment train' to head upwards, the strides the Indian economy has already made under him must be given their due. In February 2016, when the rest of the BRICS economies were tottering, Modi presented an upbeat picture of what lay ahead, 'Everyone is saying this…the World Bank, the IMF.

---

[65] BJP. 2014. 'Shri Narendra Modi Speech after his Election as Leader of BJP Parliamentary Party', *Bharatiya Janata Party*, May 20th. URL: https://www.youtube.com/watch?v=7aXK231jQwA Last accessed on February 20th, 2016

[66] TNN. 2015. 'PM Narendra Modi at Facebook Townhall with Mark Zuckerberg', *Times Now*, September 27th. URL: https://www.youtube.com/watch?v=pWh9aMycz9s Last accessed on February 20th, 2016

[67] USG. 2011. *Public Papers of the Presidents of the United States: Barack Obama, 2009, Book 1*, Washington, D.C.: Office of the Federal Register, p.460

The world is going through an economic crisis, but it is India alone that is progressing at a rapid pace. This is a unique situation when the whole world is slipping and India is growing.'[68] The Vice Chairman of General Electric, John Rice, commented around the same time that 'if five years ago it was all about BRICS, today two of them are on life support and India stands tall.'[69]

It was one of the myriad foreign endorsements of the economic attainments of the Modi Doctrine which have emanated not just from elite CEOs, but also people of different walks of life. Modi has sought rhetorical 'certificates' from corporate bigwigs, NRIs, OCIs and ordinary Indian citizens for the economic turnaround he has attempted, and received mostly resounding approvals. The broad-based, multi-stakeholder democratic spine of the Modi Doctrine is so robust that the current Indian prime minister's dream of catapulting his country from an $8 trillion economy into a $20 trillion one is realistic and is well within grasp.

---

[68] PTI. 2016. 'India Only Economy not Affected by Global Economic Crisis: PM Modi', *The Economic Times*, February 14th

[69] Borpuzari, Pranbihanga. 2016. 'Two BRIC Nations on Life Support as India Stands Tall: GE's John Rice', *The Economic Times*, January 29th

Chapter 4
'Leading' Power vis-à-vis the Great Powers

India does not need to become anything else. India must become only India. This is a country that once upon a time was called the golden bird. We have fallen from where we were before, but now we have the chance to rise again. It is my absolute belief that Indians have unlimited talent. I have no doubt about our capabilities. I have a lot of faith in the entrepreneurial nature of our 1.25 billion people. There is a lot of capability and I have a clear roadmap to channel it.[1]

Destined to Lead

Narendra Modi rarely lets up a chance to wax eloquent about India's destiny to take the lead on a wide range of issues of international concern. In 2011, when he was still a chief minister of an Indian state, he had asked, 'can India become a superpower in the world?', and had answered it himself,

'...my ten years of running Gujarat convinces me that, yes, India can rise to be a very big power. Given the capabilities that we have in India, if we set goals and nurture our abilities, it is possible. Our entire strategy must be focussed on the realisation that power is shifting from West to East in the twenty-first century. But within the "Asian Century", we

[1] CNN. 2014. 'Fareed Zakaria GPS. Interview with Narendra Modi', *Cable News Network*, September 21st. URL: http://transcripts.cnn.com/TRANSCRIPTS/1409/21/fzgps.01.html Last accessed on February 20th, 2016

are different from China. We must nurture India's three distinct qualities. Firstly, we must project our democracy and make the world acknowledge its superiority. Secondly, India has youth power when its competitors have ageing populations. This natural advantage of India must be furthered. Thirdly, our judicial system separates us from our competitors. We must bolster it. Thus, we must identify our strengths and double down on them.'[2]

In 2013, when he was nominated as the prime ministerial candidate by the BJP, he had said he was 'not depressed' and had 'full faith' that 'India will revive its past glory and become a world leader in the near future, given its strong base in spiritual and traditional values.'[3] Since taking over as the Prime Minister of India, he has extended this capability-based reasoning to project India as a global leader in numerous issue areas. Setting ambitious targets for producing solar, wind and biomass power as his 'top priority', he has extolled India as a 'world leader of renewable energy' and countered Western criticism by assuring that 'we need electricity but we will not create problems for the world.'[4] In the same vein, he has taken a dig at the Western powers 'who lecture us on environment and the use of cleaner energy but don't give us nuclear fuel', and promised that India would 'lead the world in environmental protection' and mitigating global warming.[5]

Having committed to raising the profile of traditional Indian medicinal systems like Ayurveda, Modi has urged India to 'learn from the experience of other countries, especially China, which has put in place policies and regulations for promoting their traditional medicine', and claimed that India can 'become a world leader in affordable and holistic healthcare.'[6] Likewise, Modi has advertised Yoga as 'an invaluable gift

---

[2] IT. 2011. 'Narendra Modi Speech at India Today Conclave', *India Today Conclave*, March 19th. URL: https://www.youtube.com/watch?v=SrMZJM4ybMA Last accessed on February 21st, 2016

[3] TH. 2013. 'India will become a World Leader in Near Future: Modi', *The Hindu*, September 26th

[4] NM. 2015. 'PM Modi's Speech at the Indian Community Reception at Singapore', *Narendra Modi*, November 24th. URL: https://www.youtube.com/watch?v=HYDGzrRSen8 Last accessed on February 21st, 2016

[5] IT. 2015. 'India can Lead the World in Climate Change, says PM Modi', *India Today*, April 6th

[6] PTI. 2016. 'Traditional Medicine can help India become a World Leader in Affordable Health Care: PM Modi', *Daily News and Analysis*, February 2nd

of our ancient tradition' that can assist the world to 'deal with climate change.'[7] On economic issues, as we saw in the previous chapter, Modi has often contrasted the comatose condition of much of the world with India's high GDP growth rates under his regime to paint his country as a ray of hope and a 'pillar of global growth and stability.'[8]

On security problems, Modi has promoted India as a global leader with a 'big role to play' in the 'bloodless war' going on in cyberspace by 'providing a shield to the terrified world through innovative and credible solutions.'[9] Complementary to this mandate to protect the world through cyber defence, Modi has declared that India is 'on the threshold of emerging as a manufacturing hub and a global information technology (IT) superpower.'[10] On a matter that is very close to his heart, violent extremism and terrorism, Modi has also undertaken that India would play a leading role 'at a time of crisis to save whole humanity and the world.'[11] In the maritime domain, Modi has enunciated the acronym SAGAR which means sea in Hindi, and unpacked it as 'Security And Growth for All in the Region' that can be achieved by the Indian Navy 'leading from the front' as 'a force for peace and good' in the extended Indian Ocean.[12]

Why does Modi speak in such bombastic terms as if India is exceptional and is carrying all the burdens of the world on its shoulders? It is due to his instinctive understanding of leadership as assumption of more and more responsibilities and taking on higher duties. His notion of leading is to set progressively bigger goals, initiate actions and execute them himself so as to 'set an example and make the first

---

7 DNA. 2014. 'Narendra Modi's Speech at United Nations General Assembly', *Daily News and Analysis*, September 27th

8 PTI. 2015. 'India can Become a Pillar of Global Growth', *The Economic Times*, November 15th

9 Hodge, Amanda. 2015. 'Narendra Modi wants India to Lead the Fight against Cyber Terror', *The Australian*, July 3rd

10 AT. 2016. 'India to be Global IT Superpower: Modi', *The Assam Tribune*, January 19th

11 NM. 2015. 'PM Modi's Speech at the Community Address in Wembley Stadium, London', *Narendra Modi*, November 14th. URL: https://www.youtube.com/watch?v=zCtkcfUvA2Q Last accessed on February 21st, 2016

12 PTI. 2016. 'PM Modi Flags Sea-Borne Terror, Piracy as Threat to Maritime Security', *The Indian Express*, February 7th

sacrifice.'[13] Gurcharan Das has studied Modi's leadership style and substance deeply and written that he is 'not content with laying broad policies', does 'not abdicate responsibility for implementation to those below him', and 'instead of pronouncing on strategy, he gets into the messy details of a project, monitors day-to-day performance, removes obstacles for those who were implementing it, staying close to them and motivating them.'[14] Such a hands-on leader with a personalised working methodology cannot but be exuberant in reimagining India's role in the world and being the change he wants to see in his country's international profile.

With a frontline prime minister motivated by cultural nationalist assumptions of ancient glory that must be regained, the Modi Doctrine has infused a sense of destiny in India's words and deeds in world affairs. Modi's thunder about India leading the world is not cynical or vacuous, but a conviction predicated on shrewd comparative and relative analysis of the ongoing global power shift from the West to the East and the Global North to the Global South. Raj Chengappa has shown how Modi thinks about temporal and spatial power, and where India fits into the scheme of the emerging world order, 'He believes that it is time a nation that houses one-sixth of humanity and is soon to be the world's third-largest economy, takes its rightful place under the sun. Modi also reckons that with the US on a gradual decline and the Chinese shaky, India as the world's largest democracy has the opportunity to lead the world if it plays its cards well.'[15]

Absolute faith that India's time to be a leading power has arrived and a determination bordering on urgency about not missing the bus is paramount in the Modi Doctrine. As the current Indian prime minister has remarked at a Southeast Asian business and investment summit in Kuala Lumpur in November 2015, 'most of the ASEAN economies have done their bit for Asia's resurgence. Now, it is India's turn. And we know that our time has come.'[16] In this historic mould, Modi has broadened

---

[13] Shekhar, Himanshu. Op cit. p.29

[14] Das, Gurcharan. 2014. 'It is all about Execution', *India Today*, June 20th

[15] Chengappa, Raj. 2015. 'Modi's Global Push', *India Today*, September 30th

[16] IT. 2015. 'PM Modi at ASEAN Summit: It's India's Turn Now to do its Bit for Asia's Resurgence', *India Today*, November 21st

the horizon of India's responsibilities. Addressing India's armed force commanders in December 2015, he had stated, 'our responsibilities are no longer confined to our borders and coastlines. They extend to our interests and citizens, spread across a world of widespread and unpredictable risks.' And to emphasise the dialectic between India's accumulating power and commensurate global responsibilities, he added on board a major warship of the Indian Navy, 'this aircraft carrier is the instrument of our maritime power and a symbol of our maritime responsibility.'[17]

As mentioned in the Introduction of this book, the psychological shift engineered by the Modi Doctrine is to immerse India in the quest for solutions to problems affecting geographically far-off countries. The American political scientist Thomas Volgy defines a major power as a state with 'unusual capabilities' to pursue 'unusually broad and expansive foreign policies beyond its immediate neighbourhood or region.'[18] Before Modi stormed to power in New Delhi in 2014, India did not visualise being anything larger than a subcontinental or regional power in Asia, and also lacked plans to speedily build up unusual capacities that can geographically and thematically expand its power projection. The smallness of thought and action was frustrating for a nation that aspired to be on par with China. Lacking inspiring leadership in the political class, India was stuck in bureaucratic inertia and did not proactively dream to lead the world.

The Modi Doctrine has thrown aside this anemic legacy and has undertaken to render India as a force for good that keeps lifting its teeming millions out of poverty, and simultaneously uses its diplomatic, economic and military assets to promote moderation, tolerance and welfare on a global scale. Indian policymakers, media houses and citizens are often so consumed by pressing domestic priorities and nagging social problems that it is easy to forget India's existence in a wider global context demanding greater Indian involvement and

---

[17] IANS. 2015. 'India's Responsibility not Limited to its Boundaries: Modi', *Business Standard*, December 15th

[18] Volgy, Thomas et al (eds.) 2011. *Major Powers and the Quest for Status in International Politics: Global and Regional Perspectives*, New York: Palgrave Macmillan, p.6

contribution. Charity and reform may indeed begin at home, but in a globalised and competitive international system, India cannot afford to be left behind through passivity and indifference that circumscribe its true power. This is the mental makeup of the Modi Doctrine.

Before Modi held India's reins, the principal obstacle facing its expanded role in world affairs was an ostrich-like belief that the country's problems were mainly internal, and that they needed to be fixed first to be eventually admitted into the ranks of great powers. Arguments often flowed that Indian policymakers must focus on privation within the country before doling out foreign aid or that India must manage its own domestic, communal and armed conflicts with Maoists and separatists before offering to make peace in other regions of the world. The practical import of such myopic vision was that India under-invested in its international mission. Kanti Bajpai termed it as 'foreign policy on a shoestring.'[19] Indian society took its cues from a listless state and also discouraged its youth from studying and making careers in world affairs. As a result, India underachieved in the global arena and remained on the receiving end of an external environment that was stacked against Indian desires to be influential and powerful.

All these constricting values and restricting systems have now been swept aside under the Modi Doctrine, which has woven India's domestic and international dynamics into a seamless whole. The Modi government's foreign policy team's claim that 'out-of-box thinking, boldness of vision and energetic execution' have 'reignited the India Story' and enabled India to be 'a major player in shaping evolving debates across issues, ranging from global governance reforms and climate change to trans-national terrorism and cyber security'[20], is not braggadocious. The 'three Ps'—Path-breaking, Proactive and Pragmatic—which Modi's foreign ministry now exhibits as its defining features, are not due to any overnight revolution in the bureaucracy's workings, but because Modi the doer has pushed them to be so. India is on the road to be a leading power owing to its leader and his unparalleled mobilisation of national will.

---

[19] Bajpai, Kanti. 2012. 'Foreign Policy on a Shoestring', *The Times of India*, October 13th

[20] MEA. 2016. *Diplomacy for Development: From Aspirations to Achievements*, New Delhi: Ministry of External Affairs, p.3

Sizing up the eagle

In world affairs, a nation-state's power is not absolute, but relative to that of others. Modi is aware of this comparative frame and has strived to raise India to the level where it can equal the two established great powers of our times—the USA and China. He has basically buried the thinking that India is inferior to the 'G2', as these big hitters are sometimes referred to, and will remain so for the foreseeable future. At the Wembley Stadium in London in November 2015, Modi had struck a defiant chord,

'We no longer want sympathy from the world, we want equality. And I can say after 18 months of experience that today whoever speaks to India, speaks as an equal. If they want to associate (with us) then (it is) with a win-win formula, if they want to advance (with us) then (it is) shoulder-to-shoulder and this to me is the sign of a bright future.'[21]

He repeated this theme at a gala diaspora address in Singapore, reminding the audience that 'India under him will look at the world neither with low esteem nor proudly but on equal terms. Today, the world is dealing with India on equal terms.'[22]

As discussed earlier in this book, the *Sammaan* or dignity pillar of the BJP's foreign policy is a leitmotif of the Modi Doctrine. Nowhere is this more pronounced than in the way Modi approaches the USA. Although some observers had speculated that Modi would be wary of America due to its denial of a visa to him while he was the chief minister of Gujarat, he has never been a mean politician who lets personal grudges supersede national interests. As he had told Lance Price, 'regarding the visa issue, it never bothered me. I really see these as non-issues and do not let them impact on me or my ego.'[23] Fareed Zakaria wrote in September 2014 after interviewing Modi that he was 'straightforwardly pro-American and seems to harbour little ill toward Washington.'[24] As I have analysed in a previous chapter, Modi's travels

---

21 Sonwalkar, Prasun. 2015. 'Modi says Diversity Indira's Pride as Cameron Leads Cheers at Wembley', *Hindustan Times*, November 14th

22 NM. 2015. 'PM Modi's Speech at the Indian Community Reception at Singapore' Op cit.

23 Price, Lance. *The Modi Effect*, Op cit. p.255

24 Zakaria, Fareed. 2014. 'Is India's Bold Prime Minister Bold Enough?', *The Washington Post*, September 18th

in America during the 1990s as a *prachaarak* left a positive impression in his mind about the USA's achievements. The intensity of Modi's social linkages among Indian-Americans, and his vast networking with many elements within the US corporate sector meant that he hit the ground running after becoming the prime minister of India. He could galvanise a constellation of actors within the USA to ensure that bilateral ties with India would advance enormously under his leadership.

The Modi Doctrine transcends inter-state relations and delves deep into connecting with foreign societies. On all occasions when Modi made high profile visits to the USA in 2014, 2015 and 2016, he had arranged a breadth of interlocutors, apart from summits with President Obama. His meetings ranging from mayors and governors of American cities and states, CEOs of blue-chip American companies, and corporate technological titans to the main backbone of the bilateral ties—prominent Indian-Americans—reified the phrase 'world's two largest democracies' which India and the USA often use for their partnership. Like Obama, Modi relishes non-official or popular diplomacy in the company of foreign corporates, scientists, think tanks, lobbying organizations and average citizens. Established democracies like the US have developed private spheres which cement genuine people-to-people relations with India. Modi's wooing and wowing of USA Incorporated and the American people have cemented the empathy between the two societies by reinforcing the impression that 'we' Americans are so much like 'them' Indians.

Under the Modi Doctrine, nurturing such a streak of mutual inter-societal admiration and the common language of democracy helps produce consistent votaries for ironing out the creases that keep emerging at the official government-government level. The plethora of opinion makers on both sides wishing for a rejuvenation of US-India ties, since Modi has controlled India's foreign policy, speaks volumes for how two democracies can cultivate 'thick' relations. The Modi Doctrine's 'whole of government' synthesis in formulating and executing foreign policy has been matched by a 'whole of America' strategy towards covering India's bases with different interest groups and constituents in a panoramic country called the USA.

Modi's vision from day one as the Indian prime minister has been to reset the crucial bilateral relationship with the USA to maximise benefits for India's rise. The drift in India's interactions with the USA in the final years of the Manmohan Singh era due to commercial and strategic dissonance has been offset through Modi's bold and transformative political will at the top. Americans of different hues in the government and in the private sector have come to realise that Modi, with a charismatic hold over his nation and a system-revamping pedigree, is their best bet to tap into the potential of India which had gone amiss from 2010 to 2014. Modi's promise of a qualitatively new India with a more attractive set of domestic and foreign policies provided the perfect setting for the two nations to rediscover the sweet spots and arrest the souring.

Modi being the quintessential CEO Prime Minister, the number one onus in his policy towards the USA has been to court American investors to return to India. Since the global economic crisis started in 2008 and slowed down India's GDP growth, American FDI into India had fallen from $1.3 billion per annum to merely $478 million in 2013. Smaller economies like Singapore, Japan, the UK, Netherlands and France had become bigger investors in India than the USA. Grievances against India's red tape, unfriendliness to foreign capital, stringent liability laws, taxation policies, local content requirements, intellectual property violations, land and labour regulations had scared away American investors and traders, and had created a lobby in Washington to hold India's feet to the fire.

The Modi Doctrine has succeeded in winning back American confidence in India as a fabulous market opportunity. Unlike China or Japan, where the state plays a domineering role in steering outward FDI, in the USA, Modi relies on heart-to-heart conversations with American businesses, which can channel their surpluses to India if they see value for money and a reformist governance environment. The Indian think tank Gateway House envisages a quantum leap from $100 billion of two-way trade in goods and services in 2015 to $1 trillion worth of US-India economic exchanges by 2030, provided both sides grasp unexplored opportunities such as 'affordable products and services' for India's middle and poorer classes through American innovation.[25] Modi's slogan of FDI as 'First Develop India' and the various corporate- and American

[25] Acharya, Nish. 2014. 'India-US Partnership: $1 Trillion by 2030', *Gateway House*, September 15th

government-backed initiatives to plough FDI into India's developmental strategy are acting as fresh pastures to replenish bilateral relations. As C. Uday Bhaskar had put it in 2014, bilateral ties were 'hung' until Modi came to the table and 'rebooted' them.[26]

The Modi Doctrine has succeeded in bringing back momentum in India's relations with the USA by clearing irritants and hurdles that had hitherto arrested progress. In 2015, Modi had creatively offered a government-supported insurance pool for American nuclear companies to supply atomic fuel and reactors to India to break a five-year-long impasse that had prevented American nuclear energy majors from investing in India. Obama called it a 'breakthrough understanding to elevate our relationship.'[27] The Modi government's decision in 2014 to allow more than 49 percent FDI in insurance and defence manufacturing, and to address specific 'nuts and bolts' problems of investors also enthused American corporations and restored their faith in India.[28] This was redoubled when Modi undertook big-ticket reforms of permitting 100 percent FDI in defence and civil aviation in June 2016.

Ashley Tellis, one of the architects of the India-USA civil nuclear deal during the George W. Bush and Manmohan Singh period, has underlined the impact factor of Modi's pragmatic deal-making with America as,

'Modi has demonstrated that he will not let the naysayers either in his own party or in the country get in the way of building a strong partnership with Washington—because that is, in his judgement, fundamentally in India's own national interest. It is really refreshing to be dealing at last with an Indian leader who not only believes this, but actually has the capacity to make it happen.'[29]

---

[26] Rao, Parsa. 2014. 'PM Narendra Modi's Visit Rebooted India-US Ties: Experts', *Daily News and Analysis*, October 4th

[27] Baker, Peter & Elen Barry. 2015. 'Obama Clears a Hurdle to Better Ties with India', *The New York Times*, January 25th

[28] IT. 2014. 'Modi Inspires Investor Confidence in US Visit, $42 Billion Committed', *India Today*, October 5th

[29] Haniffa, Aziz. 2015. 'It is Refreshing to Deal with Modi', *Rediff News*, February 2nd. URL: http://www.rediff.com/news/interview/it-is-refreshing-to-deal-with-modi/20150202.htm Last accessed on February 22nd, 2016

In September 2015, the US Commerce Secretary, Penny Pritzker threw light on how the Modi Doctrine was delivering when earlier Indian foreign policy attitudes had not, 'What feels new is the amount of energy that the Indian government is putting in to trying to remove the impediments that have been faced by foreign companies trying to do business in India.'[30]

That economic diplomacy is a core instrument for Modi in the process of revamping India-USA relations is evident from the rechristening of the annual Strategic Dialogue between the two countries as 'Strategic and Commercial Dialogue' from 2015 onward. One former Obama administration official, Alyssa Ayres, noted the significance of this change, 'The new structure signals a higher level of importance for economic and commercial matters. It also, notably, revises the structure of the dialogue to parallel the U.S.-China Strategic and Economic Dialogue. The U.S.-India economic relationship may be one-sixth the size of U.S.-China, but the dialogues now look similar.'[31] The urge for equality with China and the USA in status, and eventually in capabilities, is a tenet of the Modi Doctrine whose first part has already come true. Obama's highlighting of the India-USA relationship as the 'defining relationship of the 21st Century', and his record of seven personal meetings with Modi between September 2014 and June 2016 parallel the American President's hectic interactions with his Chinese counterpart, President Xi Jinping. Taken together, all these diplomatic goings-on imply that the triangular ties among the USA, China and India are most consequential for world order in the twenty-first century. Even before Modi's advent in 2014, India had already attained its position in this triumvirate through its demography, size, projected economic growth and military muscle. But the Modi Doctrine has been able to accentuate India's value in the triangle with clarity by eschewing the old role of a 'swing state' and forcing the other two sides of the triangle to treat India as a power centre of its own.

---

[30] AFP. 2015. 'India and US Renew Ever Closer Strategic Partnership', *Mint*, September 23rd

[31] Ayres, Alyssa. 2015. 'What's New in the US-India Strategic and Commercial Dialogue', *Council on Foreign Relations*, September 23rd

Triad of our times

The India-USA strategic relationship under Modi has reached levels not witnessed in earlier times. A diplomatic source involved in Modi's wide-ranging negotiations with Obama said in June 2016 that 'short of a formal alliance, the two sides are going to have the strongest ever strategic partnership.'[32] This closeness is informed by a shared concern in New Delhi and Washington of Beijing's hegemonic intent in Asia. Although the Obama administration has publicly clarified that the India-USA camaraderie is not 'aiming for confrontation with China or even to contain China'[33], there is a triangle at play which is unmissable. A diplomatic triangle is a system where the impact of relations between any two sides is felt on the third side. Just as the USA-USSR-China triangle was the defining combination during the Cold War era, the USA-China-India one has the 'make or mar' quality today for determining global power balance, institutional makeup and political outcomes. The Modi Doctrine has factored this triad into India's strategy and has entered into more geographically far-reaching planning and coordination with an eye on achieving a multipolar Asia as well as a multipolar world. The geopolitical content of India's foreign policy has mushroomed under Modi due to his sharper reading of global power politics and the manoeuvring it calls for.

The most striking shift that Modi has carried out is with regard to stretching the ambit of coordination with the USA in regions of the world where New Delhi had earlier hesitated to be marked out as a wilful actor with a defined purpose. Richard Rossow at the Center for Strategic and International Studies in Washington has argued that India under Modi is 'thinking differently about its global interests', and that it has expanded 'the number of areas where the United States and India promise to collaborate, including North Korea, Iraq, Syria, and the South China Sea.'[34] He adds that 'historically, India has avoided

---

[32] Rajghatta, Chidanand. 2016. 'With US Visit, Modi Eyes Strongest Strategic Ties', *The Times of India*, June 6th

[33] PTI. 2015. 'Obama in India: Indo-US Ties not Aimed at Containing China, says White House', *The Economic Times*, January 26th

[34] Rossow, Richard. 2014. *2015 Global Forecast: Crisis and Opportunity*, Washington, D.C.: Center for Strategic and International Studies, p.70

being this specific when it comes to identifying regions where it has strategic concerns and interests.'[35] C. Raja Mohan has echoed this view by averring that unlike Manmohan Singh, who was 'reluctant to embark on trilateral and quadrilateral partnerships with the United States, Modi and Obama have put the idea of building Asian coalitions at the centre of their regional strategy.'[36]

It goes without saying that, especially in Asia, when the USA and India appear in tandem, there will be repercussions for China's geostrategic calculations. The Joint Strategic Vision Statement for the Asia-Pacific and Indian Ocean Region which Modi and Obama released in early 2015 is a telling document because it is predicated on what the two countries call 'synergy' between India's 'Act East Policy' and the United States' rebalance or 'pivot' to Asia. The Statement's call for 'freedom of navigation especially in the South China Sea' and its appeal to 'all parties to avoid the threat or use of force and pursue resolution of territorial and maritime disputes through all peaceful means, in accordance with universally recognised principles of international law'[37] is directed at checking China's aggressive behaviour.

There was a time during Manmohan Singh's prime ministership when the USA and China had issued joint communiques to 'work together to promote peace, stability and development in South Asia'[38], which was interpreted in India as a reification of the dreaded 'G2' or group of two combine wherein the USA was extending 'an invitation to China to meddle in India's backyard.'[39] Even now, the USA and China have an institutional mechanism called 'Sub-dialogue on Central and South Asia', but this forum has lost its anti-India potential, thanks to Modi's proactive engagement with Washington. The Modi Doctrine has sold the Obama administration the idea that America needs India

---

[35] Ibid.

[36] Mohan, Raja. 2015. 'India-US Relations: Modi and Obama Begin New Chapter', *Eurasia Review*, January 29th

[37] USG. 2015. 'U.S.-India Joint Strategic Vision for the Asia-Pacific and Indian Ocean Region', *The White House*, January 25th

[38] WH. 2009. 'US-China Joint Statement', *The White House*, November 17th

[39] Polgreen, Lydia. 2009. 'China Gains in US Eyes, and India Feels Slights', *The New York Times*, November 23rd

more in light of the growing clash of interests between the USA and its nearest rival in global power stakes, China.

For a man who commenced his first term in the Oval Office as a self-proclaimed 'America's first (Asia) Pacific president', and who followed it up with a grand strategy labelled as a 'pivot' or 'rebalance' to Asia, Obama had few concrete successes to show until late into his second term in an Asia brimming with new powers, such as India, which were anxious about China's 'big country diplomacy'[40] of throwing its weight around and carving an ever enlarging sphere of influence by elbowing out rivals. Obama's finest achievements in foreign policy—the assassination of Osama bin Laden in Pakistan, the normalisation of relations with Cuba and the resort to diplomacy as opposed to war with Iran—were all in spheres extraneous to his much-touted Asian pivot policy. Under the distracted watch of the Obama administration, China grew stronger, more assertive and threatening towards smaller countries in Asia, spreading widespread doubts about America's capacity and intent to constrain the dragon.

Apart from shoring up the USA's traditional treaty allies—Japan, South Korea, Thailand, the Philippines and Australia—Obama had not done much for the bulk of his presidency to integrate non-allied partners in Asia like India. The Asian pivot under Obama, a champion of non-military multi-lateral diplomacy, was meaningless if Washington did not expand its web to literally pivotal nations such as India and Indonesia. Obama's decision to return for an unprecedented second time to India in 2015 happened in this context of a president searching for an appropriate legacy in Asia. Ironically, he had to take a leaf from his predecessor George W. Bush—a foreign policy blunderbuss in general—whose 'discovery' and embrace of India was a career highlight he can boast forever. Compared to Bush, Obama displayed less of a strategic vision and clarity about Asia and India's central role therein. But this lacuna was overcome in Obama's later years in the White House thanks to a tango partner called Modi.

It would not be farfetched to argue that Modi helped Obama redeem America's destiny in Asia, the continent that will define the

---

[40] Shi, Ting & David Tweed. 2014. 'Xi Outlines 'Big Country Diplomacy' Chinese Foreign Policy', *Bloomberg*, December 1st

shape of the world in the twenty-first century. The 'indispensable partnership'[41] which Obama hailed when he first visited India in 2010 has been raised to new heights with Modi's push. The fact that the White House assessed Modi's ingenious invitation to Obama to grace India's nationalistic Republic Day celebration in January 2015, where it proudly displays its military might, as 'a very political gesture'[42] and consented, reveals that they viewed Modi as the final chance for the US president to salvage his Asia policy. The flurry of American officials who preceded Obama in India and kept pouring in after he left India in early 2015 testified to a realisation in Washington that Modi's India is the lynchpin for the USA to manage China's assertive expansionism.

One of the milestones in the USA-India strategic partnership that Modi has personally piloted is the implementation of the Defence Trade and Technology Initiative (DTTI) via concrete projects for co-production and technology transfer of cutting-edge military knowhow. Obama's Defense Secretary Chuck Hagel spoke in 2014 of forging 'a defense industrial partnership, one that would transform our nations' defense cooperation from simply buying and selling to co-production, co-development and freer exchange of technology.'[43] Why did America climb down from its historical reluctance to offer 'groundbreaking technology' to India? Modi's business-friendly regime in New Delhi, which has liberalised FDI in defence, has whetted the appetites of the US military companies. Hagel kept repeating during his India trip in 2014 that he expected the Modi government to clear the bureaucratic delays and red tape, which had frustrated American corporations in the past.

DTTI is also a step towards fulfilling Modi's 'Make in India' thrust, which has identified military manufacturing as one of the priority sectors to develop India's indigenous industries. The Indian prime minister's statement that 'making weapons in India rather than importing them is our motto and it is the backbone of our 'Made in India' programme', and his observation that 'at present we import

[41] WH. 2010. 'Remarks by the President to the Joint Session of the Indian Parliament in New Delhi, India', *The White House*, November 8th

[42] Jha, Lalit. 2015. 'Barack Obama Invite Idea came from Narendra Modi', *Mint*, January 21st

[43] Simeone, Nick. 2014. 'Hagel Urges Expanded US-Indian Defense Cooperation', *US Department of Defense*, August 9th

weapons from other countries to equip our armed force...now, we have made it a policy that before striking a deal for weapons, the government puts in a condition in the agreement to make a part of the weapons in India'[44], are indicators to the American government and corporations that New Delhi will not be satisfied with the traditional buyer-seller model. Under the Modi Doctrine, it has to be an investor-exporter model that will generate profits for the USA, but build Indian capacities in the process.

But there is more than pecuniary calculation behind the American willingness to part with closely guarded technological secrets. The incredible rise of China in the new millennium and the relative decline of American power have left the USA's strategists scratching their heads with no rollback mechanism in sight. American reiterations of the complementarity between Modi's 'Act East' policy and the US' pivot leave no doubt that Washington wants to coordinate geopolitically with New Delhi on a much broader scale for maintaining a 'stable balance of power' (code for countering Chinese expansion). Technology transfer and joint military exercises with India have been thrown in as baits to fulfill this need. This is the underlying essence of the US designating India as a 'major defense partner' in June 2016.[45] For the US to realistically remain relevant in Asia, it needs to accommodate Indian interests and enlarge the strategic space in which India can grow and fulfill its potential. Under the Modi Doctrine, India will bargain for the best possible terms from America on a variety of issues ranging from defence co-production and nuclear liability to concessions on climate change. If the US is steadfast about not ceding Asia to China on a platter, it should not take it to heart if India votes against American positions in the UN Security Council, if Israel or France bag big-ticket military deals with India to the detriment of American competitors or if India's response on Obama's hobby horse of reducing carbon emissions is frigid. Rather than insisting on strict quid pro quos, Washington must adopt enlightened magnanimity and keep imagining new doable

---

[44] Urs, Anil. 2016. 'Weapons Manufacture is Backbone of 'Make in India' Programme: Modi', *The Hindu Business Line*, January 3rd

[45] WH. 2016. 'Joint Statement: The United States and India: Enduring Global Partners in the 21st Century', *The White House*, June 7th

projects where it can tango with New Delhi. The alternative is to stand as a mute bystander as China goes from strength to strength in Asia.

Conscious that the Chinese would scrutinise every word that the American leaders utter in India, the government of the USA often clarifies that Washington need not choose between its Asian partnerships with both China and India. But there is one unmistakable red line that goes unsaid—America has a strict ban on weapons trade and military technology deals with China. Washington also discourages Israel and European governments from assisting China's defence modernisation. US-China civilian trade and foreign investments are dizzyingly high, but they lack strategic trust to reach the stage of military give-and-take.

For that matter, even India cannot blindly rely on the USA for military supplies and knowledge exchange. Under Modi, the USA has cemented its position as India's largest arms supplier, pipping Russia, Israel and France.[46] But the Modi Doctrine is also watchful about overdependence on the USA. As a global power with a penchant for imposing economic sanctions and political preconditions on high-technology exports, America is always a high maintenance partner as opposed to Russia or Israel, which do not place policy demands on India. Suppose the alarming growth in nuclear arsenals of China and Pakistan compel India to resume nuclear testing, will the Americans understand or revert to sanctions such as the ones slapped on India after 1998? If New Delhi does not comport with America's approaches to Iran, Russia or BRICS, could such differences impinge on the US-India defence supply lines? What value are American weapons to India if some of them are also sold to Pakistan?

The Modi Doctrine intends to make America walk the talk that the India-US partnership is geared not merely towards generating bilateral gains but for sustaining the whole global order.

Modi and Obama have also committed to intensifying intelligence cooperation to combat Islamist extremism around the world. But the general propensity for military intervention and arm-twisting that the USA deploys to solve security problems in the Middle East renders India queasy. During the peak of the Ukraine crisis in 2014-2015, the Obama administration sought Indian assurances for isolating Russia. It also tried

[46] Pandit, Rajat. 2015. 'US Set to be India's Biggest Arms Supplier', *The Times of India*, July 13th

to exclude India from playing a prominent role in Afghanistan, and from permitting Iran to be involved in a lasting solution in Afghanistan. Owing to differing power capabilities and worldviews, India and the US often agree to disagree on geopolitics, and this condition has not changed under Modi who has not yielded to American pressures one bit. His pragmatic mantra is to keep aside issues that divide the USA and India and concentrate on deepening the areas of convergence such as economics, defence cooperation and management of China's rise in Asia. As the China specialist Gordon Chang put it, 'Obama's oft-discussed 'pivot to Asia' has no credibility unless Indian prime minister Narendra Modi cooperates with Washington'[47], a bargaining chip that Modi has exploited to India's benefit.

However, Modi has also set red lines that the USA cannot cross in undermining India's strategic autonomy and national interests. Unlike Manmohan Singh—who was famously obsequious to the USA, succumbed to American pressure in crucial UN votes on Iran and Sri Lanka, was docile on American cyber espionage against India and military aid to Pakistan—Modi has been far more confident to warn Washington that it can no longer hurt India in some issue areas and get away with it. This dignity-suffused 'India first' attitude flies against the reductionist reading of Manmohan Singh's National Security Adviser, Shivshankar Menon, that Modi's foreign policy has 'a strong pro-Western tilt.'[48] If *Sammaan* or national honour is Modi's creed and equality with the USA is his motto, he cannot be simplistically labelled as 'pro-Western'.

The Modi government demanded accountability from the USA for its massive cyber surveillance over private and governmental communications in India that had been revealed by the renegade Edward Snowden. Manmohan Singh was too meek on the grave threat posed to India by the US National Security Agency's (NSA) intrusive snooping. It had rightly escalated American abuse of a female Indian diplomat in 2013, but left the bigger issue of mistrust generated by the

---

[47] Chang, Gordon. 2014. 'US Sees an Indispensable Partner in Modi', *The Sunday Guardian*, September 27th

[48] Haniffa, Aziz. 2015. 'Modi Sarkar has a Strong Pro-West Tilt', *Rediff News*, July 14th. URL: http://www.rediff.com/news/special/modi-sarkar-has-a-strong-pro-west-tilt/20150714.htm Last accessed on February 23rd, 2016

NSA's hacking unaddressed. Washington took India for granted due to the non-assertive approach of Manmohan Singh, who had a strange kowtowing affection for America beyond what was warranted from the head of government of an aspiring great power. The Modi government's blunt communication to the USA that its cyber espionage of India was 'unacceptable' and that India was 'agitated and angry'[49] about it sent a clear message that India will not tolerate great power meddling.

The Modi Doctrine has also improved India's concrete preparedness to counter cyber threats from more powerful states as a demonstration of the gutsiness and toughness, which the BJP and Modi tout as cornerstones of their approach to national security. Not all Indian vulnerabilities to cyber attacks from the USA or China have been patched, but the Modi Doctrine is trying to close the gaps in Indian capabilities with the bigger players in this field like China, Russia and the USA. Given Modi's belief that India can also be a security provider for less evolved countries in this field, he has offered cyber security assistance to Mongolia, Uzbekistan and small Indian Ocean nations facing threats of Chinese penetration of their information systems, and also boosted India's cyber security cooperation with upcoming actors like Israel and Malaysia. With the USA itself, the Modi government resumed a bilateral Cyber Security Dialogue and also committed to law enforcement cooperation with China to control cybercrimes in 2015. How far it is possible for two established great powers like the USA and China and for one wannabe great power like India to have cyber truces and non-aggression remains debatable, and Modi knows that self-reliance and capacity building of India's own cyber prowess are paramount.

On American military aid of advanced weaponry to Pakistan, the Modi government has been forthright in conveying 'displeasure' and 'disappointment' to Washington on grounds that the billions of dollars of hi-tech equipment that the USA sells to Pakistan frees the latter to conventionally match India and continue unconventional cross-border terrorism against India.[50] Although the Americans refute India

---

49 PTI. 2014. 'Snooping Unacceptable, Sushma Swaraj Tells Kerry', *The New Indian Express*, July 31st

50 PTI. 2016. 'Ignoring India's Protest, US Justifies Sale of F-16 Jets to Pakistan', *The Times of India*, February 13th

by saying that their arms sales to Pakistan do not disturb the overall military balance in Asia, strategists in New Delhi see Pakistan as a tool of China to hold India down and prevent it from becoming China's equal. American reluctance to pressure Pakistan on halting Islamist terrorism aimed at India has also dampened India time and again. If the USA-China-India triangle is the main axis of world politics today, the India-China-Pakistan sub-triangle drags the USA in willy-nilly and complicates Asian geopolitics. Through its holistic strategy, the Modi Doctrine has attempted to maximise benefits from both the USA and China, and minimise tussles with the two most powerful nations on earth. But the Pakistan factor intrudes often into the triangle and reminds us of the limits of triangulation.

There are other less salient areas of disagreement between India and the USA, which Modi has not shied away from. As we saw earlier in this book, the fault lines between the two at the WTO remain in place and so do clashes over the responsibility for mitigating climate change. Obama unequivocally endorsed India's permanent membership of the UN Security Council in 2010, but his diplomats acknowledged five years later that there remain differences with India on the 'process' by which the Security Council can be reformed.[51] There are also some sensitive domestic policy issues on which India spars with the USA such as professional mobility for Indian IT professionals in America, and human trafficking and protection of homosexuals and religious minorities in India. American investors adore Modi, but still foresee tremendous practical obstacles to do business on the ground in India.

The Modi Doctrine has not papered over these cracks, but has reminded the USA that questions about China and the emerging world order are far too large to be sidelined by routine policy disputes between two mature democracies. Modi's success with the USA has been to make it stick to larger purpose and grand strategy in a way that it enables India's unstoppable rise as a leading power. The power gap between the USA and India is currently still much wider than the gap between the USA and China. Modi has tried to exploit this duality within the triangle to India's advantage. Comments by an Obama

---

[51] PTI. 2015. 'UNSC Disagreement Doesn't Mean Lack of Support to India: US', *The Times of India*, September 21st

National Security Council official, Peter Lavoy, that 'this is by far the strongest the relationship has ever been', and that 'we see a deep opening and expansion of bilateral cooperation and working together to solve regional problems and international problems'[52], testify to the acuity of the Modi Doctrine. Obama's Assistant Secretary of State for South and Central Asia, Nisha Biswal, has in fact credited the Indian prime minister's fearless diplomacy towards the USA which overcomes "the hesitations of history" as 'Modi Doctrine.'[53] The 'Mobama' personal chemistry, which was mooted earlier in this book, happened to be the interpersonal manifestation of a structural transformation orchestrated by Modi armed with his formula of 'three Ps'. Whoever succeeds Obama in the White House from 2017 onward will find that Modi has purposefully locked in a *fait accompli* of dense and multi-pronged relations which is irreversible for the foreseeable future.

Tackling the dragon

On the preeminent challenge to Indian foreign policy—China— the Modi Doctrine has evolved a carrot-and-stick strategy that does not alienate Beijing, but simultaneously duels with it grittily in spheres where it grates against New Delhi. Modi himself summed up the delicacy and intricacy of handling India's giant northern neighbour when he visited Beijing in May 2015, 'Our relationship has been complex in recent decades. I stressed the need for China to reconsider its approach on some of the issues that hold us back from realizing the full potential of our partnership. I suggested that China should take a strategic and long-term view of our relations.'[54]

He did this plain talking in the context of Beijing investing $46 billion in the China Pakistan Economic Corridor (CPEC) that passes through parts of Kashmir that India claims to be illegally occupied by Pakistan, repeated incursions of the Chinese People's Liberation Army (PLA) into land claimed by India, and China's issuance of stapled

---

[52] PTI. 2015. 'Red Tapism of Indian Bureaucracy Poses Hurdle to Red Carpet for Foreign Companies: US', *The Economic Times*, August 23rd

[53] PTI. 2016. 'US Christens PM's Vision of India-US Ties as 'Modi Doctrine', *The Times of India*, June 10th

[54] Mandhana, Niharika. 2015. 'Modi on China: From the Border to Trade, it's Complicated', *The Wall Street Journal*, May 15th

visas to residents of Arunachal Pradesh which is a part of India, but claimed by China in entirety. Sovereignty-related snubs and jabs are an integral component of contemporary Sino-Indian relations, and Modi's candid expression of concern about the seemingly 'economic' Silk Route treading on geopolitical fault lines was in that vein. Similarly, to China's repeated demand that India must reiterate its commitment to the 'one China policy' (i.e. to stay at arm's length from Taiwan), the Modi government crisply asked China to reciprocally respect a 'one India policy' (i.e. to renounce claims over Arunachal Pradesh).[55]

Modi sees himself as a history maker who can achieve a 'breakthrough' and find a path to 'early resolution' of the vexed border dispute with China. Having completed eighteen rounds of tortuous negotiations since 2003, the Sino-Indian border issue is begging for a consummation that has been frustratingly elusive. If one counts previous iterations of the current process, it goes back as far as 1981, when the two Asian neighbours began structured dialogue on the contested 4,057km-long border. Progress has been incremental, marked by backsliding from China, which reopens fronts that India considers to be done and dusted. It is a clash of national egos, will and ingenuity, with neither party willing to acquiesce on its core claims. Yet, the fact that the Asian giants stay committed to round after round of protracted talks, while averting actual military hostilities between troops tensely facing each other in the high Himalayas, conveys that the exercise is not entirely futile. Diplomacy helps avoid bloodshed, although the 'confidence' from the confidence-building measures (CBMs) often evaporates due to what India sees as Chinese slipperiness.

However, the Modi Doctrine is angling for a different outcome compared to the past. True to his foreign policy mission as a remover of obstacles, Modi has prioritised settling the Sino-Indian border as his major medium-term diplomatic target after ironing out wrinkles in the USA-India civilian nuclear agreement. Notwithstanding the complexity of the Sino-Indian negotiation framework, the solution is a simple territorial swap. China will have to drop its claim across the eastern sector of the Line of Actual Control (LAC) over 90,000 square kilometres of

---

[55] Samanta, Pranab. 2014. 'One China? What about One India Policy: Sushma Swaraj to Wang Yi', *The Indian Express*, June 12th

Arunachal Pradesh, and India in turn will disavow any claim across the Western sector on the 30,000 square kilometres of Aksai Chin, which was fully occupied by China after the 1962 war. In other words, the LAC has to be converted into a legally recognised international border with pledges by both sides to respect its sanctity. There is no other imaginable formula for peace. In September 2014, Modi's National Security Adviser Ajit Doval referred to the fact that his boss and Xi are 'two powerful and very popular very decisive leaders' who 'open possibilities' for an 'orbital jump' in bilateral relations. But he was also circumspect in adding, 'Whether it leads to solutions, nobody can be sure because that does not necessarily mean that it is only dependent on a single factor.'[56] Since then, there has been no dramatic movement towards a final settlement and both sides have hunkered down for more talks, confidence building measures and summit meetings.

Modi's eagerness for ending the territorial row with China has not been reciprocated by Xi, raising doubts as to what exactly is Beijing's strategy towards India. Does it want to keep the border dispute simmering as a pressure point against India to prevent it from cozying up excessively to the USA? Why would China, whose track record of treachery and doublespeak evoke mistrust in India, be possibly ready to compromise on its maximalist demands that have blocked genuine quid pro quo for so long? Firstly, China always measures its relative power and leverage vis-a-vis other countries and treats them accordingly. As India under Modi overtook China in GDP growth from 2015 onward, the era of China bargaining from a position of superiority with India entered its twilight. Secondly, Beijing knows that Modi is pursuing defence modernisation and building new motorable roads and infrastructure along both the western and eastern sectors of the LAC. Once the 30,000-strong Mountain Strike Corps of the Indian Army is deployed along the LAC, a new ground reality will emerge of India having conventional deterrence capability to conduct counter-offensives into Chinese-occupied Tibet or Aksai Chin.

The offensive advantage that the PLA has enjoyed and exploited through repetitive incursions across the LAC will gradually diminish

---

56 Varma, K.J. 2014. 'Narendra Modi, Xi Jinping Could Clinch Border Deal: Ajit Doval', *Mint*, September 10th

as the pace with which the Modi government has implemented landing grounds for military aircraft, strategic railway lines, tunnels, and arterial roads leading up to the LAC has been much quicker than its predecessor.[57] China should be earnest to draw up a final border before India obtains military parity under the Modi Doctrine, which has shades of the Reagan Doctrine's 'peace through strength' formula. The fact that Beijing has not yet shown the urgency suggests it may wait and see how much more powerful India under Modi can become, and close the gap with China before conceding on its claims to Indian controlled territory. Modi's determination to speedily improve India's border defence infrastructure along the LAC has provoked China to carry out more preemptive military incursions into territory claimed by India, suggesting rough weather ahead. But once the Modi Doctrine accomplishes the deterrent defence apparatus as a fait accompli, China will have to moderate its behaviour of poking and needling India in various sectors of the LAC.

American scholar M Taylor Fravel has studied the puzzle why China has amicably settled seventeen out of its twenty-three outstanding territorial disputes with various countries, and found that internal and external threats hold the answers. Whenever China feels threatened by ethnic rebellions and internal uprisings within its peripheral regions, it is compelled to offer concessions to neighbours in order to localise and isolate these internal revolts. Similarly, whenever China senses a global strategic challenge, it compromises on border disputes to deny potential allies to its global adversary.[58]

The lessons from this analysis are clear for Modi. As the host of the Dalai Lama and the Tibetan government-in-exile, India will never give up the 'Tibet card' because it is a chip to maintain internal strategic pressure on China and rebuff Chinese claims over Arunachal as 'South Tibet'. Modi's decision to invite the Prime Minister of the Tibetan Government-in-Exile, Lobsang Sangay, to his inauguration in May

---

57 Kulkarni, Pranav. 2015. 'Will Finish Building China Border Infrastructure by 2018: Rao Inderjit', *The Indian Express*, May 18th

58 Fravel, Taylor. 2005. 'Regime Insecurity and International Cooperation: Explaining China's Compromises in Territorial Disputes', *International Security*, Volume 30, Issue 2.

2014 was met with protest demarches from Beijing, but he signaled no intention to buckle under. On Chinese claims over Arunachal Pradesh, he has explicitly warned that 'the world does not welcome the mindset of expansion in today's times. China will also have to leave behind its mindset of expansion.'[59] As we saw earlier in this chapter, the Modi Doctrine has also advanced ties with the USA as a way of compelling the Chinese to be more reasonable with India in the triangular interplay. Modi's fast-tracking of the USA-India strategic partnership does alarm China, but it reminds Beijing to act fairly towards New Delhi on the border so as to blunt anti-China counterbalancing manoeuvres. Given China's increasing tensions with almost all its neighbours, showing good faith on the Indian border may earn it a much needed breather from worries of being 'encircled' by American allies.

In May 2015, Modi delivered a perceptive speech at China's premier Tsinghua University in which he reminded his hosts that 'if the last century was the age of alliances, this is an era of interdependence. Talks of alliances against one another have no foundation. Our partnership…should not be determined by the concerns of others, but by the interests of our two countries.'[60] It was in response to Chinese fears that India was aligning with the USA to contain China. For all the heralding of a 'natural alliance' between India and the USA to counter China, the Indian navy has never signed up for the US-commanded Combined Maritime Forces (CMF), a multinational naval grouping of thirty countries. Unlike Japan, which is a treaty ally of the USA and a core member of CMF, India believes in maintaining independence from American-designed endeavours that ultimately serve the USA's interests. In September 2015, India, Japan and the USA held their first 'Trilateral Ministerial' dialogue and highlighted common goals of protecting 'freedom of navigation' and upholding the 'importance of international law', while explicitly mentioning the South China Sea. The message was unambiguously directed at Beijing. In the following

---

59 Gottipati, Sruthi. 2014. 'Modi says China Must Drop Mindset of Expansionism over Arunachal Pradesh', *Reuters*, Feburary 22nd

60 PMO. 2015. 'PM Modi's Speech at Tsinghua University', *Prime Minister's Office*, May 15th. URL: https://www.youtube.com/watch?v=bq2Ur3KEg1U Last accessed on February 25th

chapter, I will analyse the Japan factor in Modi's 'Act East' strategy, and how it intersects with the American 'pivot' to Asia. Yet, the Modi Doctrine's avoidance of any formal alliance with the USA and its parallel interest in managing its rivalry and resolving outstanding disputes with China leaves room for creative diplomacy. Modi has enabled New Delhi to push back against Beijing's regional encroachment without the former having to yoke itself to Washington's agenda of trying to rope in India as an offshore balancer against China.

Neither China nor India would be doing a favour to the other by trying to bring closure to the boundary discord. They will be helping themselves if this long festering wound can be amicably healed. In 1988, China's pragmatic leader Deng Xiaoping had remarked that the intractable border dispute with India was 'for future generations to resolve.' For the Modi Doctrine, the future is now, i.e. within the next decade. Modi's desire to free India from albatrosses around the neck like the unresolved border conflict, backed up by acute reading of the Chinese psyche, means that this intergenerational border tussle is, relatively speaking, closer to resolution than before. All Chinese strategic elites I have met over the last two years believe that there is only a medium-term hope of settling the dispute over the next decade or so. Should Modi retain power and complete two terms in office, i.e. stay at the helm of Indian foreign policy until 2024, he may ultimately oversee this denouement.

Notwithstanding the strategic tensions, the Modi Doctrine has left a frisson in China surrounding enhanced economic cooperation with India. Many Chinese strategists treat Modi as 'good news because he will put the focus on economic relations.'[61] China's state-owned media have displayed wariness of Modi's nationalistic foreign policy credentials, but also welcomed him for boosting India's infrastructure and manufacturing, which create 'a myriad of opportunities for Chinese enterprises. As a right-winger in Indian politics, Modi is more likely to become India's "Nixon" who will further propel the China-India relationship.'[62] Modi's four visits to China while he was the chief

---

[61] Ward, Jonathan. 2014. 'Chinese Analysts Interpret Modi's New India', *China Brief*, Volume 14, Issue 12, p.10

[62] Zongyi, Liu. 2014. 'Modi Ready to do Business with China', *Global Times*, May 19th

minister of Gujarat to promote business links, and his eagerness as India's prime minister to attract Chinese FDI to spur the 'Make in India' campaign, have enthused Chinese elites that he will follow the modernisation lessons of Deng Xiaoping. The dramatic announcement that Modi made in May 2015 of simplified electronic visas for Chinese citizens to visit India by overruling objections of Indian security agencies has also been received in Beijing as a 'gift' and a 'big piece of news'[63] that demonstrates his seriousness about facilitating commerce, tourism and people-to-people interaction.

Even on the intractable problem of the trade deficit—which stood at a whopping $40 billion in China's favour in 2015—agreements between Modi and President Xi to reduce barriers to more Indian exports to China, and to promote large-scale Chinese Foreign Direct Investment (FDI) in India, are win-win propositions. With the Chinese economy in an extended slowdown and Western economies still in slumber, the trillions of dollars China holds as forex reserves will need a safe and sustainable outlet for investment. Modi's pitch that India is the 'next frontier of economic revolution'[64], and his avid attempts to win the hearts of giant Chinese corporations, dovetail with China's search for the next big market opportunity that will absorb its overcapacity. Just as America profited economically by outsourcing to China's factories for decades, China could do the same by investing in Modi's 'Make in India'. It is one of the little wonders of the Modi Doctrine that China, which had invested just $400 million in India from 2000 to 2014, pledged $20 billion of FDI to India from 2015 to 2020. Chinese involvement in high speed railways and industrial park development in India is set to bring the modernisation element of bilateral ties to the fore.

Yet, in spite of the 'Modi effect' on China, there is an underwhelming feel to the bilateral economic equation because of the strategic unease. In September 2014, China's Consul General in Mumbai sent expectations soaring with a magic figure of $100 billion of FDI in India over the next half decade, and adding to effect that it was 'thrice the

---

[63] Dasgupta, Saibal. 2015. 'China Cheers for Modi after E-Visa Surprise at University', *The Times of India*, May 15th

[64] ANI. 2015. 'India is the Next Frontier of Economic Revolution', Narendra Modi Tells Students in China', *Deccan Chronicle*, May 15th

investments committed by Japan.'[65] Finally though, Xi was stingier and committed merely $20 billion of FDI, with corollary implications that the gaping bilateral trade deficit has no easy solution. FDI-starved India has, of course, gratefully accepted any amount of Chinese capital coming its way. But the sharply truncated numbers were reminders that China is wary of spurring India's growth to a point where the power gap between the two neighbours narrows down. Having inched closer to the USA in power through sustained vacuuming of American private capital in the form of inward FDI, China would not sincerely facilitate India's manufacturing growth to the point that the latter becomes its economic equal.

Will China sense strategic danger in India's rising clout and subject its FDI choices to geopolitical calculations? Is it not politics that China is placing more FDI in shaky Pakistan than in stable India? Modi is not impervious to China's inscrutable motives and the trust deficit, but has followed the mantra of maximising the good and minimising the bad in this vital relationship. The former Indian diplomat Rajiv Sikri has written that 'Modi's judgement is that it is wiser to have frequent high-level engagement with China in order to douse brewing troubles at an early stage, remove misunderstandings and, wherever possible, cooperate where there is mutual interest.'[66] In the full-blown spirit of *Samvaad* or innovative retail diplomacy beyond interstate relations, Modi opened an account on Weibo, China's social media platform, and notched up over a hundred thousand followers from among ordinary Chinese citizens.[67] He has warmed up to Xi as an 'old friend', rotated a Gandhian spinning wheel with him in his native Gujarat, taken the so-called world's most powerful selfie with Chinese premier Li Keqiang at a hybrid demonstration of Yoga and Taichi which garnered 31.85 million hits, and won the accolade of 'highest ranked global leader' ahead of Xi himself from a Chinese state-owned survey institution. The

[65] Pandey, Piyush. 2014. 'China to Invest $100 Billion in India Over 5 Years', *The Times of India*, September 13th

[66] Sikri, Rajiv. 2015. 'One Year of Prime Minister Modi's Foreign Policy', in Ganguly, Anirban (ed.) *Redefining Governance: Essays on One Year of Narendra Modi Government*, New Delhi: Prabhat Prakashan, p. 131

[67] Wong, Chun. 2015. 'Hello China! Modi takes Diplomacy Directly to Weibo', *The Wall Street Journal*, May 5th

atmospherics in bilateral relations have never been better and one can attribute it to the personal diplomacy of the Modi Doctrine. It has not managed to break all the mental barriers between the two countries that go back in time, but at least opened new vistas of hope.

One of the emerging themes where Modi has ventured creatively to find common ground with China is in unconventional security. His Defence Minister, Manohar Parrikar, has gone on record stating that 'India is ready to strengthen defence cooperation with China and work hard to maintain border peace and stability. Both India and China are victims of terrorism and India hopes to stage common fight against international terrorism with China.'[68] The 'Hand in Hand' counterterrorism military exercises between the Indian Army and the PLA have grown in depth under the Modi government and have been described as 'truly "joint", comprising of joint planning, joint command, joint component units and joint action.'[69] Modi's efforts have yielded an agreement in 2015 between China and India to 'actively exchange intelligence on terror groups and their activities through a dedicated communication channel.'[70] Yet, here too, India's attempt to isolate Pakistan by getting China on board for countering Islamist extremism in the region has not yielded as much result as expected because Beijing treats terrorism aimed at Chinese controlled Xinjiang differently from terrorism aimed at Indian controlled Kashmir. China's 'all weather alliance' with Pakistan prevents the former from genuinely cooperating with India to launch a united front against jihadist groups of all hues. If the Modi Doctrine can move China even a wee bit towards pressuring all shades of Pakistan-based and Pakistan-sponsored Islamist terrorists, it would be a big feather in its cap.

In the new multilateralism for institutional reform of global financial institutions, Modi has also shown a keenness to expand cooperation with China. India is a founding member of the Chinese-led Asian Infrastructure Investment Bank (AIIB), which has been vehemently opposed by the

---

68 Miou, Song. 2015. 'Chinese, Indian Senior Officials Call for Cooperation in Fighting Terrorism', *Xinhua*, November 17th

69 GOI. 2015. 'India-China Joint Counter-Terrorist Exercise Hand in Hand-2015 Commences at Kunming, China', *Embassy of India in Beijing*, December 12th

70 Laskar, Rezaul. 2015. 'PM Modi Calls for India-China Partnership to Fight Global Terrorism', *Hindustan Times*, November 21st

USA as a threat to Western economic hegemony. China's rhetoric while weaving new multilateral economic networks is that they are 'inclusive' and helpful to spread prosperity across Asia, Africa and Europe. AIIB secured membership of dozens of countries, including India, Vietnam and the Philippines, three Asian neighbours which are quite wary of China's power and suspicious of its hegemonic intentions. Likewise, as we elaborated in the previous chapter, Beijing's proposal to create a Regional Comprehensive Economic Partnership (RCEP) trade agreement has found favour with India and other traditional Asian rivals of China.

Despite misgivings about the risks posed by a muscle-flexing and militaristic China, Asian countries including India are open-minded about the benefits of China as a regional economic dynamo. They are also frustrated by the shenanigans of West-governed financial institutions like the World Bank and the International Monetary Fund (IMF), and the limitations of the USA-Japan duo's Asian Development Bank (ADB). When the Chinese state media proclaims that 'AIIB and the US-led World Bank will be both competitive and cooperative'[71], it plays well with developing country audiences including in India that detest the Bretton Woods institutions as vehicles for American intervention and neocolonialism.

Is the AIIB's success in attracting Asian and European capital a portent of China's coming lordship of a revamped global institutional architecture? Beijing must be careful in pushing the envelope. If it overplays its hand, the so-called 'inclusive' institutional ideas it is churning out can be construed as expansionist and hegemonic. The resistance Beijing faces on the Maritime Silk Route and One Belt One Road (OBOR) concept in South and Southeast Asia holds out lessons to shed arrogance and domineering behaviour that are becoming disturbing hallmarks of Chinese foreign policy. Modi's unambiguous support for AIIB and the 'New Development Bank' of BRICS, which is headquartered in Shanghai, and his contrasting discomfort about OBOR sums up the mixed nature of the Sino-Indian relationship.

On one hand, India is happy to partake in joint endeavours with China that will deliver on India's developmental aspirations such as infrastructure ramp-up. For instance, Beijing has acknowledged that

---

[71] GT. 2015. 'AIIB will Invigorate China's Opening-Up', *Global Times*, March 19th

'unlike in the past, when it was perceived to be dragging its feet, India is now (under Modi) showing enthusiasm' on the establishment of the Bangladesh-China-India-Myanmar (BCIM) economic corridor that would link Yunnan province with the state of West Bengal and facilitate more regional trade and commerce.[72] On the other hand, India is wary of China using grandiose transnational connectivity schemes like OBOR that will strategically corner and marginalise India. The Modi Doctrine's bid to develop 'Project *Mausam*', revive the ancient 'Cotton Route', upgrade India's maritime military infrastructure, and cement economic cooperation and strategic partnerships with countries in the Indian Ocean region are explicit moves to deter Chinese domination in the Asian maritime theatre.[73] In the next chapter, I will argue that the Modi Doctrine's 'neighbourhood first' policy is also working toward vigorously pushing back against China's penetration of South Asia and resisting Chinese military expansionism in the Indo-Pacific. All these patterns confirm the dualistic strategy of the Modi Doctrine vis-à-vis China, i.e. befriend the dragon in economics, but hedge against it in the military and security domains by coordinating with the USA and Indo-Pacific powers like Japan and Australia.

Building India's sinews

Within the framework of the USA-China-India triangle, Modi is conscious that great powers only respect those countries which are their equals in capabilities or which are rising to achieve parity with them. In a tribute to the former Indian President, A.P.J Abdul Kalam, Modi lauded his dedication to amassing national military strength. The latter's obituary read, 'Strength (is) not born of aggression but of understanding. An insecure nation will rarely discover the route to prosperity. Strength commands respect. His (Kalam's) contributions in our nuclear and space achievements have given India the muscle to be confident of her place in the region and the world.'[74] That India's muscle

---

[72] Aneja, Atul. 2015. 'China, India Fast-Track BCIM Economic Corridor Project', *The Hindu*, June 26th

[73] Chaudhury, Dipanjan. 2015. 'India Plans Cotton, Ancient Maritime Routes to Counter China's Ambitions', *The Economic Times*, April 17th

[74] Modi, Narendra. 2015. 'Kalam's Vision for Nation was Anchored in Freedom and Strength', *Hindustan Times*, July 28th

needs beef is an important element of the Modi Doctrine. In August 2014, the current Indian prime minister had said while commissioning a locally constructed advanced battleship that 'our aim is to achieve such prowess in our defence capabilities that no country dare cast an evil eye on India. We can guarantee peace if our military is modernised. No country will dare challenge India.'[75]

He has put his money where his mouth is—in a large-scale Indian military modernisation programme and in ushering in a long-delayed domestic defence industrial base. When Modi became India's prime minister, he inherited a stalled and frustrating system of defence spending that had reached a fifty-year low as a percentage of GDP. He has since turned it around with year-on-year percentage increases in budgetary allocation for defence. Procurement of new weapons systems have been quickened and rendered more transparent, and the 'Make in India' precondition has dominated foreign military deals. As we saw previously, FDI limits in defence have been raised and Modi has signed major co-production deals with partner nations to impart a cutting-edge to India's military materiel. From nuclear submarines to stealth frigates, the Indian Navy has in particular received a shot in the arm under Modi and has risen in its power projection capability. He has also openly called for India to aim at 'domination of cyber space'[76] and invested heavily in improving the inter-agency coordination in the field of web-based warfare. Sudhir Mishra, the CEO of BrahMos Aerospace, a joint defence venture of Russia and India, is of the opinion that 'PM Modi has brought a paradigm shift in India's defence sphere. India will now extensively manufacture ships and helicopters. It is said that any country which can manufacture aircraft, submarines and tanks is a superpower.'[77]

Much of India's military buildup is inevitably related to threat perception from China because the two Asian giants share common geopolitical space and frequently run into each other as competitors for

---

[75] MT. 2014. 'India Welcomes its First Home-Built Warship', *Daily Mail*, August 16th

[76] Peri, Dinakar. 2014. 'Cyber Domination Crucial, Modi tells Commanders', *The Hindu*, October 17th

[77] Jain, Smriti & Ruchi Bambha. 2016. 'PM Modi has brought a paradigm shift in defence; 'Make in India' an imperative: BrahMos' Sudhir Mishra', *The Economic Times*, February 4th

influence. In May 2015, Modi shared his candid thoughts on China's rising global power and how India intended to deal with it:

'I firmly believe that there is not a single country in the world, whether its population is one million or much more, which would not want to increase its influence internationally. I think it is a very natural tendency for the nations to increase their influence in the international space, as they pursue their international relations with different countries. I firmly believe that with due regard to international rules and regulations, and with full respect for human values, I think with these two perspectives in mind each country has the right to increase its presence, its impact and influence internationally for the benefit of the global community.'[78]

It was a startling restatement of realpolitik logic mixed up with liberal ideas of welfare, and an indication that Modi sees the pursuit of power in international politics as a necessary function of leadership. All the stellar efforts he has made in bolstering India's capabilities must be seen in this light as means to obtain greater power relative to big players like China and the USA, and to wield this power responsibly.

Defence diplomacy is one of the distinguishing features of the Modi Doctrine. Professor Harsh Pant has described how India before Modi had shot itself in the foot by failing to sufficiently integrate the military into its foreign policy. 'India's lack of an instinct for power is most palpable in the realm of the military, where, unlike other major global powers of the past and the present, India has failed to master the creation, deployment and use of its military instruments in support of its national objectives.'[79] This has changed under the Modi Doctrine which has 'demonstrated a new level of confidence among India's political authorities in wielding hard power.'[80] Two episodes illustrate how defence diplomacy has multiplied India's foreign policy options and instruments under the Modi government. In June 2015, Modi had authorised a surprise cross-border military operation by India's Special Forces commandos inside the

---

[78] Gibbs, Nancy et al. 2015. 'Exclusive Interview with Narendra Modi: 'We are Natural Allies", *Time*, May 7th

[79] Pant, Harsh. 2015. 'Restraint no More: India Reassesses its Hard Power', *The Diplomat*, June 16th. URL: http://thediplomat.com/2015/06/restraint-no-more-india-reassesses-its-hard-power/ Last accessed on February 26th, 2016

[80] Ibid.

jungles of Mynamar, ambushing terrorists from the National Socialist Council of Nagaland (Khaplang faction) and the Kanglei Yawol Kanna Lup of Manipur, who were sheltering there. The level of sophistication of this foreign mission conveyed that India's capacity to deter enemies is growing under Modi. Terrorists who shelter outside India's boundaries used to brim with confidence that the Indian state cannot pursue them outside its sovereign space. Military raids cannot, of course, solve the misgovernment and accompanying socioeconomic grievances of local people along the India-Myanmar border. But they do convey that India under Modi is not a soft state that will passively absorb body blows like the killings of Indian soldiers by secessionist militants.

Since there was no outcry from the government of Myanmar after this operation, it was obvious that Modi did his diplomatic homework and secured permission from Naypyidaw to operate within specified geographical and temporal limits. Such bilateral governmental cooperation is, of course, highly unlikely when it comes to routing Pakistan-based jihadist camps. If the Modi government intends to prioritise preemption in its national security policy, it will need to train far more advanced special units akin to the American Navy SEALS that are deployable in its own neighbourhood as well as in multiple continents, wherever Indian interests are in jeopardy. But the 'hot pursuit' strike in Myanmar revealed positives that bode well for the Modi Doctrine. Pant writes that 'all sections of the government—the intelligence agencies, the armed forces, and the Ministry of External Affairs—worked as an organic whole under the leadership of the Prime Minister and the National Security Adviser. This is a rarity in Indian policy-making and should be recognized as such.'[81]

The 'whole of government' strategy of the Modi Doctrine in defence diplomacy was also evident in Operation Raahat, a commendable rescue mission by the Indian Air Force and Navy in April 2015 that evacuated 4640 Indian citizens and 960 foreign nationals belonging to forty-one countries from war-hit Yemen. India's civilian diplomats bargained for a window where the Saudi Arabia-led coalition ceased aerial bombardment to allow Indian aircraft to land and take off. Modi himself spoke to the

---

[81] Ibid.

Saudi monarch and dispatched his Minister of State for External Affairs, General V K Singh, a former Indian Army chief, to personally manage this mission from Djibouti and Yemen. An Indian strategist has observed the salience of this measure by writing that 'never has an Indian minister of Singh's political rank gone into an active war zone to conduct such a diplomatic and military maneuver.'[82] Modi subsequently praised 'seamless co-operation between organisations—MEA, Navy, Air Force, Air India, Shipping, Railways & State Govts (which) greatly helped in rescue work' and asserted that saving lives of non-Indians stuck in Yemen reflected a 'readiness to help others in distress, which is India's ethos.'[83]

That the Modi Doctrine has patented defence diplomacy in crises is also exemplified by the swiftness with which India organised humanitarian relief and rescue in Nepal after the devastating earthquake in April 2015. Banishing the old image of an elephantine India that reacts slowly and cumbersomely, Modi ordered Operation Maitri to commence work within fifteen minutes of the temblor, and earned India the enviable title of 'first responder', ahead of China or any other major world power. He was personally involved in coordinating with his Nepalese counterparts and framing this mission. He instructed his officials that 'we have to reach out to as many affected people as possible, not just Indians.'[84] Modi's emphasis on going beyond Indian citizens and his mandate to the Indian military to save foreigners was a manifestation of his self-confidence that India has the wherewithal to assume greater global responsibilities on its shoulders. The Modi Doctrine's bigheartedness and 'can do' attitude have transformed India's global image as a proactive power that leads with determination.

Notwithstanding these successes, India still has a long way to go in military diplomacy far away from its borders. The detention of thirty-nine Indian immigrants by the Islamic State (ISIS) in the northern Iraqi

---

[82] Taneja, Kabir. 2015. 'Why Operation Raahat is a Major Achievement for India', *The Huffington Post*, April 8th. URL: http://www.huffingtonpost.in/kabir-taneja/why-operation-rahat-is-a-_b_7023266.html Last accessed on February 26th, 2016

[83] PTI. 2015. 'Yemen Crisis: Modi Hails 'Seamless' Operation to Evacuate Indians from Yemen', *The Indian Express*, April 6th

[84] HT. 2015. 'PM Modi Leads from the Front in India's Response to Nepal Quake', *Hindustan Times*, April 28th

city of Mosul since June 2014 is an ordeal with long-term lessons that the Modi Doctrine must invest in special operations squads to intervene in key hotspots worldwide where there are big concentrations of Indian immigrants. A vulnerability map needs to be drawn to pinpoint unstable areas where Indians could be soft targets. Elite commando units must be trained to specialise in those regions and prepare for rapid deployment during contingencies. Modi would do well to take a leaf out of the book of Israel, which has the most advanced security planning for hostage crises involving Israeli citizens no matter where they occur on the planet. India's external intelligence agencies and diplomats cultivate plenty of levers on the ground in India's immediate neighbourhood, but Iraq is 2,000 miles away and hardly within the radar of Indian security forces. The possibility of a daring raid or rescue mission by Indian troops in insurgent-infested Iraq is at the present juncture a non-starter due to unfamiliarity with the terrain, the language barrier of Arabic, and the chaotic situation in the field, where not even the exact coordinates of the captive Indians have been certain for two years. This tragedy is a reminder that the Modi Doctrine has to build better strategic intervention capabilities to secure the Indian diaspora and foreign assets in the future.

Rising softly

If the Modi Doctrine has noticeably and purposefully lifted India's hard power capacities, it has been phenomenal in augmenting its soft power. Notwithstanding natural advantages of being a rare liberal democracy among developing countries, a non-aggressive nation in foreign policy, and a possessor of attractive cultural values such as multiethnic coexistence and management of diversity, India had not been rated highly in terms of soft power until Modi's advent. A comprehensive ranking of countries labelled 'Soft Power 30' by a London-based political consultancy, Portland Communications, in 2015 carried a rude awakening for India and spelt out the uphill battle Modi faces in his global charm offensive, thanks to a legacy of unimaginative and stolid brand building by the preceding Indian prime minister Manmohan Singh.

India was rated below the top thirty nations for universally liked culture, widely admired political values and positively engaged foreign policy. Developing countries like Brazil (ranked 23) and China (ranked 30) fared better and offered sobering lessons on where India had faltered. Portland's index gave weightage to political freedoms, civil liberties and democracy, areas where a liberal state and social system like India's would be expected to score above China, and at least equal Brazil. Yet, thanks to the ineffectiveness of governance at home and a host of other lacunae such as lack of digital diplomacy and ineffective contribution to global engagement and development, India's status in soft power was adjudged to be pathetic.[85]

Soft power—a concept and phrase coined by Harvard University professor and political scientist Joseph Nye as a means to co-opt and win followers to do what one wants without military coercion or economic inducement—is not alien to Indian policymakers and strategic elites. Yet, long after this notion has been mainstreamed as an important yardstick to measure how powerful a state is, India has been punching below its weight due to strategic neglect of soft power and dearth of ideas in officialdom about raising the nation's cachet and brand value. The silver lining, according to Portland, is Modi himself, who was allotted a special mention in the 'Soft Power 30' report as an international role model in using digital technology to communicate with the world and improve governance for Indians at home. Portland praised Modi's social media skills and 'selfie diplomacy' for not just making people around the world sit up and take notice but even for reflecting glory on other partner countries. It noted that 'one of the most interesting trends on Facebook surrounding Mr Modi's state visits is the boost that other world leaders receive on their pages following a visit of the Indian prime minister.'[86]

Modi's signature initiatives like the International Day of Yoga and Twitter campaigns like #selfiewithdaughter (to promote equality for girls and women) and #incredibleindia (to enhance awareness about India's natural beauty) were lauded by Portland for 'garnering global attention'.[87] The report concluded that 'although India did not finish in the top 30 this year, Mr Modi's India is definitely a soft power player

[85] McClory, Jonathan. 2015. 'The Soft Power 30: A Global Ranking of Soft Power', London: Portland Communications

[86] Ibid. p.35

[87] Ibid.

to watch in the years ahead.'[88] The enormous public relations benefits he generates for India by spontaneously playing on Taiko drums in Tokyo or by thumping to traditional African beats in Dar es Salaam are priceless value additions to India's soft power. As I have shown earlier in this book, no Indian leader has mastered the craft of symbolic diplomacy with flashlights shining better than Modi.

But how much burden of branding India's appeal can be left to the one-man-phenomenon of Modi? There have to be more dedicated stakeholders for India to be recognised as a genuinely likeable and praiseworthy nation, viz. the rest of the Indian bureaucracy which works on an antediluvian metric as opposed to the hypermodern Modi, and India's private businesspersons and academicians who adore Modi's forward-looking vision but are still disconnected from India's untrusting bureaucracy.

Nye identified purposeful foreign policy as a crucial driver of greater soft power. In his 2004 book, *Soft Power: The Means to Success in World Politics*, he recommended that the USA alter both the substance and the style of its foreign policy to win more favourability across the planet. Avoiding arrogant and unilateral behaviour, eschewing trade protectionism, and adopting 'broadly inclusive and far-sighted definitions of the national interest' instead of taking 'a narrow and myopic perspective'[89] were some of his substantive prescriptions to lift the sagging reputation of the USA during the George W. Bush era. On the stylistic side, Nye advocated doubling meagre American investments in public diplomacy and cultural diplomacy as part and parcel of a concerted plan for the USA to become more seductive. At least under the presidency of Barack Obama, such sound advice was heeded and America was ranked number three in Portland's index, behind the UK and Germany.

What does India need to do in foreign policy substance and style to be up there among the leading lights in soft power? The most important change has to be overturning overcautious diplomacy that refrains from attempting solutions to pressing global emergencies and problems like war and terrorism that are far from India's own borders, and other political

---

[88] Ibid.

[89] Nye, Joseph. 2004. *Soft Power: The Means to Success in World Politics*, New York: PublicAffairs, p.61

conflicts. As I have explained earlier in this chapter, the Modi Doctrine has started doing this by shouldering the burden for global public goods. But it has to go further. India is mostly known to abstain or cast its vote one way or the other in international institutions on matters of security, without taking on a bigger responsibility of joining peacemaking efforts. Indian diplomats 'discuss', 'take note of', 'express concern', 'condemn' etc., but do not proactively act to calm the maelstroms roiling the world due to shortage of personnel and a lack of leadership mentality. Under the Modi Doctrine, there is an explicitly stated ambition for India to 'drive and lead on global issues, and be active and nimble rather than neutral or risk-averse.'[90] With Modi's prodding, the MEA has partly opened its doors to outside consultants to multiply its feeble manpower and strengthen its human capital base to plan for long term outcomes and take on grander missions. These are good beginnings, but it would be absolutely essential that the Modi government inducts soft power specialists and brand management gurus from outside the career bureaucracy so that they bring in fresh thinking and new ideas to buttress Modi's creative juices.

It took just one Secretary of State, Hillary Clinton, to dramatically expand the USA's digital diplomacy reach. Modi and his foreign policy brains trust must also allocate more talent from outside government to beef up India's shoestring-budgeted Public Diplomacy division, particularly by forming India's own online 'electronic army' that can win over international public opinion on how India is providing global public goods. It is not enough for Indian officials to dish out communiques that India is a force for strategic stability and balance. In a digital era, there must be dedicated personnel drawn from outside the government to send out the right vibes. Modi has never shied away from hiring foreign branding firms to project his government's achievements and pet projects like 'Make in India'. More will be needed along these lines to push the idea that India's rise in world affairs is a case of 'responsible rise' that is to be welcome by the whole world rather than resisted or obstructed.

India's own TV channel exclusively dedicated to world news coverage, India's own Peace Corps-like volunteer force to be deployed in developing countries and India's own state-endorsed private business

---

90 AFP. 2015. 'Modi on Charm Offensive as India Seeks More Clout', *The Express Tribune*, August 19th

and academic ambassadors who take on the mantle of 'national social responsibility' are other ideas that merit due consideration. Organisation of Indian cultural festivals and art exhibitions by embassies abroad, broadcasting of Indian TV soap operas and Bollywood movies overseas will take India only so far. If the Modi Doctine is to fully realise India's latent soft power, the main reform required is in its foreign policy messaging as a compassionate leader in world politics that is admirably serving the wider interests of the international community.

The BJP's foreign policy pillars of *Sanskriti evam Sabhyata* have been aced by the Modi Doctrine, and will definitely be counted as ballast for India's soft power in years to come. The intense diplomatic lobbying and persuasion that Modi did to enact June 21 as the International Day of Yoga was nothing short of a planned operation that involved a full-court press by a select group of Indian diplomats who got China to be an early enthusiast, secured the Americans on board, and built a rare 'Beijing-New Delhi-Washington axis' which ended up securing 177 co-sponsors in the UN General Assembly in barely seventy-five days.[91] It was a stunning demonstration of the Modi Doctrine's mobilisational power and an instance of how the current Indian prime minister can gather almost the entire international community under a single banner if he prioritises a particular issue.

Like Yoga, Modi has also peddled ancient Indian traditional medicine, Ayurveda, as a cure for increasingly stressful and ailing populations around the world. Even before becoming India's prime minister, Modi was devising schemes to mass market Ayurveda to expand India's exports and had said that,

'…we have lot of talent but we need to present it to the world in the most modern manner. We need to present our technology to the world in the language in which they understand. If China is exporting it, it means there is a market. Why cannot our herbal medicines take over the world market? How can we take our Ayurveda to the world?'[92]

---

[91] Sirohi. Seema. 2015. 'How Eight Indian Diplomats Bent UN into Yoga Shape', *The Economic Times*, June 17th

[92] NM. 2014. 'Shri Narendra Modi Addressing National Ayurveda Summit 2014 at Mahatma Mandir, Gandhinagar', Feburary 25th. URL: https://www.youtube.com/watch?v=mK-HFqYdfqc Last accessed on February 27th, 2016

Peter Martin of APCO Worldwide, a multinational public relations company that has worked for Modi, has argued from the Yoga and Ayurveda cases that 'the Modi government has raised the bar on the relationship between India's soft power potential and its foreign policy. For the first time, the Indian state is beginning to make systematic use of the rich cultural and human resources that have previously developed quite independently of its policies.'[93] This strategy of calculated cultural diplomacy comports with the Modi Doctrine's philosophy of collecting all the positive facets of India, materialistic and non-materialistic, into one coherent grand strategy and narrative, which is compelling to the world as a single package called Brand India.

In May 2015, Modi was received in a packed sports stadium in Ulaanbaatar, Mongolia, amidst thousands of Mongolian citizens carrying Indian tricolour flags and displaying Indian cultural arts and traditions under the banner of the Indian spiritual organisation, The Art of Living Foundation. He recalled later that 'the way those Mongolians were introducing Indian culture was inspirational. Where a state's material might and power cannot reach, in such places soft power plays a very big role in international relations.'[94] As an old RSS *prachaarak* who knows how appealing Yoga and Indian eastern spiritual wisdom are around the world, Modi has intentionally promoted Indian non-state cultural bodies like The Art of Living and Patanjali International Yoga Foundation to become transnational forces to reckon with. To Modi, harnessing such private Indian institutions is integral to his building of a 'Team India' in international affairs.

Modi's soft power agenda also extends to finding points of commonality and mutual understanding between Indian and world civilisations, and accentuating these cultural links to make India more globally accepted. Vignettes of him squatting inside ancient Buddhist temples in Japan with folded hands, his prayers at the Mahabodhi tree in Sri Lanka, his symbolic gifts to world leaders of saplings from the

---

93 Martin, Peter. 2015. 'Yoga Diplomacy: Narendra Modi's Soft Power Strategy', *Foreign Affairs*, January 25th

94 BJP. 2016. 'PM Modi at the Inauguration of 2016 World Culture Festival by Art of Living in New Delhi', *Bharatiya Janata Party*, March 11th. URL: https://www.youtube.com/watch?v=eeRZqGw_yQA Last accessed on March 12th, 2016

original Buddhist tree of enlightenment in the eastern Indian town of Gaya, his promotion of the Buddhist pilgrimage circuit in India, and his 'unprecedented push' to conduct dozens of seminars in foreign countries to elaborate India's Buddhist past before audiences of international scholars, monks and policymakers,[95] have all elevated India's attraction as a cosmopolitan power that is reviving its ancient cultural dynamism in a modern form for the spiritual and psychological wellbeing of the planet. There is also a strategic undercurrent to Modi's Buddhist diplomacy. Chandan Nandy argues that 'competitive appropriation of the Buddha, with all of Buddhism's cultural trappings, is at the heart of Sino-Indian rivalry', and that Modi is using Buddhism to score an 'edge over China', whose reputation as a suppressor of Tibetan Buddhism and a denier of religious freedoms is notorious.[96]

In May 2016, Modi hosted the president of Sri Lanka, Maithripala Sirisena, at a mega Hindu religious festival known as Simhasth Kumbh in the central Indian city of Ujjain. Sirisena's comment there that as the leader of a country with a majority Buddhist population, 'I have special reasons to be happy' because Modi was leaving no stone unturned 'towards respecting Buddhism'[97], reflects how Modi's well-branded cultural diplomacy is yielding dividends.

Sri Lanka continues to receive economic assistance from China and could also host further Chinese naval submarine visits. However, there is nothing but total devastation of Buddhism that the former can see in Beijing. The suppression of the Dalai Lama and the cultural genocide China carried out in Tibet stands in contrast to India, where a Sri Lankan president can come and unveil a statue of Buddhist revivalist gurus and proclaim that Buddhism is safe and secure in Modi's India.

---

95 Kasturi, Charu. 2015. 'Modi Govt. Plans Buddhism Blitz in Cultural Diplomacy Refocus', *The Telegraph*, August 30th

96 Nandy, Chandan. 2015. 'For Modi Regime, Buddhism is a Soft Power Approach for Hard Power', *The Quint*, May 5th. URL: http://www.thequint.com/world/2015/05/05/for-modi-regime-buddhism-is-a-soft-power-approach-for-hard-power Last accessed on February 28th, 2016

97 MN. 2016. 'Sri Lankan President Maithripala Sirisena at International Conference on Simhastha Kumbh in Ujjain', *Mango News*, May 14th. URL: https://www.youtube.com/watch?v=Vh0J8mP7nFU Last accessed on June 10th, 2016

In parts of the world where Hindu mythology and symbolism resonate, including regions with heavy concentrations of the Indian diaspora, Modi has been equally strategic in shoring up recognition of India as the mother country from which an eclectic way of life was transmitted. The 'Ramayana trail', aimed at developing mythological spots associated with the Hindu epic in Sri Lanka and ensuring a constant influx of tourism, and the Indian government's support for conservation of monuments and modernisation of facilities at the Pashupatinath temple in Nepal are examples where Modi has won plaudits. As one Nepalese head priest said passionately, 'we see him as a mascot for Hinduism, and appreciate his efforts in saving Hindu culture.'[98]

Modi's championing of the 'Ramayana trail' and the 'Buddhist circuit' is at one level a clever contraption to boost tourism and people-to-people ties in South Asia and Southeast Asia. But at another level, it is an effort to form a combined cultural construct that would restore India's centrality in Asia. At the Global Hindu Buddhist Conclave in September 2015, the Indian prime minister had declared, 'my government is doing everything to facilitate and promote Buddhism in India'.[99] His view that 'Buddha is present in everything and everywhere and we need to follow his principles in order to rid ourselves of war'[100] speaks volumes about India's accommodative magnanimity.

Besides Buddhism, the other religious community that Modi has consciously striven to draw into the zone of his cultural diplomacy is Islam. At the World Sufi Forum in New Delhi in March 2016, he proudly remarked, 'Sufism from India spread across the world and this tradition that evolved in India belongs to the whole of South Asia.'[101] His projection of Sufism as an antidote to terrorism and extremism has

---

98 Jayshi, Damakant. 2014. 'Modi as Mascot of Hinduism, says Priest', *The Hindu*, August 5th

99 Chaudhury, Dipanjan. 2015. 'PM Modi Highlights India's Buddhist Heritage', *The Economic Times*, September 4th

100 NM. 2015. 'PM Modi at Global Hindu Buddhist Initiative on Conflict Avoidance and Environment Consciousness', *Narendra Modi*, September 3rd. URL: https://www.youtube.com/watch?v=nhPSbarbqO4 Last accessed on June 10th, 2016

101 ET. 2016. 'World Sufi Forum: With 19 References to Terror, PM Narendra Modi calls Sufism Bulwark against Extremism', *The Economic Times*, March 18th

been well received in the Muslim world, particularly in the Middle East, where the demand for moderate Indian Islamic clerics is on the rise. He has been noticed globally as a powerful votary for de-radicalisation strategies and for proclaiming that the 'ideology propounded by Sufi saints is an integral part of Indian ethos.'[102] Modi's glorification of Sufi saints from the Indian subcontinent like Kabir and Rahim as 'our inspirations'[103] and his exhortation of Islamic scholars and clerics to counter extremism through community-based initiatives and social media have clicked with an international community jittery about the spreading virus of jihadism.

Earlier in this book, I have laid out how Modi got permission for a Hindu temple to be constructed in the UAE by persuading that nation's Islamic rulers, and in the same vein also made a landmark visit to a mosque there. The export of Indian imams to the UAE is one of many markers of Modi's attempts to market India as a centre of moderate Islam in the world and Indian Muslims as role models. During his travels in the Central Asian republics, Modi has invoked India's lineage of tolerant Islam and its complementarity with Sovietised and secular Islam. Speaking in Kazakhstan in July 2015, he had argued that, 'the Islamic heritage of both India and Central Asia is defined by the highest ideals of Islam—knowledge, piety, compassion and welfare. This is a heritage founded on the principle of love and devotion. And it has always rejected the forces of extremism. Today, this is an important source of strength that brings India and Central Asia together.'[104] All these symbolic words and acts of cultural diplomacy have burnished India's image. The usual bromides in diplomatese about historical bonds and cultural commonalities, which are routinely mentioned in bilateral events, now have a concrete leverage value in India's foreign policy thanks to the Modi Doctrine.

Is it not ironic that a man berated by his critics as a Hindu fundamentalist has managed to present a convincing picture of an India with diverse ancient truths to the wider world? Before Modi,

---

102 Ibid.

103 Roy, Amit. 2015. 'PM holds Aloft India's Diversity but Makes Reference to Islam and Gun', *The Telegraph*, November 14th

104 PTI. 2015. 'Islamic Heritage of India, Central Asia has Rejected Extremism: PM Narendra Modi', *The Economic Times*, July 7th

India's leaders—most of whom donned a 'secular' tag—had practically no achievements to boast of in cultural diplomacy, barring mouthing clichéd lines about India's 'age-old relations' with various nations. The paradox of a so-called 'Hindu nationalist' winning the hearts and minds of non-Hindu countries and communities globally is explained by Modi's uninhibited and uncomplicated attitude towards religious expression. Instead of hiding behind a facade of repression and avoiding of public references or associations with religion and spirituality, he has engaged openly with all faiths and upheld their positive traits and contributions. India's soft spiritual power is on the rise as Modi exudes confidence in being a Hindu who deeply respects and nurtures all other denominations with a sense of equality.

Apart from cultural diplomacy, Modi has also championed the formation of an International Solar Alliance (ISA) as a coalition of 120 solar resource-rich countries lying between the Tropics of Cancer and Capricorn to unite for alternative energy solutions. The universal scope of ISA and its wide acceptance in the international community reconfirm that India's convening power has grown manifold times under Modi. Likewise, although India had been campaigning for the adoption of a counter-terrorism convention at the UN for years, Modi has also made interventions at the G-20 to 'involve religious leaders, thinkers and opinion makers for a social movement against extremism, particularly addressed to the youth…in countries where it is most prevalent'.[105]

At the policy level, Modi has enhanced India's cooperation with Iran on the latter's proposal for a 'World Against Violent Extremism' (WAVE) and has been applauded by President Hassan Rouhani as an 'essential' partner for 'eradication of terrorism in the region.'[106] By situating India as an indispensable actor in addressing a pressing challenge like religious extremism, the Modi Doctrine has built up reserves of international goodwill which are crucial to combat unconventional threats to global security. In the next chapter, I will outline how these intangible gains in world public opinion are enabling India to isolate Pakistan on terrorism

---

105 Mehra, Puja. 2015. 'Delink Terror and Religion, Modi Tells G20 Leaders', *The Hindu*, November 16th

106 TNA. 2015. 'Indian PM Hails Iran's Role in Regional Security, Anti-Terror Campaign', *Tasnim News Agency*, July 9th

and forge new coalitions of the willing to weaken violent non-state actors. Here, it is sufficient to note that the soft power that Modi has begun to accumulate is a boon for India's overall capabilities and comprehensive national power. Ideas and actions, impressions and capacities, feelings and powers have all fused in the Modi Doctrine to produce a stronger India in international affairs.

Power in institutions

Modi is as savvy with the nuts-and-bolts of one-on-one bilateral diplomacy as with complex multilateral forums with many countries trying to coordinate their respective national interests for larger, collective purposes. Having understood the moral and material power vested in international institutions and regimes, he has tried to present India as a leading state within them, and has attempted to shape the debates in these bodies with a barrage of new ideas and proposals. There is an X factor about Modi when he is in multilateral settings due to international expectations that he would show the way or offer fresh vistas to steer the international community in futuristic directions. Buoyed by high GDP growth at home, a well-earned reputation as a strong political leader, and the perception that India is transforming to become a top power, Modi has justified the tag of a global celebrity with a razor-sharp mind and practical bent. In November 2014, *The Guardian* called Modi the 'political rock star' of the Brisbane G-20 summit who was 'one of the most popular figures…a leader others want to see, and be seen with.'[107] Even after the novelty value of a recently elected Indian prime minister with a historic parliamentary majority faded, Modi has managed to remain the cynosure of all eyes in multilateral summits due to his insertion of India as a rule-maker, his digital diplomacy and famous personal touch with foreign counterparts. To argue that the Modi Doctrine has promoted India from a has-been into a happening power in the portals of multilateral institutions is no exaggeration.

The main difference Modi has made to multilateralism is injecting a creative spirit to institutions that may be losing steam and need rejuvenation. For example, from his very first appearance at the BRICS

---

[107] Doherty, Ben. 2014. 'Narendra Modi: From International Pariah to the G20's Political Rock Star', *The Guardian*, November 14th

summit in Fortaleza, Brazil, in July 2014, Modi began to try and steer this important formation of emerging market economies towards becoming a more coherent and impactful political bloc. His call for BRICS to 'contribute to international efforts to address regional crises' and security threats so as to 'restore a climate of peace and stability in the world' was in tune with his own foreign policy activism and desire to be shaping the big outcomes of world politics.[108] Dissatisfied with BRICS as a merely economics-centered institution, Modi envisions this institution taking up the role of resolver of wars and terrorism, alongside its traditional mandate of economic advancement. Despite having heads of state level summits since 2009, BRICS shied away from joint diplomatic or military action to overcome regional armed conflicts and tensions. Modi is egging on BRICS to formulate a mechanism that can go beyond their routine statements or communiqués which condemn violence or intrusion into sovereign nations' internal affairs by interventionist Western powers. As leaders of their respective regions or sub-regions, BRICS countries could anoint local point persons for Africa, Latin America and Asia and offer undiluted support to these designated countries to douse wars, rebellions and other calamities befalling their neighborhoods. For instance, if a situation like the Islamist threat to Mali arises again, South Africa or Nigeria should be the point person backed unequivocally by all BRICS countries to be the decisive factor that paves the way to a solution. Likewise, the intractable crisis in Afghanistan might be tackled by India and China if they form a troika with Russia and win the consent of the other regional neighbors, which are not sanguine about what the Americans have done in the last fifteen years.

Modi's message to fellow BRICS leaders that 'the region stretching from Afghanistan to Africa is experiencing turbulence and conflict and remaining mute spectators to countries being torn up can have grave consequences'[109] is a clear sign that he intends to proactively mould its evolution. Just as he has sounded the death knell to the old India as

[108] PTI. 2014. 'Narendra Modi Nuances Foreign Policy Approach Ahead of BRICS Summit', *The Economic Times*, July 13th

[109] ET. 2014. 'Prime Minister Narendra Modi Pitches for United Terror Fight at BRICS', *The Economic Times*, July 16th

a passive and reactive player in world affairs, he wants BRICS to be refitted with a broader and more political purpose. With the ingenuity of the Modi Doctrine as a propulsion force, BRICS can forestall the culture of neocolonial interference by the USA and European powers in the guise of firefighting in the Global South. Imagine what a sea change we could witness in international security if there were, say, a BRICS Peacekeeping Force that would work along with the UN and regional organisations as an independent troubleshooting entity which could deploy in select unstable parts of the world. How refreshing would it be if there were BRICS diplomatic missions, consisting of high level representatives of the five nations, to go on fact-finding assignments, avert catastrophic wars or invasions, and even broker peace between warring parties?

Hiding behind resource constraints and leaving the field to the Americans and the Europeans as the sole peace brokers and conflict managers is not a respectable option in Modi's mind for BRICS, if it fancies itself as a motor for global leadership. Surrendering to the West or riding piggyback on Western global governance structures is a status quo-ist strategy that does not behoove of the revisionist BRICS. Modi sees India as furthering the BRICS' shared goal of working towards a multipolar world order as a serious responsibility. Given India's high economic growth rates while the rest of the BRICS have suffered declines, Modi knows that his words and proposals for reforms have higher cachet in this institution and is determined to leave his imprint on it.

Another aspect on which Modi is navigating BRICS in unheralded ways is his emphasis on decentralising its agenda by going 'beyond summit and leader-centric deliberations and championing subnational level exchanges between our states, cities and other local bodies.'[110] Arguing that BRICS have 'horizontal influence to compel the world to take notice', he has urged the grouping to deepen 'vertical bonds' through people-to-people engagements and formation of new entities like a BRICS university, a BRICS young scientists' forum to nurture innovation, BRICS language schools, a BRICS healthcare platform, a

---

110 Ibid.

BRICS mechanism for promoting small and medium businesses and a BRICS framework for promoting tourism.[111] In 2015, Modi went further and mooted a BRICS clean energy project, a BRICS digital initiative, BRICS research centres on agriculture and railways, a BRICS sports council, a BRICS film festival, a BRICS business information platform and a BRICS trade fair.

By its very definition, a great power is one which shapes its external environment as per its domestic preferences. Modi's flurry of ideas to diversify BRICS' ambit and modus operandi shows how India is assuming a leadership role with a plethora of suggestions. In 2016, the Chairmanship of BRICS passed by rotation to India placing the onus on it to amalgamate the interests of all the other member countries and forming the locus of the organisation's priorities. But even without the chairmanship, Modi sees India as the lodestone of BRICS. The CEO of the IT giant Cisco, John Chambers, has echoed this vision by saying that the 'possibility and probability of India being the very top emerging BRICS country under the leadership of Mr Modi...are extremely good.'[112]

Power within international institutions comes not just from economic and military might, but also from diplomatic initiative and agenda-setting. Under the Modi Doctrine, India is maximising its weight within multilateral bodies and thereby accruing significant power in the international system. Historically, India has seen itself as a defender of the underdogs and a fighter for equity and justice in multilateral institutions. Under Modi, that line remains intact, but he has walked the talk better on India's role as an equaliser, which is also assuring weaker member states through its presence and verve. For example, when the BRICS were brainstorming the launch of their ambitious New Development Bank (NDB) in 2014, the massive asymmetry between China and the rest of the members triggered anxiety among smaller members that the NDB may turn out to be a Sino-centric version of the Western-dominated Bretton Woods institutions. After all, with China

---

111 Iyer, Vaidyanathan. 2014. 'Go Beyond Summit, Decentralise to put BRICS in Fast Lane: Modi', *The Indian Express*, July 17th

112 PTI. 2015. 'India may Become Top BRICS Nation under Modi: Cisco Chief', *The Economic Times*, June 10th

alone accounting for more than half of the total GDP of BRICS, the fear of the institution being suborned as a multilateral facade for Chinese interests to be advanced is rational.

In such a stark situation, Modi played his cards forcefully and resisted China's offer to 'contribute more than its share to the bank, which would give Beijing greater control over its affairs.'[113] His tough negotiation on equal capital contributions and equal voting powers for all members in BRICS blocked the Chinese intent to hegemonise or bully the institution. In the process, he found common ground with Brazil and other smaller BRICS nations to corner China into accepting the egalitarian formula. Modi eventually had his way in the design of the NDB as an antidote to the IMF and the World Bank models where the nations with the most money and power run the show. With an Indian IT and financial notable, K.V. Kamath as the first President of NDB and Modi's preferences for lending to green technologies embedded within the bank as a focus area, it is obvious that India has negated the Chinese drive to lord over BRICS.

The Modi Doctrine leverages India's strengths and projected growth in international forums by contrasting them with global vulnerabilities. With BRICS nations slowing down economically in the last few years even as India is chugging along briskly, Modi has legitimately avowed that, 'if there is anyone standing with vigour in BRICS today, it is the "I".'[114] Even in the larger G-20 bloc of twenty largest major economies of the world, Modi has been accorded due importance because he is able to deliver on GDP growth at home and automatically attracts attention with fresh ideas. In 2014, he grabbed eyeballs by pushing for a G-20 agreement to tighten screws on black money and tax havens that had a central hand in the global economic crisis since 2008, and which had bothered many member countries. He struck a chord by attacking 'excessive banking secrecy' and seeking 'greater international

---

[113] Boehler, Patrick & Teddy Ng. 2014. 'Indian PM Modi Praised for Rebuffing China's Power Play on BRICS Development Bank', *South China Morning Post*, July 7th

[114] TNN. 2015. 'Narendra Modi at SAP Center San Jose, California - Full Speech', *Times Now*, September 27th. URL: https://www.youtube.com/watch?v=8V_uwSOlgak Last accessed on March 3rd, 2016

cooperation for return of illicit money to the country of origin.'[115] Modi's domestic credentials as a clean politician lent credibility to his advocacy for 'zero tolerance for corruption', have helped enhance increased information sharing among countries to prosecute financial chicanery and given life to the G-20's Anti-Corruption Implementation Plan. The current Indian prime minister's trademark personal diplomacy and active lobbying abilities have yielded other fruits. References to transparency and accountability in tax rules, which were not initially included in the draft of the G-20's formal statement in November 2014, were 'incorporated in the final communique after Prime Minister's (Modi's) strong intervention.'[116]

At a time when security problems have peaked in terms of mass violence, atrocities and forced displacement, Modi stands out in the G-20 with catchy concepts like his 'ten-point formula' to counter terrorism. For a G-20 that has limited itself to global economic management to shift gear and also take on security problems, it needs active votaries among upwardly mobile member states. Modi has not only campaigned for India's standard assertions that states which sponsor terrorism (like Pakistan) must be isolated or that the UN must adopt a Comprehensive Convention on International Terrorism, but also offered new insights into how the G-20 can counter radicalisation of youth and the extremist ideologies which prey upon them. Modi's assertion that terrorism 'calls for a comprehensive global response' and that 'combating it must be major priority for G20'[117] have strengthened India's position internationally and paved the ground for robust joint action against this scourge.

On the economic front, Modi has rejected neoliberal nostrums of fiscal austerity and preached at the G-20 for major public investments to stimulate GDP growth and infrastructure modernisation. The formation of the 'Global Infrastructure Hub' in Sydney in November 2014 to serve as a clearing house and powwow facility for needy governments and wealthy investors to sit across the table and strike deals was

---

115 Roy, Shubhajit. 2015. 'Overseas Black Money: Global Cooperation Needed for Return of Illicit Money, says PM Modi', *The Indian Express*, November 17th

116 HT. 2014. 'G20 Supports Modi's Pitch on Black Money', *Hindustan Times*, November 17th

117 Jaipuria, Timsy. 2015. 'G20 Leaders Talk Paris, Modi Calls for Global Response to Terrorism', *Hindustan Times*, November 15th

enabled by direct personal diplomacy between Modi and his Australian counterpart, Tony Abbott.[118] Modi has also marketed at the G-20 his signature domestic initiatives like 'Make in India', 'Skill India', 'Digital India', industrial corridors and smart cities as employment-focussed policies that 'will be a source of strength for the global economy.'[119] Under the Modi Doctrine, the sky is the limit for India to don the role of a locomotive for global growth and a true leader of the G-20, which is now the established domain for deciding on the world economy.

At the UN too, Modi has made a splash and considerably advanced India's prominence as a leading power which is inventive in diplomacy and responsible in carrying along the interests of the international community. The UN Secretary General Ban Ki-moon has 'expressed his admiration for the Prime Minister's focus on improving the socio-economic well-being of all Indian people'[120] and has applauded Modi's commitment to solar power as 'the kind of bold leadership the world needs to reap the benefits of the clean energy revolution.'[121] On the long-pending matter of reforming the UN Security Council (UNSC), Modi has accelerated bridge-building with large regional blocs of countries so as to overcome objections to India's permanent membership. His mobilisation efforts to ensure that 'India and Africa must speak in one voice'[122] on this issue, and his inroads with small Pacific Island nations who have the collective power of fourteen votes in the UN General Assembly (UNGA) within the 53-member Asia-Pacific Group[123], convey a razor-sharp Modi Doctrine which is determined to get India its long-denied place at the high table of world politics. Modi has also elevated the 'G-4' coalition consisting of India, Japan, Germany and Brazil to

---

[118] PTI. 2014. 'Tony Abbott Calls PM Narendra Modi to Talk G-20; Says Keenly Waiting for Him', *The Economic Times*, November 7th

[119] PTI. 2015. 'G20 Summit: Narendra Modi Seeks Greater Public Investments to Boost Growth', *Deccan Chronicle*, November 16th

[120] PTI. 2014. 'UN Secretary General Ban Ki-moon Thanks India for Contribution to UN Peacekeeping Efforts', *The Economic Times*, September 28th

[121] PTI. 2015. 'World Desirous of Narendra Modi's Bold Leadership for Clean Energy: Ban Ki-moon', *The Economic Times*, January 11th

[122] Roy, Shubhajit. 2015. 'India-Africa Forum Summit: PM, African Leaders Push for UNSC Reforms', *The Indian Express*, December 25th

[123] Bagchi, Indrani. 2015. 'Eye on UNSC Seat, India Woos Pacific Islands with Investments', *The Times of India*, August 22nd

a heads-of-state level institution that will confabulate and strategise on their stalled bids for UNSC permanent seats. The adoption by the UNGA of a method of text-based negotiations for UNSC reform in September 2015 was hailed by the Modi government as 'historic' and 'pathbreaking', testifying to a new momentum behind India's bid.

Even if the UNSC expansion process does not proceed quickly as it is contingent upon a myriad permutations and politicking in New York, the Modi Doctrine has invested sufficient time, energy and resources into amassing India's overall hard and soft power so that it becomes increasingly indispensable in every relevant intergovernmental body. Modi has redoubled India's contributions to the UN's core functions and it is not a matter of 'whether' but 'when' India finally gets in as a permanent member. He has reinforced India's role as a leader of the Global South in the UN system. The adoption of the sustainable development goals (SDG) by the UN in September 2015 was shaped by Indian diplomacy, which fought on behalf of the G-77 group of developing nations to ensure that richer countries do not chicken out of their responsibilities for development finance and capacity building.

On reforming UN peacekeeping, Modi is striving to increase the decision-making power of troop contributing countries (of which India is a giant) in all aspects of mission planning. For too long, the agenda-setting of the mandate and limitations of peacekeepers on the ground has been determined by donors and major powers, rendering senders of blue berets into obedient servants carrying out orders. Modi is fighting to engineer a shift in the balance of power in the peacekeeping regime in favour of developing nations that bear the brunt of the work in conflict zones. He has also innovatively paired up with the USA to train UN peacekeepers from six African nations and, in characteristic style, has proposed that India would fund the establishment of a UN Peacekeepers' Memorial Wall in the UN headquarters. He has also introduced at the UN emerging concepts like the 'Blue Revolution' to whip up multilateral consensus on preserving oceans and small island nations, and 'G-1' or 'G-All' to unite various sub-groupings at the UN for realising the Indian ideal of the world as one family and genuine interdependence rather than zero-sum-games.

Powering the future

In atmospherics, punch lines and concrete outcomes, the Modi Doctrine has qualitatively and quantitatively enhanced India's power in the international system. It has moved India from a 'swing state' to a leading state, a subcontinental to a pan-regional player, and an emerging to a major power. India is still not a great power in the ranks of China or the USA, but the Modi Doctrine has set the tone for this eventuality. It has shed past diffidence that marked India as hesitant and unsure, and has embarked India on a road to achieving parity with the big two. If Modi is given time of one decade in office by India's population, the probability of a 'G-3' of the USA, China and India becoming the triumvirate of acknowledged great powers is high. In November 2014, after attending five summits and twenty bilaterals in the Indo-Pacific, Modi wrote, 'I noticed one thing—that the world is looking at India with renewed respect and immense enthusiasm! I see a global community that is tremendously keen to engage with India.'[124] This appetite for India has been sustained by the Modi Doctrine's hard and soft power accomplishments.

The current Indian prime minister has consistently kept his eye on the ball on India's material and non-material capabilities, which are the building blocks for power in international politics. Apart from spurring economic growth and military modernisation at home, his diplomatic proactiveness and reordering of relations with China and the USA are paramount factors as India aspires to great power status. The triangle I elaborated in this chapter is presently such that China is wary of India's rise because that would mean the latter catches up with the former, while the USA is wary of China's rise. The mathematical concept of transitivity states that if A is greater than B, and B is greater than C, then A is also greater than C. The larger power gap between the USA and India is favourable to India because it means that Washington is not interested in preventing or blocking India's rise, at least not for the foreseeable future. But the urgency of containing China through the 'pivot' and other means is obvious in the American strategy because the former is a lot closer in power to the USA than India. The Modi Doctrine

---

[124] ANI. 2014. 'The World is Looking at India with Renewed Respect and Immense Enthusiasm, says PM Modi', *Business Standard*, November 21st

has read this dynamic better than preceding Indian governments, and it is also prepared to take advantage of the fact that whoever replaces Obama as the next American president will be even more likely to turn her or his attention to stopping the Chinese juggernaut. But instead of bandwagoning with the USA to counterbalance against China, the Modi Doctrine has adroitly kept China interested in India's growth through commercial diplomacy and is, thus, freeing India somewhat from absolute Chinese strategic pressure.

In this chapter, I have explained how Modi has created more buy-in for India's economic growth in China even as he remains circumspect about Chinese strategic intentions. The path to great power status has historically been overlaid by hegemonic wars and demonstration of rising powers' victories in iconic battles.[125] The Modi Doctrine is, however, charting out a strategy of India rising responsibly without being halted on its tracks by preventive or pre-emptive wars by China or its proxies. China has vowed to turn a page in history and avoid wars even with the USA via a 'new model of great power relations.'[126] But the intense competition between Washington and Beijing for global influence and control has only begun and is going to deepen in the decades to come. The Modi Doctrine's achievement is to avoid head-on collisions with either of the big two powers and to simultaneously amass more power in India's hands until it grows into their equal.

Having astutely managed the triangle, India is still not guaranteed to be a great power. Doug Bandow of the Cato Institute in Washington has argued in *Forbes* that Modi is losing the chance to make India the next great power by failing to undertake structural economic reforms.[127] Peter Hartcher has similarly contended in *The Age* that India has 'the prospect of greatness on one side', but it may 'relapse to the status of a country that cannot provide toilets to its schools' on the other hand if Modi fails to deliver on domestic governance and infrastructural

---

[125] Gilpin, Robert. 1981. *War and Change in International Politics*, Cambridge: Cambridge University Press

[126] Wertime, David. 2015. 'Unpacking Xi Jinping's Pet Phrase for US-China Ties', *Foreign Policy*, September 23rd

[127] Bandow, Doug. 2015. 'India Losing Opportunity to Become Next Great Power? Narendra Modi's Faltering Revolution', *Forbes*, July 30th

promises.[128] Analysing Modi's internal policies and their pros and cons is beyond the ambit of this book, but it is undeniable that he has rectified India's external strategy and set it on course to maximise power for his country. Some of the bottlenecks at home will actually be set right through the incoming benefits produced by his foreign policy such as FDI and technology transfer. Parallely, India's claim to great power status will be judged by how solid its domestic ship is. The Modi Doctrine is vested in connecting India's domestic and foreign odysseys into a comprehensive national strategy. There are numerous factors beyond the Modi Doctrine's reach which will ultimately determine whether India will rise fast enough and deep enough to reify 'G-3'. As a practitioner of world politics, Modi knows that India acquiring and wielding power is contingent upon how other states and non-state actors react and respond. He has so far made the best of this field, although infinite tasks remain to be done.

---

128 Hartcher, Peter. 2015. 'India Still no Rival to China's Super Powers', *The Age*, April 21st

Chapter 5
Omnipresent India: Extending the Arc and Ambit

In international relations, today India is playing a crucial role on the basis of humanity and concern for all. Today, we have a government in Delhi which is visible every second and in every place of the world.[1]

360-Degree Foreign Policy

Wherever Narendra Modi travels, it is counted by the host nation and observers as a milestone in terms of the time gap between the last time an Indian prime minister set foot in that country and his arrival. In March 2015, he became the first Indian head of government to step into Sri Lanka since twenty-eight years. In August 2015, he became the first prime minister to visit the UAE in thirty-four years. In September 2015, he scored another first by being the first Indian leader to visit Ireland after fifty-nine years. When he landed without prepping anyone in Lahore in December 2015, it was a landmark as no Indian leader had been to Pakistan in twelve years. The list goes on and on: the United Kingdom after ten years, Nepal after seventeen years, Australia after twenty-eight years, Fiji after thirty-one years, Seychelles after thirty-four

[1] TNN. 2015. 'PM Modi's Full Speech in Dubai', *Times Now*, August 17th. URL: https://www.youtube.com/watch?v=w-AhA-yjeho Last accessed on March 4th, 2016

years, Canada after forty-two years etc. To his credit, he is also the first ever Indian prime minister to go to Mongolia and is scheduled to make history by visiting Israel.

For an indefatigable former *prachaarak* who has clocked unbelievable globetrotting travel records like crisscrossing 60,000 km within thirty days,[2] if one were to draw a map of Modi's overseas peregrinations, it would hold a mirror to India's ambitions of being omni-directional and omnipresent. If one added to his foreign visits the beeline that foreign leaders have made to be hosted by him in India, the map would thicken with many more lines in all directions. To be where no Indian leader has been in ages or never before is to declare intent of the Modi Doctrine that India is now engaged to its fullest capacity in developing foreign relations. The era of neglect of international affairs, insularity and inaction, which typified Indian foreign policy under the former Indian prime minister Manmohan Singh, has been reversed by an activist Modi who is eager for what the BJP terms as *Samvaad* with large and small countries from far and near.

A leading power should be one that is not just visible in every domain from land, air and water, but also have an impact on the principal issue areas of interest to the international community. Under the Modi Doctrine, India is doing just that. Barring a few misguided critics in India who have been indulging in petty calculations of how much public money Modi has spent on his foreign visits, Indians in general have been supportive of his frenetic foreign relations calendar because of the tangible and intangible gains it generates. They are the silent majority who believe Modi when he says India's time has come to rise in world affairs. Given the effects of economic globalisation and exposure of many Indians to what is happening around the planet due to the internet and the news media, Modi's globalised foreign policy is seen by them as a long-overdue and much-needed effort to leap into the ranks of great powers.

Thanks to relentless public diplomacy, the linkage between India's domestic, economic and developmental priorities on one hand and its foreign policy has also been better explicated and implemented under the

---

[2] Haidar, Suhasini. 2015. 'Modi set to Travel 60,000 km in 30 Days', *The Hindu*, October 16th

Modi Doctrine than by previous Indian governments. Deepa Ollapally of George Washington University has argued that Modi's foreign policy does not fit a 'hard nationalist script' based on India's military might and expansionism, but is rather focussed on India's development and informed by a 'globalist mindset privileging regional and global economic integration, with a diplomatic approach for settling security conflicts.'[3]

In other words, Modi's mantra of 'India First' is not a blunt or crude jingoism that would face instant resistance and counterbalancing by other countries, but a sophisticated nationalism suitable to the milieu of globalisation with plenty of liberal content and ideas in it to appeal to Indians at home and to the world at large. Modi has softened much of the world to look at India's rise as an opportunity rather than a threat and has converted many formerly sceptical countries to see India in a new light as a provider of global goods. Under the Modi Doctrine, India is rising softly, responsibly and non-confrontationally. Firmness and toughness are embedded in the Modi Doctrine, but only used where they are absolutely required. The bulk of the foreign policy work is guided by Modi's 'three Cs' of culture, commerce and connectivity, which have excited and attracted the world to India's corner.

Neighbourhood First, Acrimony Last

Any aspirant country to great power status knows that the crux lies in managing its own backyard to be friendly and cooperative. If it faces hostility and threats all around its immediate vicinity, the chances of that nation asserting itself on the global stage are zilch because it gets tied down in its sub-region. There is also a compelling economic logic to ensure a calm and conducive neighbourhood. As I have mentioned in Chapter 3 of this book, the principal trading partners and investors of great powers tend to be their own neighbouring countries owing to the advantages of geographical contiguity and ease of moving goods and capital back and forth. For maximising both security and economic gains, a major power must have a reasonably consolidated neighbourhood that can act as the first layer of its international influence rather than

---

[3] Ollapally, Deepa. 2015. 'His Own Diplomacy', *The Indian Express*, February 3rd

an albatross around its neck. The USA in the Western Hemisphere and China in East Asia have never had fully smooth sailing, but they were historically most powerful when their neighbours went along with their ambitions instead of ganging up against them.

Map of South Asia

There are essentially two pathways identified by scholars and practitioners of foreign policy for a major power to achieve a favourable regional order. The first is the realpolitik tradition that proffers complete domination over neighbours as necessary for a state to be secure and to exert power in the world. The ancient Indian guru of *raison d'état*, Kautilya assumed in his *Mandala* theory of concentric circles that, 'every state bordering on yours is an enemy and every state that does not touch yours but is a neighbour of your enemy is a potential ally.' Writing in the fourth century BC in the context of perpetually warring states, his advice to sovereigns was, 'if one's country is stronger than a neighbouring kingdom, a king must attack; if a neighbour suffers a calamity, one must attack; if a treaty is no longer useful, one must attack.'[4] The notion that one must militarily conquer or subjugate one's near neighbours is also present in contemporary realist writings of John Mearsheimer, who argues that attaining regional hegemony is the principal aim of a great power and that this goal is met through increasing its relative power over neighbours, waging war, resorting to blackmail, and keeping rivals tied down in protracted conflicts.[5]

There is also the liberal tradition of promoting regional integration through the efforts of a leading country's state and social actors in order to generate economic and welfare gains for all the involved countries. This school does not presume that relations among neighbours are inherently conflictual, and believes that focussing on trade, commerce, investment and connectivity can ultimately tame territorial and political disputes and suspicions in a region. In the words of the nineteenth century French liberal philosopher, Frédéric Bastiat, 'when goods cannot cross borders, armies will.'[6] A liberal great power should, therefore, strive to bind its neighbouring nations in a virtuous cycle of mutually beneficial economic and people-to-people cooperation and

---

4 Boesche, Roger. 2003. *The First Great Political Realist: Kautilya and his Arthashastra*, New York: Lexington Books, pp.108-109

5 Mearsheimer, John. 2001. *The Tragedy of Great Power Politics*, New York: W.W. Norton

6 Roche, George. 1971. *Frédéric Bastiat: A Man Alone*, New York: Arlington House, p.49

free itself from strategic pressure and debilitating military competition in its surroundings.

Narendra Modi may never have studied theories of statecraft, but he instinctively adheres to the age-old wisdom of converting neighbours from challenges into opportunities. The Modi Doctrine is definitely intent on leveraging India's neighbourhood for economic prosperity. Its commercial diplomacy aspect, which I elaborated in Chapter 3 as a fulfilment of the BJP's *Samriddhi* pillar of foreign policy, naturally endeavours to bind South Asia in a web of economic interactions. Modi's approach to neighbours is, indeed, predicated on what the Australian scholar, Rory Medcalf terms as, 'closer integration of Indian business and diplomacy.'[7] Modi rightly 'sees a big market in India's neighbourhood and one that the previous governments have not been able to harness to the country's benefit.'[8] The fact that SAARC remains the least integrated region with high barriers to movement of legitimate goods, services and people is an affront to the Modi Doctrine, which thrives on economic interdependence and interaction.

The developmental agenda that Modi nurses as his prime responsibility to fellow Indians cannot be accomplished if South Asia is stuck in a pre-globalised pattern of mistrust and jealousy. The emphasis on connectivity and commerce in South Asia that he has given is also a reflection of his confidence in India's economic vitality and its ability to spread public goods to its smaller neighbours. India cannot grow in isolation and nor can its neighbours rise if India slows down economically. This is the win-win commercial logic that Modi wants to universalise in South Asia. Already, the business dividends of the Modi Doctrine in India's neighbourhood are apparent. In April 2015, South Asia became the number one destination for India's high-technology exports, recording a ninety percent growth over the previous year, and accounting for over fifteen percent of India's total shipments in this sector. The head of the Engineering Export Promotion Council (EEPC) of India has observed that, 'when Europe and

---

[7] Medcalf, Rory. 2014. 'Under Narendra Modi, there will be Closer Integration of Indian Business and Diplomacy', *The Economic Times*, May 27th

[8] Pandey, Vikas. 2014. 'Can India's Modi Integrate South Asia?', *BBC News*, May 29th. URL: http://www.bbc.com/news/world-asia-india-27572992 Last accessed on March 5th, 2016

several other parts of the world are posing challenges, finding a handsome growth in the neighborhood was a pleasant surprise. The development gels very well with the policies of the government to give top priority to our neighbours in the foreign policy."[9] As the Indian economy motors along, South Asia will find even more resonance in Modi's developmental goals.

At the same time, there is also an element of realpolitik in the Modi Doctrine's neighbourhood strategy, which is watchful and wary about growing Chinese penetration of South Asia. Hence, it has invested heavily in military diplomacy and manoeuvring to keep the dragon at bay. One sees a trace of Kautilya in the way Modi has rediscovered the *Mandala* theory, wherein India is at the centre of a wave of concentric circles, the nearest and most critical being immediate neighbours. But unlike the one-dimensional Indira Doctrine, which I mentioned in the Introduction of this book as centred on security, the Modi Doctrine combines liberal trade and commerce with a hawk-like alertness to meeting the competition from China to weaken India's numero uno status in South Asia.

Modi's coronation as India's prime minister in May 2014 was an unprecedented moment for South Asia, with heads of government of India's neighbours attending that ceremony in Delhi on his special invitation. The message he sent through this symbolic event was that the neglect of South Asia by previous Indian governments, which had squandered leverage and goodwill through neglect and unimaginative repetitions of hackneyed policies, was over. Under Modi, India has returned with a bang in its neighbourhood. Barring Pakistan, whose hostile military establishment still threatens India with jihadist terror, the Modi Doctrine has succeeded in overcoming nagging past failures with the rest of the South Asian fraternity. It has crafted a largely benign environment in its backyard which will enable domestic and transnational economic exchanges.

Modi's conclusion of the Land Boundary Agreement (LBA) with Bangladesh in May 2015, which had been prepared, but not implemented by the Manmohan Singh government due to domestic political obstructionism, is the diplomatic equivalent of a slam dunk that

---

9 "Ghosal, Sutanuka. 2015. 'PM Modi's Neighbourhood First Policy: South Asia Leads in Indian High-Tech Products', *The Economic Times*, June 9th"

will ensure India regains its stature as a benevolent and accommodating lynchpin on its sensitive eastern flank where the Chinese shadow has been lengthening. During their very first meeting In September 2014, Modi requested his Bangladeshi counterpart Sheikh Hasina to 'have faith in me'[10] to seal the long-stalled LBA. The gamesmanship with which Modi then convinced political parties and state governments at home to amend the Indian Constitution and ratify the LBA, and the grace with which the Modi government accepted the adverse verdict of the Permanent Court of Arbitration in July 2014 to settle the Bangladesh-India maritime boundary dispute have converted sceptics and won hearts in South Asia. In both these instances, India was a net loser which gave up more land and water resources to its smaller neighbour. But from a broader perspective, India was a net winner by reshaping perceptions in Bangladesh, where the mood has turned into adulation for Modi across partisan lines.

It is worth recognising that the traditionally India-baiting opposition outfit, the Bangladesh National Party (BNP), proclaimed in 2015 that it will 'never be anti-India.'[11] BNP's supremo and former Prime Minister Khaleda Zia herself took the initiative to write Modi a letter expressing a desire to meet him in Dhaka—a volte face from her earlier cold-shouldering of Indian dignitaries. The BNP has turned over a new leaf and is eyeing India with a positive lens as a force for equitable economic cooperation and a role model democracy. The old charge that India is an exploitative bully is losing steam, so much so that the Chinese state media have speculated whether Modi went to Bangladesh in June 2015 to 'reduce China's influence on South Asia.'[12]

Modi has engineered an identity shift by presenting India as a large-hearted power capable of delivering on its words and making strategic concessions to promote South Asian harmony. In the words of his External Affairs Minister, Sushma Swaraj, India has shrugged off the damaging tag of 'arrogant big brother' and replaced it with

---

10 Roy, Shubhajit. 2015. 'Aap Mujh Pe Bharosa Rakhiye, PM Narendra Modi Told Sheikh Hasina', *The Indian Express*, May 8th

11 DNA. 2015. 'BNP Welcomes Modi's Visit, says its Stance not Anti-India', *Daily News and Analysis*, May 27th

12 Mali.2015. 'Modi's Bangladesh Visit to Strengthen Bilateral Ties', *Xinhua*, June 3rd

'caring elder brother.'[13] The success of the Modi Doctrine lies in a deft combination of personal touch diplomacy and framing issues in the language of mutual economic gain. The Modi magic works in India's neighbourhood because he talks pragmatic and gives foreign interlocutors a sense that they can benefit from India's rise.

Sheikh Hasina's foreign policy adviser, Gowher Rizvi, has argued that as India and Bangladesh bury most bilateral hatchets (with the Chief Minister of the eastern Indian state of West Bengal, Mamata Banerjee, in tow, Modi is keen to also find an amicable conclusion to the Teesta river water row), the time is ripe to 'go forward and tackle sub-regional or trilateral issues, where much of our hope lies.'[14]

Just as Germany and France halted bilateral bickering and slowly wove the rest of Europe in a web of liberal interdependence around their rock solid partnership, India and Bangladesh are approaching a level of coordination to form a vector for fusing the entire SAARC community. The high politics in SAARC has for decades intruded and crippled commoners whose livelihoods depend on access to markets and technology across borders. The Modi Doctrine is now clearing these hurdles and presenting a new politics where diplomacy serves the masses. Unfortunately, Pakistan remains a cantankerous spoiler to the South Asian economic virtuous cycle spearheaded by India and Bangladesh. By harping on the 'unfinished agenda of the partition' of the subcontinent, Islamabad is stuck in an outmoded mindset at a time when boundaries have transformed into conveyors and facilitators rather than confiners. Winds of change are blowing in India's east. Those on its west who remain impervious are hacking at their own feet.

Modi has conveyed this 'don't-miss-the-gravy-train' message to Pakistan, often, since assuming office as India's prime minister. His decision to re-start comprehensive bilateral dialogue with Pakistan in December 2015, despite no cessation in its terrorist activities aimed at India was a statesmanlike gesture that established India as the initiator

---

[13] ENN. 2015. 'India Playing Elder Bro, not Big Brother to Nepal: Sushma', *The New Indian Express*, December 8th

[14] PTI. 2015. 'PM Modi's Trip to be Turning Point in Regional Cooperation: Bangladeshi Official', *The Economic Times*, June 4th

and driver of regional peace and economic integration. His shock visit to Lahore at the end of 2015 caught the whole world unawares and showed that Modi is an innovator and unconventional strategist when it comes to neighbourhood diplomacy. Although serious doubts exist about whether or not Pakistan will reciprocate Modi's olive branch, he has given Pakistan a chance to clasp India's hand and help itself out of a deep self-inflicted economic and security morass. Far from appeasing Pakistan or turning a blind eye to its propensity to use terrorist violence as a tool of foreign policy, Modi has aimed to shore up the wider Asian landmass on India's west and shame Islamabad to shun its negative ways. By talking to Pakistan in both bilateral and multilateral settings, Modi is pressuring Pakistan to realise that the old game is up.

This strategy was evident in Sushma Swaraj's statement in Islamabad in December 2015 that, 'the heart of Asia cannot function if its arteries are clogged'—a challenge thrown at Pakistan to stop stymieing regional progress and muddying the waters in Afghanistan by arming anti-India terrorists. Pakistan's intransigent stand against the Motor Vehicle Agreement of SAARC blocked Indian trucks carrying products from reaching the Afghan market, thereby putting paid to Modi's vision articulated by Swaraj of 'interlinked trade, transit, energy and communication routes' as lifelines for cash-starved Afghanistan.[15] The Afghan President Ashraf Ghani, who has grown totally disillusioned with Pakistan's continued sponsorship of Taliban proxies and double-dealing on peace talks, sounded almost identical to Swaraj as he pictured Afghanistan as, 'the roundabout of Asia, a place through which ideas, people and goods flow.'[16]

India and Afghanistan are inevitably reverting toward closer strategic alignment, and this geopolitical correction gives the former an upper hand in dealing with Pakistan's narrow-minded military-dominated establishment. Much as Pakistan, backed by China, would wish to be the arbiter of Afghanistan's destiny, Modi has unambiguously situated India as the fulcrum that can transform the fate of South and even Central Asia. He has thrown the ball in Islamabad's court to moderate its behaviour to partake in collective gains.

---

15 PTI. 2015. 'Time for India, Pak to Display Maturity to do Business: Swaraj', *India Today*, December 9th

16 Ibid.

What if Pakistan does not get the drift of its failing economy and ignores Modi's invitation to do business and strengthen regional trade and cooperation? Worse still, what if Pakistan refuses to kick its old habit of projecting destructive menace in its neighbourhood via religious extremism and terrorism? Pakistan will need to incur costs for acting as a spoiler for it to change its behaviour. Modi has dispatched India's NSA, Ajit Doval, for secret meetings with his Pakistani counterpart, General Naseer Janjua, at surprise neutral venues out of the media glare. Their confabulations have centred on terrorism, the fragility of the Line of Control (LoC), and Kashmir. In these 'candid' exchanges, Doval would have conveyed how Pakistan could practically suffer if it did not completely halt sponsorship of jihadist violence against India.

With Pakistan embroiled in two debilitating counter-insurgencies against secular separatists in Balochistan and jihadists in Khyber Pakhtunkhwa, India is in a much stronger bargaining position regarding Kashmir now. Gone are the heydays of jihadist mayhem where Pakistan and its Kashmir Valley-based minions could proclaim themselves as unavoidable interlocutors who had to be consulted for a final settlement on the issue. If the Modi government has agreed to discuss all outstanding issues including Kashmir in the composite dialogue with Pakistan, it is not out of weakness, but rather self-confidence that the insurgency in Kashmir cannot be revived to its former peak ever again. Modi talks to Pakistan so that it recognises this fait accompli and climbs down from its maximalist dreams of annexing Kashmir.

Modi knows the lesson of history that no amount of American persuasion can alter the Pakistani military's jihadist mentality. The USA's Deputy Secretary of State Antony Blinken's advice to Pakistan in December 2015 to go after both 'inwardly directed and outwardly directed terror groups'[17] was a sound counsel, but Modi remains wary of the fact that the USA continues to deliver Pakistan hi-tech weapons worth billions. Dependence on Washington to tame the terror machine in Pakistan is old hat that never worked for India. By directly engaging Pakistan, Modi is self-confidently stepping up one gear and trying to steer India's worst neighbour into a positive dynamic. Modi is not naive about an intrinsic

---

[17] PTI, 2015. 'Pak Must not Distinguish Between Terror Groups: US', *India Today*, December 8th

change of heart in Islamabad, but he is extending a powerful unclenched fist, which the other side can disregard to its own disadvantage.

Yet, the brooding shadow of terrorism and the backlog of mistrust mean that Modi's attempts to 'try and turn the course of history' with Pakistan is just the beginning of a turbulent and unpredictable process. For India, how far the constructive turn goes depends singularly on whether Pakistan will kick its terrorist addiction. Disturbing attacks on Indian military installations by Pakistan-based jihadists, violations along the LoC and infiltration of jihadists into Indian-controlled Kashmir and Punjab have left Modi fuming that India will 'judge progress on their (Pakistan's) commitments on terrorism.'[18]

Since civilian leaders are not in control of Pakistan's national security apparatus, the billion-dollar question on everyone's lips is whether or not the terror tap will be turned on top gear by the Pakistani Army and the Inter-Services Intelligence (ISI) as the bilateral dialogue sought by the Modi Doctrine hurts their vested interests. Previous Indian prime ministers have been deceived by bonhomie from civilian counterparts in Pakistan who could not carry along their hard-line military and allied Islamists. To skeptics, Modi is destined to end up chastened by the visceral anti-India attitude which defines Pakistani nationalism and Islamist outlook. But by securing India's homeland better against terrorist attacks, and ushering in normalcy in Indian- controlled Kashmir, he can be in a stronger position to do business with liberal-minded elements of the Pakistani polity.

The ISI and its spoilers cannot wreck the peace process at their whim and fancy, despite characteristic malevolent intentions, if their capacity to harm India is blunted due to reordered priorities of facing domestic counter-insurgencies in Balochistan and Khyber Pakhtunkhwa, as well as through India's own proactive internal and cross border security measures. Modi's thaw with Pakistan needs to rest on this realistic liberalism akin to Reagan's 'peace through strength' formula.

Notwithstanding mistaken caricatures of Modi as a Hindu fundamentalist who adopts a hard line against Muslims and Muslim countries like Pakistan, Modi's persona and convictions are geared to believing that systems prone to failure can be made to change through

[18] PTI. 2015. 'Talks with Pakistan is to Try and Turn Course of History: Modi', *The New Indian Express*, December 15th

determined human effort rather than abandoning them. He realises that he must try to reverse the negative tide with Pakistan while retaining healthy skepticism about its military establishment. Protracted and bitter bilateral conflicts rarely yield instant peace, and the best one can hope for is that India and Pakistan will move forward on some issues where there is a win-win liberal logic, and keep channels of communication open on harder topics where their presently defined national interests clash.

Modi has no reason to be complacent that the Pakistani military will restrain itself. His peace and 'three Cs' policies can only succeed once Indian security agencies prevail and completely eliminate the threat of jihadists massing across the border. Strengthening internal security and also enhancing India's covert operations against jihadists inside Pakistani territory are necessary for the Modi Doctrine to work in the case of this obstreperous neighbour. There is no contradiction between continuing bilateral talks and developing an understanding with moderate elements of Pakistan's state and society on one hand, and going after notorious terrorist leaders on the other. Jihadists will continue to hurt India even if its agents assassinate their bigshots in Pakistan, but the message will be sent that India does not softly absorb blow after blow and carry on with business as usual. New Delhi must impose a psychological price on Pakistani hardliners intent on 'bleeding India with a thousand cuts'. The sooner the Modi Doctrine establishes and deploys such deterrence mechanisms, the better the chances of dismantling the terrorist empire in Pakistan and yielding a sustainable peace dividend. When India attains an impregnable position to ward off jihadist threats, it would by default also gain credence as a true great power in world politics.

Since Pakistan is currently a special case not amenable to the rational win-win propositions of the Modi Doctrine's 'neighbourhood first' mantra, it may remain one of the rare cases where Modi does not achieve big breakthroughs. The suicidal jihadist logic of the Pakistani military establishment, which Professor Christine Fair of Georgetown University has described as Pakistan never acquiescing to India and suffering 'any number of military defeats' in its efforts to weaken 'Hindu-dominated' India[19], is alien to the appeals for

---

[19] Fair, Christine. 2014. *Fighting to the End: The Pakistani Army's Way of War*, Oxford: Oxford University Press, p.4

economic interdependence and developmental diplomacy that Modi champions. For the mullahs and their military patrons in Pakistan, Modi's hand of friendship is a stratagem to devour and destroy Pakistan and its conservative Islamic values.[20] Modi may have to be satisfied with simply avoiding war with Pakistan rather than decisively ending this congenital struggle that started the day Pakistan was created by partitioning India in 1947. In India, there is a tendency in the mass media and popular imagination to focus obsessively and disproportionately on Pakistan, and to judge any government's foreign policy almost entirely on how it is performing in relation to this troublesome Western neighbour. Modi is sensitive to this narrative and has taken extraordinary personal and political risks to try and heal the war of attrition with Pakistan, which has corroded the heart of South Asia.

Nevertheless, as a pragmatist, Modi is not waiting in vain for Pakistan to reform itself for the rest of his 'neighbourhood first' priorities to fructify. In August 2015, he declared that, 'we have decided to strengthen connectivity in SAARC countries. Some have tried to block talks, but let them be, the rest of SAARC will move ahead on it.'[21] He has floated new concepts of 'SAARC minus one' (i.e. without Pakistan), and has mooted new common market ideas like BBIN, which I have described in Chapter 3 of this book. India's infrastructural aid and road and rail connectivity with its northern and eastern neighbours is growing on a fast-track basis. Indian private sector entrepreneurs have been prodded by the Modi government to invest more in the SAARC economies. Bangladesh, Bhutan, Afghanistan, Nepal and Myanmar have witnessed increases in Indian assistance to speed up physical and digital links and raise the quality of commercial infrastructure. That this pattern is part of a well-defined and articulated strategy of the Modi Doctrine is clear because most of the countries which have seen a hike in development

---

[20] Yadav, Yatish. 2015. 'Hafiz Cries Tauba, Tauba; Pak TV Asks if Modi had Visa to Enter', *The New Indian Express*, December 27th

[21] NM. 2015. 'PM Modi's Address to the Indian Community at Dubai', *Narendra Modi*, August 17th. URL: https://www.youtube.com/watch?v=spPKk79yO0k Last accessed on March 5th, 2016

assistance have also seen a visit by prime minister Narandra Modi in the past year.[22]

In late 2015, the Modi Doctrine was severely tested in Nepal during an unfortunate phase of internal social divisions and turmoil in that country over the promulgation of its new Constitution. India was caught in the crossfire between agitating Madhesis from the Terai area of Nepal and the dominant hill elites. A humanitarian and economic crisis resulted from stoppage of supplies along the India-Nepal border, which was labelled by many Nepalese politicians and people as a deliberate blockade by New Delhi. Diplomatic history is rife with examples of tempers fraying in the heat of the moment, when allegations fly and every action by one side is taken amiss by the other. In those times, many leaders become blinded to the long-term interdependence and the symbiotic links that bind two nations together and tend to focus on the immediate tensions for narrow political gains. This was the delicate condition of Nepal and India when the Madhesi issue was at its peak in 2015. Nepalese elites interpreted India to be stoking Madhesi protests to blackmail them, and Indian elites believed that they were being scapegoated for Nepal's inability to resolve their intramural ethnic fissures and counterclaims. In the words of the then Nepalese Prime Minister, K.P. Oli, 'misunderstandings' crept up with India surrounding the Constitutional logjam.[23] Critics of Modi in India slammed him for a foreign policy failure. His government's inability to counter the anti-India sentiment that had suddenly crested in Nepal seemed to suggest absence of a single line or strategy towards Nepal.

However, the Modi Doctrine has a unique way of recovering lost ground by appealing to reason over emotions. Through patient backdoor diplomacy and dialogue, India began to reset relations with Nepal from early 2016 by going back to the playbook of the 'three Cs'. Modi's persuasion that it is pointless to keep debating as to which side 'won' or 'lost' from the confrontation, who blinked and who held his

---

22 Bagchi, Indrani. 2016. 'India Boosts Aid to Other Countries', *The Times of India*, March 4th

23 PTI. 2016. 'Indo-Nepal PMs Talk it Out; K.P. Oli says no Misunderstandings Now', *The Times of India*, February 20th

ground got through to Nepalese decision-makers. It is Modi's belief that foreign relations, especially among geographically contiguous and culturally similar states like India and Nepal, cannot be left to raw emotions and one-upmanship games. A certain maturity of thought, modesty in words and perspective in action are necessary to step back from brinkmanship and to coordinate policies for mutual welfare of the two societies that benefit from friendly relations.

When the fracas around the Constitution erupted, there was consternation in Nepal around 'Who is the real Modi?', viz. the one who had initially won all hearts in 2014 including those of the Communists and the Maoists or the one who was painted as a diabolical Big Brother using strong-arm tactics to trample Nepalese sovereignty? Dire circumstances and political crises generate stark negative stereotypes and make people forget the essence of the other side. The truth is that Modi is different from previous Indian leaders in getting the smallest of countries to feel comfortable due to his egalitarian mindset. He can motor entire South Asia out of chronic underdevelopment if there are willing partners in neighbouring countries. By 2016, Nepal realised this potential and expressed a desire to 'move in a new direction' with a 'focus on inviting Indian investment in Nepal.'[24] Modi has since then moved with Nepal towards completing construction of two hydroelectric power projects worth $1 billion, laying cross-border electric transmission lines, road building in the Terai area, construction of a second airport and a state-of-the-art hospital, technical education schools and a university.

Nepal is the classic case in South Asia where India sees the threat of Chinese influence lengthening. Nepal has reasons to believe it can counterbalance Indian pressure by joining the Chinese One Belt One Road (OBOR) initiative. Like any small state sandwiched between two competing giants, Nepalese foreign policy has tried to play off India against China and maximise leverage for its own interests. However, Modi is not insecure about this ploy and understands its logic. But he is hoping that Nepalese elites of all partisan hues realise the tremendous economic potential of the BBIN idea when it fully materialises. If Nepal wants to have the Chinese cake and eat the Indian one too, it

---

[24] IANS. 2016. 'Nepal PM to Focus on 'Clearing Misunderstanding' with India', *Business Standard*, February 16th

is not a loss for Modi because he is confident of the geographical and cultural affinities between India and Nepal that no other power can reproduce. When Modi wore orange robes and performed prayers at the Pashupatinath Temple in Kathmandu in August 2014, the cultural diplomatic advantage was clearly with India. If Modi enables Nepal to set up a university on the traditional Indian medical system of Ayurveda, he would again be reinforcing the non-materialistic bonds that make Nepal so dear and special to India. In my own travels in Nepal after the Madhesi crisis, I heard local interlocutors say that Modi must recognise active pro-India elements within Nepalese society and activate them to counter negative stereotyping of India. Such identification of 'assets' on the ground is usually the preserve of the Indian embassy, but the retail diplomacy of Modi has raised expectations that he himself and the office of India's prime minister should directly intervene to turn around the tide in Nepal back in India's favour.

Sri Lanka is another neighbouring country which has posed a strategic challenge to the Modi Doctrine. When Mahinda Rajapaksa was the Sri Lankan President until January 2015, he invited Chinese submarines to dock in the Colombo harbour and deepened Chinese economic investments in his country as a deliberate ploy to counter Indian interests in creating an ethnically pluralistic and just post-war Sri Lankan society. Rajapaksa's electoral defeat to Maithripala Sirisena in early 2015 was a surprise victory which removed a thorn in the flesh for India. But this outcome was hardly a lucky break that fell in Modi's lap. Allegations from Rajapaksa's camp about 'a deep campaign by foreign elements'[25] to dethrone him have kindled speculation that the Indian government wilfully schemed behind the scenes to ensure the authoritarian leader's fall.

Given the plausible deniability in intelligence operations and the cloak-and-dagger politics of Sri Lanka, the truth is anyone's guess. But if Sirisena did benefit from Indian help in organising a common opposition platform that prevailed in the elections, he surely knows inside his heart and treasures India's assistance to civil society groups that coalesced to oust the dictatorial Rajapaksa. Sirisena often stresses

---

[25] Chalmers, John & Sanjeev Miglani. 2015. 'Indian Spy's Role Alleged in Sri Lankan President's Election Defeat', *Reuters*, January 17th

'shared values of pluralism and democracy' that bind Sri Lanka to India. It is a deliberately chosen phrase. Sri Lanka's identity as a democracy, which has to be restored after it was mauled and tattered by Rajapaksa, is inextricably linked to furthering partnership with free India rather than autocratic China.

Sirisena's desire to 'elevate engagement' with India 'to greater heights'[26] is, thus, an existential need as he tries to steer Sri Lanka away from the dark past of a heavy-handed state apparatus that crushed human rights and suppressed minorities. Despite New Delhi's traditional reluctance to promote democracy in its foreign policy, India has always been an inspiration and a spur for forces of moderation in Sri Lanka by virtue of being South Asia's strongest pluralistic democracy. The Modi Doctrine has not shied away from capitalising on India's democratic strength in countries where it matters, and sets India apart from China. For example, in addressing the parliament in a Bhutan making a transition to democracy in June 2014, he lauded India's democratic polity as a blessing for SAARC nations and averred that, 'a strong and stable India is needed to make sure that we can help our neighbours with their problems.'[27]

Modi knows that among all foreign players, only India has sufficient historical and contemporary connections and networks in Sri Lanka to enable it to counter conservative and fundamentalist resisters of reforms. By associating Indian diplomacy with tolerant groups, the Modi governmentis trying to limit the Buddhist Right wing and militaristic Sinhalese elites which had been Rajapaksa's backbone. Sri Lankan intellectuals and activists have thrived on mutual learning from their Indian peers. But regularised and concrete mechanisms to expose Sri Lankans more to India's multicultural ethos, methods of coopting armed separatist movements, and achievements in post-war reconciliation, are still missing. Modi must initiate a bilateral knowledge exchange programme involving students, professionals, journalists and farmers to consolidate India's comeback in Sri Lanka. Just as the 'Colombo Plan' for transfer of technology and skills for economic development was initiated

---

[26] PTI. 2015. 'Lanka Looks Forward to Elevating Engagement with India', *The New Indian Express*, February 9th

[27] IT. 2014. 'Modi Addresses Bhutan's Parliament, says a Stronger India Better for Bhutan Too', *India Today*, June 16th

by the Indian diplomat K.M. Panikkar in 1949, Modi must launch a new Colombo Plan for strengthening civic institutions and key constituencies in Sri Lankan society.

The Ceylon Chamber of Commerce has recommended that Sri Lanka's economic growth model should shift from infrastructure-driven to an exports and FDI-led strategy. It is in India's interests to second this redirection because the omnipresence of China in India's backyard relies on infrastructure-based GDP growth patterns, wherein Beijing muscles into countries like Sri Lanka and Maldives via mega construction contracts.

Sri Lankan industry bodies are clamouring for 'deeper economic ties with India beyond the current Free Trade Agreement.'[28] The bilateral trade imbalance in India's favour reflects inadequate export capacity in Sri Lanka, a lacuna that Modi can help redress through accelerated investments in the teardrop island nation which is India's gateway to the strategically located Indian Ocean. Sri Lankan leaders after the fall of Rajapaksa have touted a 'balanced foreign policy', implying that China cannot be wished away after it gained the position of Sri Lanka's largest foreign investor during the Rajapaksa period. But China's sway can be limited through targeted Indian investments in Sri Lanka, which has a skilled workforce and low transportation costs due to geographical proximity. Unlike Pakistan, Modi's gospel-like faith in commercial diplomacy has a fantastic willing laboratory in Sri Lanka.

Afghanistan is not India's immediate neighbour, but a member of SAARC which relies on Indian support for its stability and reconstruction after decades of crippling foreign military interventions by the USSR, the USA and Pakistan. The Modi government has overcome the vacillating policy of the Manmohan Singh era, and has boldly decided to supply the Afghan government with long-sought lethal military aid. The attack helicopters donated by India have proven to be crucial for the Afghan state to repel Taliban and allied militants answerable to Pakistani masters. General John Campbell, the commander of American forces in Afghanistan, admitted that Modi's gifts to the fledgling Afghan Air Force were 'making a great difference'

---

[28] ENS. 2015. 'Lanka Opportunity', *The Indian Express*, February 17th

in Afghanistan's war against terrorism.[29] The Modi Doctrine's departure from the feeble and indecisive approach of the Manmohan Singh era is based on confidence about India's capabilities to withstand any blowback effect from Pakistan in retaliation for enhanced Indian security support for Afghanistan.

Like in the rest of the SAARC community, Modi is watchful of the growing Chinese presence and diplomatic games in Afghanistan. Since 2015, China has escalated its role as a moderator or guarantor in peace talks between the Afghan government and the Taliban. China's bosom ally, Pakistan, and even the USA have welcomed Beijing's deepening involvement in Afghanistan's peace process. Modi's reiteration that India endorses only an 'Afghan-led and Afghan-owned process', and his veiled criticism of Pakistan in calling for a 'positive and constructive approach from neighbours, including an end to support for violence'[30], leave little doubt that India is now fighting back with multiple levers against its marginalisation in Afghanistan. Modi's quip in Kabul in December 2015 at the newly inaugurated Afghan Parliament built with Indian aid that, 'India is here to contribute, not to compete; to lay the foundations of future, not light the flame of conflict; to rebuild lives, not destroy a nation',[31] speaks of a new determination to differentiate India from other players in this geostrategically vital country. The fact that Afghan President Ashraf Ghani first tried wooing Pakistan as a necessary partner for ending the war in his nation, then denounced Pakistan, and reverted to clasping Modi's hand as a morale booster says much about the Modi Doctrine's resilience in keeping Indian influence alive in the hardest of circumstances. Where geopolitical competition is intense, the Modi Doctrine has the reserves to survive and emerge with an enhanced profile for India.

The tiny archipelago of Maldives is another SAARC member where China has been steadily encroaching, posing one more trial to the Modi Doctrine. The Maldivian President Abdulla Yameen has

---

[29] PTI. 2016. 'Indian Helicopters Helped War Against Militants in Afghanistan: US General', *The Indian Express*, February 3rd

[30] Roche, Elizabeth. 2015. 'Narendra Modi backs Ghani's Plans for Afghanistan Peace Process', *Mint*, April 29th

[31] NM. 2015. 'PM Modi's Speech at the Inauguration of the New Parliament Building of Afghanistan', ***Narendra Modi***, December 24th. URL: https://www.youtube.com/watch?v=oJAk4kOadGY Last accessed on June 15th, 2016

endorsed China's OBOR and has offered huge land concessions for Chinese companies to swarm the island country. Chinese Air Force and Navy vessels have been invited to the Maldives to deliver humanitarian aid. Although Yameen wrote a letter to Modi in August 2015 assuring him that he will not allow his country to be militarised, Beijing does not need fulltime military bases to call the shots in foreign countries. Hence, Indian naval patrolling and manoeuvring in the Indian Ocean must prepare and plan for signalling and deterring temporary, but continuous Chinese inroads. Since the Chinese are unrivalled masters at physical infrastructure, and given that India's land reclamation companies would be handicapped by the anti-India dispensation in Male, the Modi government needs to make a bigger concerted effort to nurture the Maldives' social and human capital, which holds the key to swaying public opinion.

Indian intellectuals should offer maximum advice as consultants to raise the subpar capacity of the nascent Maldives National University. The scholarships and training that India gives to Maldivian youth and civil servants must be multiplied several fold. The Maldives has a majority Muslim population, which is of South Indian origin, holding tremendous potential for enhancing India's natural educational and cultural links, something that the Chinese cannot artificially generate the way they effortlessly reclaim barren islands. In tourism, where China has virtually taken over the Maldives, there must be an Indian government-guided effort to promote the Maldives as a prime holiday destination for India's itinerant upper-middle class, whose size and discretionary spending are growing, but whose gaze is fixated on the Thailand, Malaysia and Singapore routes.

The Modi Doctrine's multi-pronged instruments of culture, commerce and human resource capacity building are all being deployed to avoid India being sidelined in the Maldives. In October 2015, Modi sent Sushma Swaraj to the Maldives and 'produced a blueprint for re-energizing ties—from health to economy to tourism and skill development.'[32] This trip helped set 'strained ties back on track.'[33]

---

[32] Roche, Elizabeth. 2016. 'Maldives Looks to Host Indian Prime Minister Narendra Modi this Year', *Mint*, February 18th

[33] Ibid

Politically, the injustice meted out to opposition party activists in the Maldives is certainly a cause of concern and deserves Indian advocacy. Modi was scheduled to visit the Maldives in March 2015, but this was cancelled when the Yameen regime forced the judiciary to persecute the pro-India former President Mohamed Nasheed. However, since then, Modi has also reached out to Yameen, and has placed on the table whatever benefits he hopes to get from India. India has overcome old reluctance to engage in weapons exports and supplied Maldives with light helicopters, radars and increased maritime surveillance exercises with the Maldivian military.

Under the Modi Doctrine, India has tried to avoid being typecast as a foreign power identified only with one party, ideological camp or ethnic group, a phenomenon that has in the past cost New Delhi dearly in Sri Lanka, Nepal and Bangladesh. This multi-vectoral diplomacy is an important instrument in Modi's toolbox in shaping South Asia to suit India's vision of an integrated and economically dynamic sub-region. To sum up, the Modi Doctrine has resuscitated India in South Asia with diplomatic prioritisation and innovation. It is not paranoid about Chinese expansionism in its backyard, but is alert to Beijing's shenanigans. It is not aiming to project India as a substitute to China in South Asia, but is working towards maintaining and extending India's leadership in the region. In cases where there have been setbacks to Indian interests in the neighbourhood, the Modi Doctrine has displayed strategic patience to stick it out and to work quietly to regain a foothold. Because of the balance between realpolitik and liberal economic principles in the Modi Doctrine, and the rapid GDP growth that India has registered under Modi, he has more options to throw at a problem in South Asia. If the political relations plummet with a neighbour, he has an economic salve. With the plethora of regional public goods that an economically booming India can offer in South Asia, Modi has many levers on hand. If economics is going well, but security is still undercooked, he can fall back on India as a net provider in defence. As India's military production and exports are augmented under the Modi Doctrine in years to come, one can expect the 'neighbourhood first' policy to score more successes.

The Modi government's claim that, 'India continues to shine brightly as a beacon of hope for democracy across the world',[34] and its willingness to play the democracy card more strategically also added to the arsenal in handling what has always been a delicate neighbourhood. Modi's ingenious ideas for launching a SAARC satellite, setting up a special purpose facility in India to finance infrastructure projects in South Asia, offering long-term business travel cards for SAARC citizens, and holding annual exercises of SAARC rescue teams and doctors to minimise damage during natural disasters, are other platforms through India has shown that it is finally leading in its backyard. Professor Harsh Pant's assessment is worth citing here, 'South Asia is passing through a phase where Pakistan is getting increasingly isolated and India under Modi is making its presence felt around the world. Modi's proactive diplomacy has expanded the strategic space for India to manoeuvre in South Asia and beyond.'[35]

Without resorting to the militaristic methods favoured by Kautilya, Modi has grasped the nettle of what the original master of realpolitik would call prevailing in India's 'first concentric circle'. The reason Modi's neighbourhood policy has delivered in overall terms is that he has approached it as if it were a system rather than a haphazard array of India's bilateral equations with seven other SAARC member countries. It is the hallmark of a doctrine to have a systemic treatment of regions and issues with a distinct set of policies for each region and cluster. India lacked a punch in South Asia as long as it was devoid of the big picture thinking and a far-reaching doctrine. Modi has at last filled the void.

Defending 'India's Ocean'

Narendra Modi has reminded the world that,'India is, and has always been, a maritime nation' with a 'glorious maritime tradition' as reflected in ancient Sanskrit texts and the Indus Valley civilisation.[36] For a country inured to viewing regional security and power politics with a land-based, territorial strategic outlook, he has wrought a new self-image by

---

[34] MEA. 2015. *Breakthrough Diplomacy: New Vision, New Vigour*, New Delhi: Government of India, p.6

[35] Pant, Harsh. 2015. 'PM Modi's Proactive Diplomacy is Changing South Asia', *The Daily Mail*, December 10th

[36] ANI. 2016. 'India Will Host First Ever Global Maritime Summit in April: Modi', *Deccan Chronicle*, February 7th

going back aeons to a period when Indian merchants, sailors and navies roamed the high seas for wealth, commerce and empire. Researcher Aakriti Bhutoria of Australia's Griffith University has observed that, 'under Prime Minister Modi's leadership the Indian Ocean has assumed great importance, signalling a shift away from the "continental mindset" of the previous governments. To be sure, India still continues to grapple with territorial border intrusions from China and Pakistan in the north but over the last two years the oceans have attracted the focus of the foreign policy establishment in an unprecedented manner.'[37]

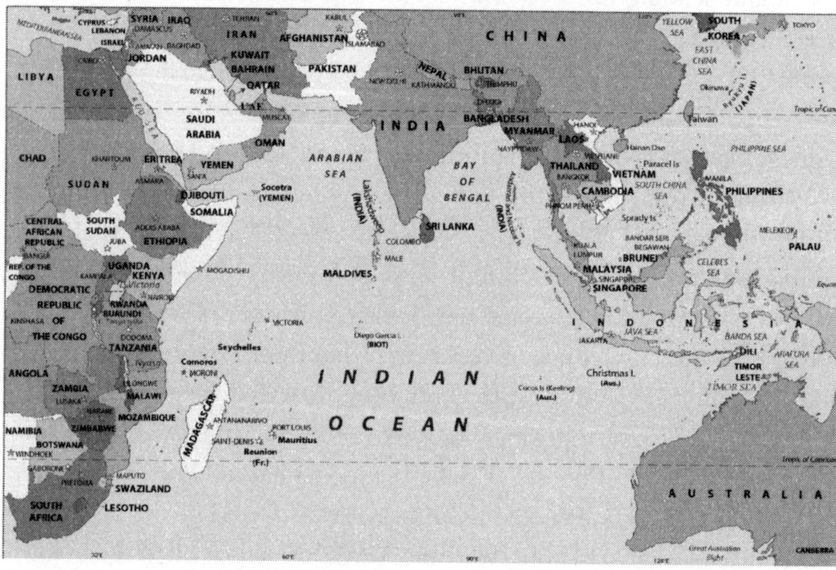

Map of the Indian Ocean Region

The Modi Doctrine's goal of establishing India as a leading power has to inexorably pass through the medium of water, which is fluid and open to rising powers to stake new claims than land or air, which are already marked out in political geography and are parcelled out among existing great powers. For India to alter the power configuration of the international system in the twenty-first century, mastery over the seas is the only viable path.

[37] Bhutoria, Aakriti. 2016. 'Indian Foreign Policy and the Second International Fleet Review', *Australian Institute of International Affairs*, February 12th

Modi's explicit emphasis on the Indian Ocean Region (IOR) as 'one of my foremost policy priorities'[38] has sounded India's determination to focus on what Robert Kaplan terms as the maritime space that is the 'center stage for the 21st century'[39] where 'the new Great Game in geopolitics' will be played.[40] The framework put forth by the Modi Doctrine in the IOR is encapsulated by the acronym SAGAR (meaning sea in Hindi), which Modi has expanded as Security and Growth for All in the Region. His stress on the IOR as the 'extended neighbourhood which is vital for India's security and progress'[41] conveys that there is both a commercial and military connotation to the way the Modi Doctrine is attempting to raise India's salience in this crucial waterway. Modi himself has spelt out why the IOR matters to India and the world in lucid terms while commissioning an Indian-built naval patrol vessel for the National Coast Guard of Mauritius in March 2015,'This Ocean bears two-thirds of the world`s oil shipments, one-third of its bulk cargo; and half of its container traffic. Over three-fourths of its traffic goes to other regions of the world.'[42] This ocean, the only one in the world to be named after a country due to India's ancient dominance in these waters, carries eighty percent of China's oil, sixty-five percent of India's oil, and sixty percent of Japan's oil. It is basically the lifeline of Asia, and is hence also heavily militarised and contested by major powers. The Modi Doctrine realises that the IOR is the modern-day jugular vein that will determine power struggles and supremacy, as well as economic welfare of 2.5 billion people living in thirty-six littoral states in an arc stretching from the east coast of Africa to the West coast of Australia. Accordingly, it has fielded diplomatic, military and corporate assets to ensure that India remains the hub of all developments in the IOR.

---

38 NM. 2016. 'PM Modi at the International Fleet Review in Vishakhapatnam, Andhra Pradesh', *Narendra Modi*, February 7th. URL: https://www.youtube.com/watch?v=qUdTVaULlLQ Last accessed on March 6th, 2016

39 Kaplan, Robert. 2009. 'Center Stage for the 21st Century: Power Plays in the Indian Ocean', *Foreign Affairs*, March/April

40 Kaplan, Robert. 2011. *Monsoon: The Indian Ocean and the Future of American Power*, New York: Random House, p.13

41 GOI. 2015. *Sagar Yatra: The Ocean Voyage*, New Delhi: Government of India, p.1

42 PMO. 2015. 'PM in Mauritius: Commissioning of Offshore Patrol Vessel Barracuda', *Prime Minister's Office*, March 12th. URL: https://www.youtube.com/watch?v=lS7wXltU9xE Last accessed on March 6th, 2016

Modi's SAGAR strategy has infused fresh energy into India's mantle as the fulcrum of stability in the IOR. It has signalled India's intent and capacity to ward off extra-regional challengers and emerge as a net security provider in these strategically seminal sea lanes. India stands geographically, ideationally and potential-wise bang in the middle of the IOR littoral. Other capable countries like South Africa, Iran, Indonesia and Australia are also members of the IOR family, but none of them has the centrality or attraction like India to assume regional leadership. Modi's visits to Seychelles, Mauritius and Sri Lanka in early 2015 affirmed that India is not only the historical lodestone of the Indian Ocean, but is also the contemporary leader with the wherewithal to safeguard and develop the littoral region. He has served notice to China and the US, the two external superpowers prowling the Indian Ocean for influence, that India will not let its comparative advantages to go to waste.

Modi's messaging to tiny maritime nations in the IOR is that India has the firepower and scientific prowess to support what he respectfully and affectionately dubs as *chhote chhote taapu* (small islands), and which he goads as true leaders capable of producing stability by tagging with India. Shedding the reticence of his predecessors, Modi boldly trumpets India's military rise as beneficial for these little countries. Small states lying on the maritime edges of a great power can feel vulnerable when the latter flexes military muscle. For example, China's revolution in military affairs (RMA) concept has frightened the wits out of its weaker neighbours in the East China Sea and the South China Sea, where disputes over islands and mineral rights are escalating. The Modi Doctrine is a different cup of tea altogether, wherein India will never mount any territorial claims over its Indian Ocean cohabitants. Rather, India will do everything to strengthen the defence sectors of these countries to ward off traditional challenges like powers from outside the region and non-traditional foes such as seafaring pirates, religious extremists and terrorists.

On the Western flank of the IOR, the African writer Alioune Ndiaye has flagged India's 'Varuna triangle' strategy of reinforcing Seychelles, Mauritius and Madagascar through naval diplomacy, opening of listening posts, and securing India's external trade and countering growing Chinese presence in the region.[43] On the eastern flank, there is increasing interoperability of the Indian navy and select Southeast Asian and Australian navies as a part and parcel of Modi's 'Act East' policy. Although the Manmohan Singh government had been moving in this direction on both ends of the IOR, it is only under the Modi Doctrine that substantial progress has been made in military diplomacy. The distinct Indian vision of a security umbrella in the Indian Ocean is reflected in two landmark agreements signed by the Modi government with Seychelles and Mauritius, whereby New Delhi acquired infrastructure development rights in Assumption Island and Agalega Island—two vital listening posts. By operating and sharing surveillance systems on these islets, India aims to help their host nations 'access the moves of unsavoury elements in the region.'[44]

During Manmohan Singh's rule, Seychelles had offered refueling and docking facilities to Chinese warships involved in anti-piracy operations. Sri Lanka, too, had hosted Chinese submarines for re-supplying en route to anti-piracy missions near the Horn of Africa. Cognisant of the expansionist mindset of the Chinese navy, which is preparing to push many more 'naval escort missions' into the Indian Ocean 'in accordance with the situation',[45] and the ever-present American navy which has hunkered down in India's backyard with heavy paraphernalia, Modi is pursuing robust arrangements for India to remain a 'preferred partner' for the security of Indian Ocean neighbours. He has sought to expand India's traditional trilateral maritime security arrangement with Sri Lanka and Maldives to include Mauritius and Seychelles to form an 'IO-5' grouping which will train forces jointly for maritime operations and domain awareness. He has also ramped up a Defence Cooperation Agreement with the UAE and launched a 'strategic security dialogue' with that country so that the Western portion of the Indian Ocean is not conceded to the Chinese navy, which is prowling the waters there in the guise of countering maritime piracy.

---

[43] Ndiaye, Alioune& Pooja Jain. 2015. 'Africa-India: Stakes of a Win-Win Partnership', *The Herald*, November 10th

[44] ANI. 2015. 'India-Seychelles Engage on Cooperation in Maritime Security', *Daily News and Analysis*, March 11th

[45] MOD. 2015. 'Defense Ministry's Regular Press Conference', *Ministry of National Defense, The People's Republic of China*, January 29th

Is India behaving like other neocolonial powers by chasing after exclusive defence pacts and leases? Has Modi shed India's old diffidence and anti-colonial perception about acquiring foreign military bases? Does he covet foreign military power the ways the USA has built it up and what China has begun to do by taking its first overseas military 'support facility' in Djibouti on the north-Western edge of the IOR? We must distinguish what the Americans have done in the Diego Garcia atoll of the Indian Ocean and what India is accomplishing in Assumption and Agalega Islands. The former was unethically snatched from Mauritius by Britain, and was then handed over to the USA as a naval base in 1966. Nationalistic Mauritians have been demanding for decades that the Chagos Archipelago, which contains Diego Garcia, be rightfully returned back to their sovereignty. American diplomats have insinuated in Wikileaks cables that Mauritius is entering into 'willing subordination to India' over Agalega.[46] But the cultural closeness and trust that Modi has evoked in Mauritius confirms that the Indian model of security and economic cooperation is not imperialistic. As I have mentioned in Chapter 1 of this book, the cultural diplomacy card that Modi has played in Indian Ocean countries with large ethnic Indian diasporas has been a big force multiplier for New Delhi. The receptivity for Modi's ideas of cooperation to advance the 'blue economy' or 'blue revolution' and to arrest climate change also echoes in the so-called 'Vanilla islands' whose people as well as governments want an agile and proactive India on their shores and soils.

The 'blue economy' concept has been maxed by Modi to a positive effect in the IOR. It connects the Sagar Mala scheme of developing India's domestic coastal infrastructure for trade and commerce, which I have described in Chapter 3 of this book, and a chain of production, trade and investment throughout the IOR to sustainably tap into aquaculture, shipping and seabed mining. The Modi government has defined the blue economy as a reconceptualisation of 'oceans as development spaces where spatial planning integrates conservation, sustainable use, oil and mineral wealth extraction, bio-prospecting, sustainable energy

---

46 Brewster, David. 2014. *India's Ocean: The Story of India's Bid for Regional Leadership*, London: Routledge, p.75

production and marine transport.'[47] True to his legend as a *prachaarak* diplomat who makes the smallest of actors feel honoured and self-important, Modi has highlighted Mauritius as the pivot for the blue economy which can mobilise all the littoral states by virtue of it being the headquarters of the Indian Ocean Rim Association (IORA). Modi's comment in August 2015 in the presence of the President of Seychelles that 'we should look at small island countries as large ocean states with vast potential'[48] is a clincher that attracts IOR littoral states which fear Chinese and American bossiness and heavy-handedness. It resonates across the region that India is not an exploitative or extractive actor, but an empowerment vehicle which can spur economic growth without trampling over ecological conservation of marine resources.

Yet, much endeavour lies ahead if the Modi Doctrine is to reap the benefits of this vast goodwill in the IOR. India's capacities to match China in building ports and other seaworthy infrastructural projects in the region are still limited. The Modi government has attempted to respond to what military strategists label as China's 'string of pearls' game plan of surrounding India by speeding up construction of the Sittwe deep-water Port in Myanmar on the Bay of Bengal, and by investing in developing the Chabahar Port in Iran, which helps to counter the Chinese-built and controlled Gwadar Port in the Arabian Sea. But India lacks the deep pockets of China to finance many more such strategic projects. A Sri Lankan analyst Nilanthi Samaranayake argues that, 'until India approaches maritime economic policy in its neighborhood more proactively and demonstrates the appeal of its own investment and construction capabilities, it will continue to react with alarm to each new manifestation of China's inexorable reach into the Indian Ocean.'[49]

Beijing's $20 billion 'Maritime Silk Road' initiative poses a long-term problem for New Delhi because it aims to increase Chinese

---

[47] IANS. 2015. 'Cabinet Nod for Blue Economy Cooperation with Seychelles', *Business Standard*, October 7th

[48] PIB. 2015. 'Text of PM's Statement to the Media with President Michel of Seychelles', *Government of India*, August 26th

[49] Samaranayake, Nilanthi. 2015. 'India's Key to Sri Lanka: Maritime Infrastructure Development', *The Diplomat*, March 31st. URL: http://thediplomat.com/2015/03/indias-key-to-sri-lanka-maritime-infrastructure-development/ Last accessed on March 6th, 2016

building of oceanic infrastructure all along the IOR. Yet, this yawning gap with China is likely to be filled in the years to come as India under Modi clocks high GDP growth and its foreign exchange reserves multiply, even as China slows down and is unable to maintain humungous foreign aid budgets and fulfil mega regional corridors at the same stratospheric levels. There are also other political means that the Modi Doctrine can utilise to mitigate China's expanding maritime designs in the IOR. In February 2016, Bangladesh scrapped the Chinese funded Sonadia Port project on grounds that it lacked financial viability, even as it has gone ahead with a Japanese-developed Matarbari Port. Indrani Bagchi has argued that this cancellation was an example of 'Asian allies synergising converging interests' and 'clearly a strategic decision by Bangladesh, doubtlessly helped along by India, Japan and the US.'[50] Had Sonadia gone into China's ambit, it would have brought Beijing's civilian and military assets closer to India's Andaman and Nicobar Islands and completed one eastern node of the 'string of pearls' to contain India.

The Modi Doctrine has recognised the geographical merit of the Andamans as a bulwark against Chinese trespassing and intrusions into the IOR. Modi's strategic vision is to develop these islands as the eastern maritime frontier and line of defence of India against the Chinese navy, as opposed to the Coromandel Coast, which is within mainland India. By shifting the front 1400 km to the east of India's east coast, India is adopting a forward posturing against Chinese penetration. The military head of India's Andaman and Nicobar Command (ANC) exuded confidence in the Modi Doctrine's commitment to defence modernisation in early 2016 stating,

'It will be a different story in the next five years. Over the last twelve months, there has been more infrastructure build-up than ever before. The mindset is changing now. Additional forces have been promised. There are efforts to develop both military and civil infrastructure. There has been a lot of improvement along our strategic sides. In the next few years, the archipelago will have formidable defences.'[51]

---

[50] Bagchi, Indrani. 2016. 'Dhaka Cancels Port to be Built by China, India Eyes Another', *The Times of India*, February 8th

[51] Gupta, Jayant. 2016. 'PLAN Ships Continue to Prowl Around Andamans', *The Times of India*, February 26th

Quadrilateral naval exercises with Japan, Australia and the USA and mammoth events like the International Fleet Review that India organised off its eastern coast in Vishakhapatnam in February 2016, where Modi spelt out his SAGAR vision in the present of warships from fifty nations, also convey that New Delhi is not just awake, but is also proactively trying to shape the IOR's security. Modi's decision to host the first ever Global Maritime Summit in India in early 2016 is another show of his determination to lead the IOR in his desired way. Senior officials in the Modi government have been cited as saying that 'from Mozambique to the Marshall Islands, and Tanzania to Tuvalu, the Prime Minister's outreach is couched in traditional ties but rooted in specific strategic concerns linked to China's incursions in the Indian Ocean and rising tensions in the Asia Pacific.'[52] Modi's NSA, Ajit Doval, has obliquely attacked China by reminding IOR nations of a UNGA resolution of the 1970s 'calling upon great powers not to allow escalation and expansion of military presence in the Indian Ocean.'[53]

Modi himself does not speak openly about the Chinese threat because of his parallel track of gainful commercial diplomacy with China and other considerations of political decorum for a head of government. But his Defence Minister, Manohar Parrikar, has not minced words by averring in India's Parliament that 'we are responding' and 'taking counter measures along maritime areas' to check the growing influence of China in the IOR.[54] Defence analyst Chietigj Bajpaee has also noted that, 'naval discourse in India increasingly places emphasis on sea-control and competitive naval diplomacy while moving away from a traditionally defensive maritime posture' due to the apprehension that China will repeat its militarily aggressive bulldozing behaviour in the IOR just as it has done in the South China Sea and the East China Sea.[55]

---

52 Kasturi, Charu. 2015. 'Modi Ocean Overdrive with Eye on China', *The Telegraph*, August 4th

53 Srinivasan, Meera. 2014. 'Indian Ocean has to Remain a Zone of Peace: Ajit Doval', *The Hindu*, December 1st

54 PTI. 2014. 'India Taking Steps to Deal with China's Influence in Seas: Government', *Daily News and Analysis*, December 19th

55 Mazumdaru, Srinivas. 2015. 'Naval Buildup Reflects India's Ambition to Project Power', *Deutsche Welle*, February 23rd. URL: http://www.dw.com/en/naval-buildup-reflects-indias-ambition-to-project-power/a-18275292 Last accessed on March 6th, 2016

In turn, Chinese military specialists have watched the Modi Doctrine unfurling and warned that India should not view the Indian Ocean as its own, and that New Delhi's analogy of a 'backyard' is dangerous because Beijing treats the IOR as open seas and the Chinese navy is geared for 'open sea protection' to ensure freedom of navigation.[56]

The battle lines are thus drawn. How well India can hold its ground in the IOR will be a litmus test for the Modi Doctrine. From defence diplomacy to the blue economy, Modi has shown variety and steeliness in preserving India's influence in the IOR against both China and the USA. But he would admit that the real proof of the pudding for his IOR strategy is in unleashing economic and cultural synergies. As I have demonstrated earlier in this book, the Modi Doctrine's speciality lies in identifying what are India's mojos in a particular region or issue area and capitalising upon them. Leveraging the 'three Cs' is where India can keep its lead over China and the USA in the IOR. The cultural content in Project *Mausam* has to be fully realised to revive the ancient Hindu and Buddhist religious pilgrimages and travel circuits that connected India with the entire littoral basin.

Capacity building of poorer IOR countries, especially African nations like Mozambique, Tanzania and Kenya, to benefit from the blue economy is another promising avenue. The Indian navy and Indian corporations have to work in tandem to support eastern African nations in fisheries, offshore oil and gas and hydrographical science. Modi has also shown heartfelt empathy for the climate change-related existential risks facing little nations in the IOR and the Indo-Pacific. In November 2015, he had remarked, 'there are small island nations which fear that they will be drowned by global warming. We will not let that happen. India will do whatever we can (to combat climate change) as we believe in *Vasudhaiva Kutumbakam* (whole world is one family).'[57] Raising the human capital in the IOR in the field of renewable energy and conservation of marine ecosystems is a low-hanging fruit awaiting Indian inputs.

---

[56] PTI. 2015. 'Indian Ocean Cannot be Backyard of India: China', *The Economic Times*, July 1st

[57] EWD. 2015. 'PM Modi in Singapore: Today, World Looks Towards India with Great Faith', *The Indian Express*, November 24th

Modi's popular personal chemistry with leaders of small countries has to also ultimately produce a sub-system in the IOR where India is the leader and others are its partners and followers. The Australian scholar David Brewster has argued that Modi is 'breaking some long-standing taboos in Indian foreign policy' and is trying to form a 'grouping with the island states' towards 'a new multilateral alignment in the Indian Ocean, with India at the centre.'[58] He adds that, 'for India it would represent an important psychological step beyond its traditional adherence to nonalignment, which could have much broader implications.'[59] Shashi Tharoor, the Chairman of India's Parliamentary Committee on External Affairs, has echoed these thoughts by noting that under Modi, 'India is waking up to the importance and potential of its own position in the middle of the Indian Ocean' and that this 'awakening is being translated into action.'[60] As I have pointed throughout this book, placing India in the middle and augmenting it as an independent pole in the international system is the primary aspiration of the Modi Doctrine. If Modi follows up on his Indian Ocean strategy to its optimal limits, this goal will be nearer to realisation.

Acting East, Breaking Ground

Although successive Indian governments had sported a 'Look East' policy since 1991, it is only after Modi became India's prime minister in 2014 that the vocabulary has changed to 'Act East' and the scope and activities have also grown manifold. Danielle Rajendram of the Lowy Institute in Australia posits that Modi's shift from 'looking' to 'acting' is not a cosmetic rebranding, but is a 'message that India is becoming increasingly willing to play a more active and prominent strategic role, exemplified by enhanced defence diplomacy in East and

---

[58] Brewster, David. 2015. 'Modi Builds India's Sphere of Influence in the Indian Ocean', *The Interpreter*, March 17th

[59] Ibid

[60] Tharoor, Shashi. 2015. 'Modi's Indian Ocean Tour Shows that India's Watching China', *The Huffington Post*, May 11th. URL: http://www.huffingtonpost.com/entry/modi-indian-ocean-tour-china_b_6849936.html?section=india Last accessed on March 6th, 2016

Southeast Asia.'[61] She adds that it is motivated by Modi's 'intention to pursue a more ambitious foreign policy agenda, including carving out a greater global role for India.'[62]

Map of the Indo-Pacific/Asia-Pacific Region

[61] Rajendram, Danielle. 2014. 'India's New Asia-Pacific Strategy: Modi Acts East', *Lowy Institute for International Policy*, December, pp.2-3

[62] Ibid

Just as the waters of the Indian Ocean and of the Western Pacific Ocean are a continuum, India's 'strategic' turn to the maritime space on its right side under Modi's Act East policy is driven by concerns about China's thrust into South Asia and the IOR. In crude terms, it is a tit-for-tat on China amounting to 'you poke me in my backyard and I will return the favour in your sphere of influence.' The Indian strategist Rajeev Srinivasan contends that Modi is pursuing 'an emerging "reverse string-of-pearls" strategy by India, Vietnam, Japan, Australia, and Russia' to 'have a significant containment and chilling effect on China's global ambitions.'[63] In the same vein, Professor Harsh Pant from King's College writes that there is a 'turf war' informing Modi's Act East policy, wherein 'if for China the Indian Ocean is not an Indian lake, New Delhi's imperative is to contest impressions in Beijing that the waters east of Malacca automatically fall under the latter's sphere of influence. India's naval engagement in the East, therefore, has also been a reaction to China's expansion in the Indian Ocean region.'[64] Modi's partnering with the USA and Japan to verbally and militarily jab at Chinese aggressiveness in the South China Sea, his publicly taking sides with Vietnam and the Philippines in their struggle against China's coercive behaviour, and his reported enthusiasm to work with Vietnam and Japan in a trilateral security format, have all been read by analysts as indicators that the Act East policy has shed past Indian governments' ambiguity and is confidently headed towards counterbalancing Chinese hegemony.[65]

However, there is a larger ambition informing the Modi Doctrine in East Asia, which is to insert India as a fulltime resident power that will be a net provider of security and a partaker of prosperity in that region. The Modi government's frequent adoption of the phrase 'Indo-Pacific' over the traditional 'Asia-Pacific' constitutes an attempt to

---

63 Srinivasan, Rajeev. 2014. 'Modi's Overseas Ambitions: Vietnam and the Reverse 'String-of-Pearls' to Contain China', *Firstpost,* October 31st. URL: http://www.firstpost.com/world/modis-overseas-ambitions-vietnam-and-the-reverse-string-of-pearls-to-contain-china-1781389.html Last accessed on March 6th, 2016

64 Pant, Harsh. 2016. 'A New Maritime Balance in Indo-Pacific Region', *The Japan Times*, March 4th

65 PTI. 2015. 'India's Act East Policy Balancing China in the Region: Think Tank', *The Indian Express*, July 24th

give India a vantage point to position itself as a hub for the frenetic economic and political networks being spun through integration of the Asian landmass and waterways. 'Indo-Pacific' originated from Indian and Australian opinion-makers as an update of 'Asia-Pacific', which conceptually separated the IOR from the Pacific Ocean area. Viewing the vast littoral stretch from the eastern coast of Africa all the way to Australia as one shared space with common challenges is a radically different perspective from the conventional compartmentalised notion of South Asia, Southeast Asia, Northeast Asia and Australia as separate entities. Under the Modi Doctrine, India has altered its gaze from dealing individually with each sub-region as if they were in silos to treating the whole marine and territorial expanses to its east as an interconnected entity where India has a broader systemic role to play as a stabiliser.

In acting east, the Modi government has broken new ground by jettisoning circumspect and feeble attitudes of its predecessor. It is more self-assured in committing to and investing in key relationships in the Indo-Pacifc, and less worried about whether such actions would displease China. Modi's muscular and nationalistic 'India first' geostrategy is not obsequious to Chinese or, for that matter, American wishes. He dreams of India setting the terms and rules of the Indo-Pacific theatre rather than bending to external pressures. Beijing is, of course, far ahead of New Delhi in its power attributes and connectivity diplomacy in this region. China's grand strategy is premised on reviving the historical Silk Route by road, rail and sea. In November 2014, Chinese President Xi Jinping announced a $40 billion Silk Road infrastructure fund to break the connectivity bottleneck in Asia. China's ambitious vision is to keep itself as the centre of an expanding economic zone of prosperity that is buttressed by Chinese-financed super expressways, train lines and ports across the Indo-Pacific, which Beijing continues to call 'Asia-Pacific' as a reminder that India cannot barge in. As a far larger manufacturing and trading power than India, China has both the moolah and the strategic blueprint to utilise its Asian Infrastructure Investment Bank (AIIB) and other bilateral channels of aid to remain the economic arbiter of the Indo-Pacific.

However, the Modi Doctrine is accurate in reading that China's strength and success can, ironically, also be its limitations. The overwhelming economic and political shadow that China has cast in ASEAN and Australia has hit such epic proportions that the latter countries wish there were other big players that can help reduce their dependence or helplessness vis-a-vis the dragon. The USA has for decades acted as a go-to substitute that can generate public goods in the Indo-Pacific, while attenuating Chinese domination. But doubts about Obama's 'pivot to Asia' and the USA's economic vitality have clouded the security landscape among smaller nations in the region. Without overtly touting India as an alternative to China or the USA, Modi's 'Act East' policy rides subtly on the sentiment that there is a seat on the Indo-Pacific table which seeks to be filled. India is nowhere close to being as industrially competent, financially generous or efficient in infrastructural project implementation as China, but it can play on the anxieties of smaller countries and secure a strategic red carpet for itself as a medium-weight 'Other' to China not only in economics, but also in politics and culture.

For example, Modi's meeting with Myanmar's democracy icon Aung San Suu Kyi in November 2014 symbolically indicated how India, as the world's largest democracy, can possibly succour countries undergoing political transitions. Likewise, with Fiji moving in a democratic direction, Modi's visit to this tiny Pacific island with a large ethnic Indian population was meant to also help move its political process forward. China holds the unbeatable edge in rotating business flows throughout the region, but India has the parliamentarians, media persons and civil society activists without any of the colonial baggage of America or Europe. Depending on the internal political evolution of different countries in the Indo-Pacific, the Modi Doctrine has harped on India's democratic credentials wherever they may resonate. Modi is realistic to know that no country can shove aside or replace China from the status of lodestone of the Indo-Pacific. But his implicit message is that India is stepping up to the plate and widening the room for manoeuvre in a region partially renamed after it.

In the realm of cultural diplomacy too, Modi has emphasised the need to raise the salience of the Buddhist travel, educational and pilgrimage circuits which bind India and East Asia. By harping on

Buddhism, Modi has tacitly conveyed a message that the Indo-Pacific has never been an entirely Chinese Confucian civilisational zone. His insistence on 'drawing up a Buddhist connect as part of Act East policy'[66] has been used to build bridges with mainland China itself, but also to stage a comeback for India as a font of civilisational wisdom in the entire Indo-Pacific. Modi's claims during the 'Global Hindu-Buddhist Initiative' in New Delhi in September 2015 that, 'India is taking the lead in boosting the Buddhist heritage across Asia' and that it is 'a nation that is extremely proud of its Buddhist heritage'[67] were meant to especially hammer home to the ASEAN countries that their materialistic present may be overwhelmingly defined by trade and commerce with China, but their historical identities were nurtured through India's spiritual exports. As I have explained in Chapter 2, Modi has also harnessed the Indian diaspora in Southeast Asia, particularly in Singapore and Malaysia, in the cause of thicker and emotionally binding relations in this region.

On the practical side, Modi has sought to deepen Indian presence within ASEAN by means of road connectivity to facilitate easy movement of goods, services and people through the 3,200 kilometre-long India-Myanmar-Thailand trilateral highway corridor, which he is speeding up to be completed in 2018.

The economic aspect of Modi's renewed courting of ASEAN is captured by another 'Modi-ism'—the 'five Ss' of 'scaling up trade and investment; speeding up connectivity; smart cities; skills development; and state focus.'[68] According to the Asian business intelligence consultancy, Dezan Shira, there is a 'rising tide of trade' between India and ASEAN due to 'India's "Act East" policy, which has reaffirmed India's plans to engage more substantially with the economies of its Southeast Asian neighbours' and Modi's 'range of programs intended to make the country a more attractive investment

---

[66] Haidar, Suhasini. 2015. 'Buddha Link High on PM's Eastern Foray', *The Hindu*, April 3rd

[67] Chaudhury, Dipanjan. 2015. 'PM Modi Highlights India's Buddhist Heritage, Takes a Swipe at Pakistan', *The Economic Times*, September 4th

[68] BS. 2015. 'Modi's Singapore, Malaysia Visits to Boost Defence Ties', *Business Standard*, November 19th

destination to foreign countries.'[69] Modi's clarion call to the ASEAN heads of state and business titans to 'come and see the winds of change in India' at a time when 'the world economy is not exactly doing well'[70] is a barely disguised pitch that India can pick up the slack from the slowing Chinese economy, which has for long been the guiding light for ASEAN's economic growth. For ASEAN to diversify away from overreliance on China, India is the only large economy that beckons.

On the burning problem of the South China Sea dispute which has torn apart ASEAN and created a low intensity conflict with China, Modi has been quite forthright in backing Vietnam and the Philippines. The American and Indian strategic analysts Patrick Cronin and Darshana Baruah have explained how significant this policy departure is from the Manmohan Singh era:

'While India has always maintained that freedom of navigation through international waters is crucial, New Delhi usually refrains from making a direct comment on disputes outside of its territories. What is of significance is Modi's choice of platforms in bringing up the issue. He first mentioned it in his joint statement with Obama, then with his Vietnamese counterpart during his trip to Vietnam and at his maiden presence at the East Asia Summit and the India-ASEAN summit in 2014. His call for a binding Code of Conduct in the South China Sea reflected a willingness to assure India's friends and key players in the region that India may finally be ready to take on the role of a security provider that the region demands.'[71]

As a member of the East Asia Summit that includes ASEAN countries, India under Modi can play a decisive role in mustering alternative structures to work together to check expansionist tendencies of China. India's state-owned oil major, ONGC Videsh, has entered into cooperative business deals with Petro Vietnam in the South China

---

69 DS. 2015. 'The Future of ASEAN-India Trade Looks Bright', *ASEAN Briefing*, August 10th. URL: http://www.aseanbriefing.com/news/2015/08/10/the-future-of-asean-india-trade-looks-bright.html Last accessed on March 8th, 2016

70 PTI. 2015. 'PM Modi at ASEAN Summit: India's GDP Growth is Up, Inflation is Down', *The Indian Express*, November 21st

71 Cronin, Patrick & Darshana Baruah. 2014. 'The Modi Doctrine for the Indo-Pacific Maritime Region', *The Diplomat*, December 2nd. URL: http://thediplomat.com/2014/12/the-modi-doctrine-for-the-indo-pacific-maritime-region/ Last accessed on March 7th, 2016

Sea despite Chinese objections. Joint maritime business consortiums that rope in companies from smaller claimants who are being harassed by China will be worthwhile investments for Modi to propose and initiate. The region needs to be able to offer the proverbial 'equal and opposite reaction' to China's actions, if the Asia-Pacific is to breathe easier. Fearlessness is in the DNA of the Modi Doctrine and the acme of its Act East policy would be a series of formations that would check Chinese aggression and reassure smaller actors.

Obama's 'pivot' or 'rebalancing' to Asia had envisaged deploying more than half of the USA's naval assets to the Indo-Pacific to leash China's maritime expansion. But as of 2015, Washington had 289 ships, of which only fifty-eight were prowling the Western Pacific.[72] Modi is no vacillator when it comes to China, but Obama has been more cautious. Therefore, China has often called the American bluff by breaking free of its previous bounds of 'offshore defence' to pursue 'open-seas protection', that is, with a blue-water navy that can prevail far away from its coastline in the IOR and beyond. The calculation that the Americans may huff and puff but lack the resolve to force China to backtrack lies at the heart of the insecurity enveloping Asia. It is simultaneously a crisis and an opportunity for the Modi Doctrine.

With one big shark, the USA, in effect passing the baton to the other big animal, China, are the smaller nations in the Indo-Pacific region doomed to become subservient fish in a new Sino-centric pond? Emboldened by its unstoppable momentum, Beijing has fired shots across the bow to New Delhi, demanding that the latter must 'first get approval from China' before exploring for energy off the coast of Vietnam.[73] What are the options for weaker parties in the light of the USA being past its prime and China on the rampage in its reclamation over disputed territories? The Australian think-tank, The Lowy Institute, has called for 'minilateral' coalitions of middle powers like India, Indonesia, Vietnam and Australia to enhance indigenous capacities and

---

[72] WSJ. 2015. 'Kaiser Xi's Navy', *The Wall Street Journal*, May 29th

[73] Parashar, Sachin. 2015. 'No oil hunt in South China Sea without Nod: Beijing to Delhi', *The Times of India*, May 31st

inter-operability for upholding balance in a region undergoing rapid flux and power transition.[74]

The need of the hour is alternative security institutions involving smaller nations warily watching the Sino-American tussle, where the final outcome could be a Chinese victory. India—which is not a party to the South China Sea fracas, but whose Act East policy and primacy in the IOR are being pressured by advancing Chinese flotillas—must take the lead in forging new security permutations, norms and understandings among lesser regional actors. Pinning hopes on the USA to rein in China is wishful thinking. Two parallel shifts demand India to step up to the plate. First is the reluctant, but evident abdication of a weakening USA in favour of a resurgent China. This trend may be arrested after Obama remits the White House, but it is not a matter of specific individual American Presidents, but a reflection of relative decline of American power in the world. The second shift is the endeavour of medium-ranked powers in Asia to catch up with ascendant China and equalise their terms of interaction. With deft diplomacy, the Modi Doctrine can steer this dual change.

India lags behind China and the USA in military firepower and economic muscle. But it can parlay this disadvantage into an attraction by convening new 'plurilateral' institutions of the underdogs in the Indo-Pacific, just as it once floated the Non-Aligned Movement (NAM) during the Cold War period. Modi's initiation of forums, dialogues and joint exercises will be welcomed at the present juncture in ASEAN, as New Delhi lacks the means and intentions to dominate the region. The South China Sea tinderbox, with a sharp USA-versus-China binary, has an opening for a non-threatening third force to strengthen a spirit of regionalism that reduces dependency of the minnows on the whims of hegemons. Doubts persist over whether India, hobbled by an understaffed career diplomatic corps notorious for its overcautious foreign policy, can sense its chance and play a proactive role as a gatherer of like-minded countries and a moderator of new security communities in the Indo-Pacific.

The saving grace is the boldness of Modi, who has a king-size ambition to convert India into a great power. Given the top-down nature

---

[74] Medcalf, Rory & Raja Mohan. 2014. 'Responding to Indo-Pacific Rivalry: Australia, India and Middle Power Coalitions', *The Lowy Institute*, August 8th

of India's bureaucratic apparatus, a concerted push from Modi is infusing creativity and fresh blood into its diplomatic arsenal. For too long, India had contemplated defensively about whether to catch or drop the ball of rules and institutions conceived and proposed by other countries. It had wilted nervously whether China would take askance at what India does in the former's backyard, and how it might boomerang on India in its border dispute with China or in Chinese expansion in the IOR. Under Modi, the onus is on India to develop and throw the ball in the Indo-Pacific, and to mobilise smaller countries not so much like a military bloc, but as a networked security community with shared threats.

Of all the revamped security relationships that Modi has sculpted via his 'Act East' policy, Japan stands out as a *primus inter pares*. Japanese Premier Shinzo Abe, who has the closest personal rapport with Modi among all world leaders, is almost like India's unofficial ambassador in the Indo-Pacific. Abe has written that 'hand in hand with Prime Minister Narendra Modi I intend to make the "Confluence of the Two Seas"—the Indian Ocean and Pacific Ocean—open, peaceful and abundant, and we shall further advance peace and prosperity in the Indo-Pacific.'[75] Abe had envisaged an alliance of democracies in Asia even before Modi rose to India's pinnacle, 'whereby Australia, India, Japan and the U.S. state of Hawaii form a diamond to safeguard the maritime commons stretching from the Indian Ocean region to the Western Pacific.'[76] However, the Manmohan Singh government had been a lot cagier about any such alliance with an overt intent to contain China. Under the Modi Doctrine, Abe has come the nearest to realising his 'diamond' dream. Modi has willingly forged an unabashed alignment with Japan to shape the balance of power and prospects for economic stability in Asia.

Few world leaders share the level of mutual admiration that Modi and Abe have for each other. The Japanese Prime Minister famously follows only three persons on his Twitter account—his wife Akie Abe, the historian Naoki Inose and Modi. The glue that binds this duo is a

---

75 Abe, Shinzo. 2015. 'India, Japan: Natural Partners', *The Times of India*, December 11th

76 Abe, Shinzo. 2012. 'Asia's Democratic Security', *Project Syndicate*, December 27th. URL: http://www.project-syndicate.org/commentary/a-strategic-alliance-for-japan-and-india-by-shinzo-abe?barrier=true Last accessed on March 9th, 2016

sense that both these charismatic politicians are kindred souls entrusted with similar challenging missions in life—reviving the sagging economies and piloting the international ascent of their respective countries. Pro-business instincts, nationalistic outlooks and a belief in reforming outmoded and hidebound ways of running government are other traits that lend an air of inspiration to the Modi-Abe pair. Both of them see that a new spectre looms over Asia in the form of a colossus named China. If any two countries can ensure through coordinated diplomacy and defence cooperation that the rise of China can be managed to avert hegemonic instability, it is Japan and India.

Modi has deepened bilateral military exercises, weapons procurement and production, and transfer of technology with Japan. Abe's radical move to reinterpret the American-drafted Japanese Constitution's pacifist clauses has freed his hand to assign a more proactive role for the Japanese self-defence forces in East Asia and beyond. This pivotal shift dovetails with India's own quest to become a 'net security provider' in the Indo-Pacific theatre, where assertive Chinese military actions have provoked fear and handwringing. With Japan and India increasingly acting in concert, the security assurances it generates for smaller players like Vietnam and the Philippines, which are struggling to ward off Chinese pressure, are invaluable. Prior to the Modi Doctrine being implemented in Indian foreign policy, India's global image had a lacuna of not engaging with political and strategic matters concerning distant regions and confining itself to trade, investment and cultural diplomacy. By partnering with a hyperactive diplomatic actor like Japan that wants to make the world strategically safer, Modi is redressing this weakness and raising India's power projection.

One of the Modi Doctrine's most consequential moves is to invite Japan as a permanent third participant of the annual naval wargame exercises codenamed Malabar, which had been hosted under a bilateral framework since 1992 between India and the USA only. For the Japanese Maritime Self Defence Force (JMSDF), entering the Malabar drills on a full-time basis brings benefits of capacity-building as it tries to fulfil the enlarged role envisaged by Abe for his military. Transitioning from a defensive and minimalist navy into a proactive one cannot be accomplished unless the JMSDF is exposed to what Malabar's organisers label as 'complex high-end warfighting' experiences.[77]

The evolution of India's position on who is 'in' and 'out' of these multilateral naval simulations explains much about the changing nature of its diplomacy and force posturing. In 2007, when Japan, Australia and Singapore first joined Malabar as guests upon India's invitation, China issued a robust diplomatic protest against it as a manoeuvre by the USA's allies and friends to gang up and contain China's ascent. Beijing's peevish reaction worried New Delhi and forced the Manmohan Singh government to reduce the multinational character of Malabar in subsequent iterations. The defensive and overcautious Indian establishment of that time decided against military moves of a scale and dimension that could anger China and disturb peace and tranquillity between Asia's two biggest nations.

But Indian deference to Chinese preferences has now been eschewed in response to three transforming strategic realities, viz. the blossoming partnership between New Delhi and Tokyo, New Delhi's ambition to shape the Indo-Pacific maritime order, and Beijing's eschewing of previous restraints to strong-arm its neighbours over territorial and natural resource disputes in the East China and South China Seas. Modi dreams of India setting the terms and rules of the Indo-Pacific theatre, instead of bending to external pressures. If the Manmohan Singh government silently suffered from a palpable inferiority complex with regard to China, the Modi Doctrine has set out with the belief that Chinese hegemony over Asia and the developing world is not inevitable, and that India must act in concert with other powers to avert this outcome.

In the economic sphere, Modi has also leapfrogged the India-Japan partnership to heights never seen before, with record levels of FDI and trade in the offing. Motivated by the zeal of a CEO-in-chief who had earlier experienced the magic of Japan as the chief minister of Gujarat, he has intensified Japan-India economic exchanges as a crucial external pillar on which India's national modernisation dreams can soar. Modi reveres Japan for its technical pedigree and wants to maximise economic advantages for India through cutting-edge technology obtained via

---

77 PTI. 2015. 'India, US, Japan Navy Unite for 'Malabar Exercise', *The New Indian Express*, October 14th

smart foreign policy. In December 2015, Modi and Abe issued a joint statement referring to 'the synergy between India's Act East policy and Japan's Partnership for Quality Infrastructure' (PQI). The latter is Japan's version of China's OBOR. While Japan has been aiding developing nations in infrastructure for decades, under Abe there is a strong strategic emphasis on the same and Modi has carved out space for India to benefit from it.

The sister city agreement between Modi's parliamentary constituency of Varanasi or Kashi and Japan's ancient-yet-modern Kyoto is a case in point. From water and sewage to transport and building, Kashi is undergoing a facelift with Japanese knowhow in pursuit of Modi's vision of a 'smart heritage city', where historical aesthetics, ecological conservation and advanced technology go hand-in-hand, the way Kyoto has been designed and maintained to universal acclaim. All aspects of the blossoming Japan-India partnership are turning out to be unprecedentedly 'glocal', i.e. international cooperation that is shaping local transformation. Apart from the pairing of Kyoto and Kashi, Abe and Modi are overseeing collaboration for superfast bullet trains that will revolutionise India's land transportation system. Japan's Shinkansen network of high-speed railways is legendary not just for velocity, but also for a spotless record in terms of safety and reliability. Shinkansen beat the rival China Railway High-speed (CRH) for the Mumbai-Ahmedabad sector, thanks to the former's reputation for accident-free functioning, higher quality, workmanship and superior terms of low-interest and long-duration financing to India.

For Japan whose economy has remained sluggish despite the strenuous efforts of 'Abenomics', helping India modernise is a win-win project, which creates demand for its world-class products and services. India's infrastructural ramp-ups generate customer orders for Japanese firms, giving a much-sought push to Japan's GDP growth, which keeps stumbling every few quarters. Japan is, thus, not doing charity to poor India, but gaining market access on an equal footing. There are still some remnants of overseas development assistance (ODA) that Japan dispenses as aid to India, but the relationship today is fundamentally different from the giver-recipient mode of yesteryears. Abe describes India under Modi as the 'most attractive investment destination'[78] based on the calculation that Japan gets vast material gains from being India's best friend. Modi's pride in Japan allocating $12 billion for the implementation of 'Make in India' is a reflection of the enormous enthusiasm he himself has seeded among Japanese businesses by creating a special window for clearance of their investments.

That there is a distinct 'Modi effect' in taking Japan-India ties to sublime heights is evident from the way New Delhi has pulled off a miracle in getting Tokyo to sign a memorandum on civil nuclear cooperation in December 2015 as a first step to a full deal. Owing to the catastrophic atomic bombings of Hiroshima and Nagasaki, Japan has an ingrained opposition to nuclear weapons and an automatic deference to the nuclear non-proliferation regimes. Since India became a de facto nuclear weapons power in 1998, carving out an exception for India and engaging in civilian nuclear commerce with it has been anathema in Japan, despite its alertness to the larger importance of the bilateral relationship. Vexing negotiations had been on since 2010, but it is only now under Modi that Japan has overcome ingrained psychological reservations and inched forward to giving India what the USA had offered relatively quickly.

Japan is the only country designated by Modi's India as a 'special strategic and global partner', which is an upgrade over the clichéd 'strategic partner' label that India has conferred on more than twenty nations. The emphasis laid by both Abe and Modi on the 'global' dimension for securing the Indo-Pacific maritime region is the crux of the matter. Here, the discomfort both of them share about Chinese hegemony is one obvious driving factor. Another motivation is the business potential for India as a site for manufacturing Japanese submarines and aircraft, turning India into the first big market since Abe lifted Japan's longstanding ban on weapons exports. China's thoroughly anti-Japanese state-owned media has reacted harshly to burgeoning military cooperation between Japan and India by

[78] PTI. 2015. 'India has Become Very Attractive Investment Destination for Japan: Abe', *Hindustan Times*, December 12th

alleging that it would 'make all peace-loving countries in the world feel worried.'[79] But this bluster from Beijing is in itself a reason for Modi to celebrate the achievements of the Japan-India tag team in raising the quality of their average people's lives and deterring Asia's takeover by a single power.

If Japan is entrenching itself as a close strategic partner of India, can its main neighbor South Korea stay far behind? The Modi Doctrine has targeted Seoul as a high potential country to enable 'Make in India', especially in railways, shipbuilding and other infrastructural goals. In May 2015, during Modi's East Asia travels, the Indian scholar Tridivesh Maini argued that 'while all eyes will be on Modi's China sojourn, it is the robust relationship with South Korea that could help India get its economy back on track and consolidate its position in Asia.'[80] The challenge for the Modi Doctrine in South Korea will be to raise the strategic content of this relationship. Much to Washington's chagrin, Seoul has moved closer to Beijing in recent years owing to historical disputes with Tokyo. If Modi can use economic and military incentives to try and wean South Korea away from complete dependence on China, it would be an achievement for India's influence in Northeast Asia. Since New Delhi and Seoul share common concerns about the North Korean nuclear and missile misadventures, which have in the past involved illicit cooperation with Pakistan, there is scope for India to be more useful to South Korea in the strategic sphere and dent China's dominant hand in Seoul.

Of all the gains that the Modi Doctrine has engineered under the 'Act East' policy, the embracing of tiny Pacific Island nations is remarkable. Before Modi hosted a unique summit for heads of state of these fourteen mini-states in August 2015 in the Indian city of Jaipur, most Indians had never heard of countries such as Tonga, Tuvalu, Nauru, Samoa, Vanuatu, Niue, Micronesia or the Marshall Islands. But by bringing them all together in India, he has raised awareness and

---

79 Yue, Zhang. 2015. 'Japan's Considerations Behind Eagerness to Break into the International Arms Market', *China Youth Daily*, December 11th

80 Maini, Tridivesh. 2015. 'The Significance of Modi's South Korea Visit', *The Diplomat*, May 16th. URL: http://thediplomat.com/2015/05/the-significance-of-modis-south-korea-visit/ Last accessed on March 9th

elevated their strategic importance in Asia. That size is not the be-all and end-all in world affairs is dawning on people in India, thanks to Modi who has personally visited weeny states such as Fiji, Seychelles and Mauritius to draw them closer to New Delhi. Modi's claim that India 'does not operate with the haughtiness of being stronger but on the principle of walking shoulder-to-shoulder with other nations'[81] has gone down well with foreign interlocutors, particularly in the Pacific Islands. They have enthusiastically welcomed India's offers of tele-medicine, tele-education, space cooperation, and technical aid for bolstering democracy and community activities. Reciprocally, as a sizeable voting bloc in the UNGA, they have indicated support for India's bid to secure permanent membership on the UNSC. The collective power of fourteen Pacific Island votes is crucial for India, as it wants to ensure adequate numbers within the fifty-three-member Asia-Pacific Group of the UN.

Despite being a self-avowed admirer of China's modernisation, Modi has stressed areas of cooperation where India can be more helpful to the Pacific Islands than China. As I have shown earlier in this chapter, Beijing has a huge lead over New Delhi in physical infrastructure construction overseas and in doling out massive foreign aid. But Modi is demonstrating advantages which India can offer in enhancing human capital, environmental protection and democracy promotion in the Pacific countries. In courting small and needy countries like the Pacific Islands, the Modi Doctrine is in a way taking a leaf out of the Chinese foreign policy book of selectively chasing after sub-regions of the world that are lacking in military and economic power, and where there are vacuums or imbalances that can be filled by emerging actors.

Like a buyer of distressed or underrated assets, China has made the Pacific Islands integral to its grand strategy of accessing underwater minerals, checking the sway of the United States and its regional allies such as Australia and New Zealand, and achieving the reunification of Taiwan. Yet, as the Chinese scholar Jian Yang has written, China has negative image problems in the Pacific and cannot

[81] TNN. 2015. 'PM Narendra Modi's Full Speech in Dubai', *Times Now* Op cit.

turn into a genuine hegemon there.[82] Herein lies an opportunity for the Modi Doctrine, which is redefining India's core national interests on a geographically wider canvas and projecting India as a leading power to push for strategic balance and stability in Asia. Just as Modi has skillfully leveraged Mongolia and Central Asian nations' search for a 'third neighbour'[83] to break free from the stranglehold of the traditional superpowers in that regions, namely Russia and China, his breakthrough with the Pacific Islands is a reification of his vast ambition and a sign that Indian foreign policy is percolating into the nooks and corners of Asia. The 'Act East' policy is a feather in the Modi Doctrine's cap and a harbinger of greater accomplishments to come in the Indo-Pacific.

Look West, the Supreme Juggle

If Modi's embrace of Japan is a quantum leap in Indian foreign policy, then his unapologetic cultivation of a special partnership with Israel is a paradigm shift in the way India has handled the Middle East or West Asia. Until Modi's advent, India had been coy about the burgeoning defence diplomacy with Israel. The hush-hush nature of India-Israel military cooperation under Manmohan Singh was augured by domestic political considerations that his government would lose the support of India's over 170 million Muslim citizens who were assumed to be all sympathetic to the Palestinian cause. Fear of being seen to be betraying the Palestinian cause for self-determination, and also of upsetting Arab states in the Middle East had tied up New Delhi in knots for more than two decades since it normalised relations with Tel Aviv in 1992. Once Modi came on to the scene in 2014, these cobwebs of doubt and incertitude were quickly set aside and a new vigour and energy took over what used to be a promising, but publicly awkward relationship.

---

82 Yang, Jian. 2011. *The Pacific Islands in China's Grand Strategy: Small States, Big Games*, New York: Springer

83 Soni, Sharad. 2015. 'The 'Third Neighbour' Approach of Mongolia's Diplomacy of External Relations: Effects on Relations between India and Mongolia', *India Quarterly*, Volume 71, Issue 1

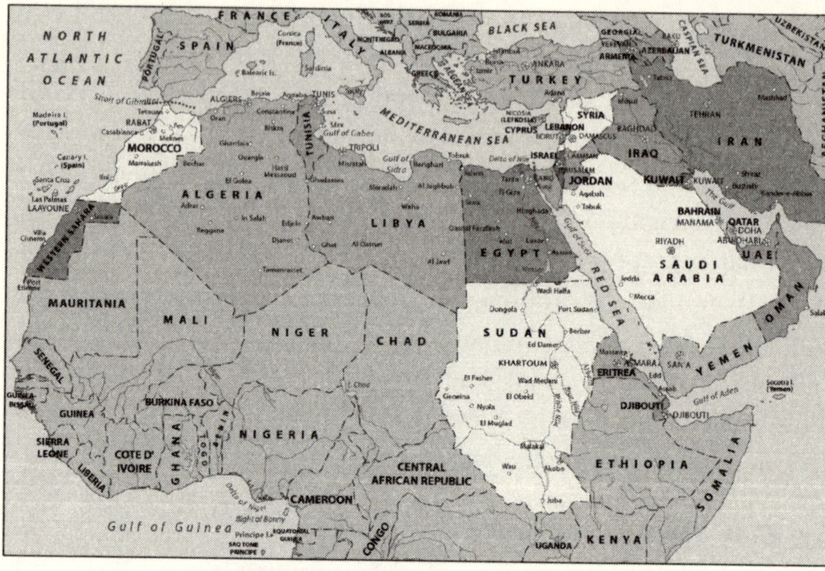

Map of the Middle East/West Asia

Modi's decision to send the President of India for the first time ever to Israel in October 2015 and his intent to be the first Indian prime minister to set foot in Israel, are two high-level signals that he does not carry the defensive and politicised baggage that stunted the full potential of the relationship in the past. Free from domestic religious vote banks, and convinced that Israel is crucial for India's national security and economic modernisation, Modi has altered India's gingerly strategy in the Middle East with a 'Look West' policy in which Israel is overtly a building block for India to become influential in that region. Under the Modi Doctrine, every part of the world is studied with a gimlet eye to identify building block states that will be conveyors and transmitters of Indian influence. Israel is now considered one such fundamental partner in whom India would invest heavily, rather than a liability or a closet friend whose liaison must be hidden from the world.

Under the Modi Doctrine, India and Israel have advanced intelligence sharing about jihadist outfits threatening both nations. Modi's NSA, Ajit Doval, is believed to have personally toured Israel's Negev nuclear facility near Dimona in August 2015,[84] and he has

---

[84] Kasturi, Charu. 2015. 'Secret Trips to West Asia', *The Telegraph*, September 7th

publicly professed admiration for the willpower and mental strength of Jewish people facing multiple threats and discriminatory attitudes. The elite Special Forces of both nations also scheduled to conduct joint exercises, an idea that took 'more than two decades to fructify'[85], thanks to Modi's proactive interest in this relationship. Defence sales, manufacturing and co-production agreements in sensitive systems like anti-tank guided missile, battleship missiles, aerial drones and electronic border management tools have also mushroomed under Modi. The Modi government chose to buy Israeli Spike missiles worth $525 million over American Javelin missiles in October 2014, clearing a deal that had been originally proposed in 2010, but which had gotten stuck. When Modi strategically dropped into a pavilion of Israel Aerospace Industries in Bangalore in February 2015, the Israeli Defence Minister Moshe Ya'alon, another first such office holder to travel to India since the countries established diplomatic relations, was on hand. Ya'alon remarked that, 'we are open to more or less [selling] anything' to India.[86]

Appreciative of Israel's expertise in defence technologies, Modi has warmed up to Prime Minister Benjamin Netanyahu's proclamation that 'Israeli industries, including the defense industries, could "Make in India", and thereby reduce costs of manufacturing products and systems developed by Israel.'[87] The impetus given by the Modi Doctrine has attracted a beeline of small and medium Israeli companies to partner with Indian firms under the principle of joint ventures with technology transfer built in. As I have mentioned earlier in this book, Modi envisions defence as one of the frontline sectors for the 'Make in India' campaign to lift off. To Modi, Israel will be a lynchpin for India to eventually become self-reliant and even an exporter of weapons, perhaps far more than Russia or the USA.

Is the Modi Doctrine lurching too far to the right of the ideological spectrum in its unencumbered snuggling up to Israel? Has it thrown

---

85 Datta, Rahul. 2015. 'India, Israel to Lift Defence Ties Veil', *The Pioneer*, October 7th

86 Harel, Amos. 2015. 'Israel-India Strategic Ties are No Longer a Secret', *Haaretz*, February 18th

87 Ningthoujam, Alvite. 2014. 'Reinvigorated Indo-Israeli Military Ties: The Modi Phenomenon', *The Jerusalem Post*, November 19th

India's principled support for the Palestinians into the dustbin? This is not so. India has not abandoned its traditional backing for Palestinian statehood and it continues to offer assistance for state-building projects in the West Bank. Moreover, the Modi Doctrine has expanded India's relations with the Arab monarchies of the Gulf Cooperation Council (GCC), particularly Saudi Arabia, the UAE and Qatar, to a much greater level than was the case with the Manmohan Singh government. India's equations with these Arab states now transcend the welfare of India's vast diaspora, remittances and oil supplies. They include hitherto untrodden territory such as deepened cooperation on counter-terrorism and inward FDI from Arab sovereign wealth funds for 'Make in India'. The Saudi Foreign Minister Adel al-Jubeir was asked in March 2016 as to how India and his country moved beyond oil and sped up the security component of bilateral relations. He had replied that 'trust' had increased, and that 'the recognition that we should cooperate, in order to be effective to fight terrorism and extremism' made it 'natural' to quicken engagements in this hitherto untouched domain.[88] To deepen counter-terrorism cooperation with GCC countries, which have a dubious record of sponsoring Sunni extremism and Islamist ideology in the Middle East and around the world might look quixotic. But the steady flow of anti-India terrorists being apprehended and handed over to Indian security agencies by these nations suggests that India is benefiting from courting them on security matters.

The Modi Doctrine has artfully shelved the 'either-or' dilemma of India partnering with Israel and Arab countries. It has managed to de-hyphenate the two, while maximising gains from each, a feat enabled by the fact that Sunni Arab states and Israel have controversially, but surely aligned closer with each other owing to common animosity towards Shia Iran. In 2015, it came to light that India had become one of five international venues for secret back-channel talks between Saudi and Israeli officials to 'discuss the threat posed by Iran.'[89] The Modi Doctrine

---

[88] Bagchi, Indrani. 2016. 'India is Our Strategic Partner, Pak Historic Ally: Saudi Mantri', *The Times of India*, March 10th

[89] PTI. 2015. 'Israel, Saudi Arabia Hold Secret Meetings over Iran's Nuclear Programme', *The Economic Times*, June 5th

has made the best of both worlds—Jewish and Arab—not only due to this strategic realignment within the Middle East, but also because of growing competition between the USA and its GCC allies for oil and gas markets. With the Americans having lifted their long ban on energy exports, they are business rivals of their own Sunni Arab allies for market share. The Indian strategist, Sanjaya Baru, has written of a 'structural change in the global energy market with West Asian oil and gas increasingly heading to South and East Asian markets rather than to the Trans-Atlantic markets.'[90] This transformation has lent meaning and substance to the GCC's own 'Look East' policy, which dovetails perfectly with Modi's 'Look West', and leaves India in an advantageous position.

Does the Modi Doctrine's dual focus on bonding with Israel and Sunni Arab countries endanger India's third leg in the Middle East, i.e., its strategic closeness to Shia Iran which is the prime adversary of both Israel and the GCC nations? On the contrary, Modi has not left any stone unturned to upgrading New Delhi's links with Tehran, especially in light of the USA-Iran entente and final settlement of the row over the latter's nuclear programme. Modi's NSA, Doval, has praised Iran's 'brilliant role in fighting terrorism and its positive role in restoration of stability and security in West Asia and called for expansion of all-out cooperation between the two countries.'[91] Like a contemporary replay of Kautilya's *Mandala* theory, the Modi Doctrine has attempted to leverage the 'enemy of my enemy', i.e., Shia Iran which faces Sunni jihadist threats from Pakistan. In August 2015, Doval is reported to have 'discussed the possibility of a more long-term base for the Indian navy' in Iran[92] as a means to pressure Pakistan on its Western flank. In early 2016, the Modi government approved a $150 million investment to develop the Iranian port of Chabahar as a connectivity imperative for India's sea-land access to Afghanistan and Central Asia. Indian strategic coordination with Iran has irked Pakistan and weakened the latter's bargaining power over the war in Afghanistan. Comments by

---

[90] Baru, Sanjaya. 2015. 'The Sprouting of the 'Look West' Policy', *The Hindu*, August 19th

[91] IANS. 2015. 'Iran, India are Key Partners for Peace', *Business Standard*, February 10th

[92] Kasturi. 2015. 'Secret Trips' Op cit.

the Iranian Ambassador to India in 2015 that 'there is immense scope of strategic cooperation between Iran and India' and that the two countries 'have cooperated with each other in Afghanistan and are still doing so'[93] leaves little to doubt that the Modi Doctrine expects to make India a more consequential power in the Middle East by riding on Iranian coattails.

Will the animosities among Israel, Arab states and Iran ever intrude on Modi's proactive multi-partisan diplomacy in the Middle East, and force India to make uncomfortable choices? As long as New Delhi is not a defining power in that region with vast military or economic stakes, this risk is not going to materialise because each of these three sides has independent mutually beneficial bilateral goings-on with India. Kadira Pethiyagoda of the Brookings Institution argues that geopolitical winds in the Middle East are shifting due to American decline and that this is creating room for newcomers like India to grow in strategic heft, especially in the northwestern corner of the Indian Ocean that abuts the Persian Gulf. His counsel that New Delhi must *ipso facto* 'adopt a long-term vision, targeting states and actors most important for India's strategic ascendance and increasing engagement commensurately'[94] is a sound one on which the Modi Doctrine is already pegging away.

Despite India's abject dependence on the Middle East for oil and remittances from its diaspora, it has not yet acquired corresponding political leverage for helping to resolve ongoing armed conflicts and turbulence in that region. The Modi Doctrine should aim to ultimately admit India into the core security management formations like the 'Middle East Quartet', and other institutions that behoove of true great powers. If there is a scenario which Modi detests, it is when India is excluded and out of the picture in any region that is vital to its economic growth and security. In the years to come, the goal of his 'Look West' agenda should be to not just keep juggling the contradictory balls of Israel, Arab states and Iran, difficult as it is, but also to insert India into

---

[93] Johny, Stanly. 2015. "Modi's Iran Visit will be a Milestone in Bilateral Relations', *The Hindu Business Line*, April 3rd

[94] Pethiyagoda, Kadira. 2015. 'Modi Looks West: India and the Middle East', *The Brookings Institution*, June 16th. URL: http://www.brookings.edu/blogs/order-from-chaos/posts/2015/06/16-modi-looks-to-middle-east-pethiyagoda Last accessed on March 9th, 2016

the problem-solving camp for that region. If New Delhi can be a net security provider in the IOR, then it has the inherent worth to also be one in the Middle East. Modi's bold foreign policy does not accept the bureaucratic language of limitations and constraints. It functions on the premise of opportunities and capabilities. The Middle East is a prime test case of his dream to make India an omniscient power.

'Bright Spots' of South–South Cooperation

For the Modi Doctrine to attain the holy grail of India as a leading power in world affairs, Africa and Latin America inexorably feature as essential spaces without which the grand strategy will flounder. These are rising continents with youthful populations carrying soaring aspirations and boundless natural wealth, headed to take their rightful places in the international system after centuries of colonial suppression. Together, they constitute a whopping eighty-seven member countries of the UN. As I have mentioned in Chapter 3 of this book, Modi has correctly spotted Africa and Latin America as growth areas and 'bright spots' for diversifying India's trade and investment avenues. He has also realised that the time has come for India to deal with each of these continents as a single large opportunity domain rather than as a set of disjointed countries with whom India has one-on-one equations.

The Modi Doctrine's big picture logic, which has enlarged the focus of Indian foreign policy, is most visible in Africa. In October 2015, New Delhi looked like the capital of the Global South as heads of government of forty-three countries converged for the third India-Africa Forum Summit (IAFS). It was a landmark event in the history of relations among emerging powers. India had never seen such a massive gathering of leaders from a rising continent on its soil, confirming an unprecedented elevated stature for India as a leading developing nation under Modi. Unlike the duration of the Manmohan Singh era, when New Delhi used to selectively invite a little over one dozen African leaders for these summits under the so-called 'Banjul Formula', Modi wanted a king-size summit to demonstrate to the world India's pan-African reach and scope. He had tweeted at that time with national pride that, 'level of engagement for @indiafrica2015 has been tremendously scaled up.' Only China, the number one external power in Africa over the last two decades, has been able to host summits attended by more African presidents. Modi is making the world sit up and take note that India has arrived on the big stage when he says, 'we will help connect Africa from Cairo to Cape Town, from Marakesh to Mombassa.'[95]

IAFS-III sported an inspiring logo showing the African lion and the Indian lion merging along with the two landmasses that were once conjoined as Gondwanaland, but now separated through geological drift. The imagery of Africa and India teaming up with courage and boldness to be 'on the prowl'[96], as the Modi government advertised, signifies a confidence and optimism that formerly downtrodden, colonised and racially discriminated peoples have an unstoppable momentum today. In characteristic systemic fashion, Modi has also made a departure from previous Indian leaders by initiating dialogue on 'core global issues such as climate change, information technology, education, healthcare, skill development, economy, terrorism etc. that affect both India and Africa.'[97] Treating Africa as a bottomless mine of natural wealth has been the Western and the Chinese outlook. The Indian one, which Modi is finessing, is based on respecting Africa as a dialogue partner for solving international problems. Rajrishi Singhal of the Indian think tank, Gateway House, has correctly argued that there is a 'new policy stance—Modi's push to forge a united front with African nations for a common, but differentiated, negotiating framework in multilateral institutions.'[98] Instead of looking down upon and exploiting least developed countries (LDCs), which has been the tragic behaviour of great powers in history, the Modi Doctrine is proposing to forge a union based on solidarity of the past but also new economic synergies.

According to Infinite Potentials Consulting, Africa's consumer market will reach $1.4 trillion by 2020, surpassing Indian and Chinese

---

[95] NM. 2015. 'PM Modi at Inaugural Session of India-Africa Forum Summit 2015', *Narendra Modi*, October 29th

[96] IANS. 2015. 'Proud, Bold and on the Prowl - The India-Africa Forum Summit Lion', *Business Standard*, August 13th

[97] Gupta, Arushi. 2015. 'India-Africa Forum Summit: A New Twist to Modi's Foreign Policy', *The Financial Express*, October 19th

[98] Singhal, Rajrishi. 2015. 'Modi Resets India's Africa Strategy', *The Hindu Business Line*, November 17th

market sizes.[99] The rising middle classes and young people of the continent are, therefore, prized customers for Indian exports, services and investments. As the Ghanian High Commissioner to India put it, Africa is 'the new frontier', and Modi's India should 'source raw materials from Africa, Make in India and sell in Africa.'[100] On the other side of the ledger, many African leaders have asked Modi to help them to 'Make in Africa' as well. Modi's promise at IAFS-III that India would 'help develop your infrastructure, power and irrigation; help add value to your resources in Africa; and, set up industrial and information technology parks'[101] has made waves on the continent and raised expectations. This is especially felt on the east coast of Africa, where the enthusiasm for Modi's 'blue economy' idea is paramount. I spoke to Mozambican diplomats in early 2016, and found them in a state of excitement about Modi's upcoming visits to Africa. They were chafing under Chinese 'takeover' and eager to have the Indian state and private sectors step up gears and 'show intent and action' in Africa.

What the Modi Doctrine needs to do in the coming years in Africa is to not only strengthen the African Union (AU)-level institutions, but also tighten partnerships based on sub-regional peculiarities with African groupings like the East African Community (EAC), the Southern African Development Community (SADC) and the Economic Community of West African States (ECOWAS). The launch of an ambitious African Standby Force (ASF) in 2015 to reduce the continent's dependence and vulnerability to Europe and North America in times of wars and crises is a path-breaking initiative to which India must contribute. India has more experience in peacekeeping than the South African military, which is driving the ASF. Combining India's global acumen and South Africa's regional leverage can relieve Africa from nefarious external interventions that have often destabilised the continent. Given India's

---

[99] IPC. 2014. 'Africa's Consumer Market will Reach $1.4 trillion by 2020, Surpassing India and China', *Techmoran*, June 12th. URL: http://techmoran.com/africas-consumer-market-will-reach-1-4-trillion-by-2020-surpassing-india-and-china/ Last accessed on March 10th, 2016

[100] Dutta, Indrani. 2015. 'Africa sees Investment Opportunities in Modi's Make-in-India Initiative', *The Hindu*, July 30th

[101] TNN. 2015. 'India-Africa Summit: Read Full Text of PM Narendra Modi's Speech', *The Times of India*, October 29th

own desire to be a net security provider from one end of the IOR to the other, it makes sense for Modi to also contribute to the Africa Integrated Maritime Strategy (AIMS), which aims to establish 'regional centres of excellence in training in maritime safety and security' but has 'yet to secure adequate funds to achieve its ambitious goals.'[102] Modi's defence diplomacy has a huge entrée window in Africa.

Politically, India stands tall as a role model for Africa where dictatorships are already on the retreat and democracy is slowly turning into a norm. The usual Indian diplomatic reticence and diffidence about offering conflict resolution and democratisation assistance to Africa has to be replaced by a more proactive posture that does not wait to be asked by Africans, but prods Africans as to whether they want our advice and expertise on how to forge multiparty competitive polities, multi-ethnic coexistence and peaceful transfer of power after elections and during transitions. I often hear laments among African social activists that India is an evolved democracy and a stable polity that is reluctant to transfer these achievements to the continent. Under Modi, India is not bashful about its strengths and should, therefore, be more forthcoming with practical suggestions and plans for political development on the continent.

Without abandoning India's trademark humility and non-hegemonic attitude, Modi can catalyse Africa's renaissance. He is a master at importing good ideas from the Global North for India's domestic modernisation and economic development, but there is also a converse responsibility on India to engage in policy transfer diplomacy with Africa in spheres where India has progressed. This cannot be limited to vocational training, crafts and skills. India must assist socially and politically in Africa, not just through technical means like election assistance and observation, but also through civic engagement on the continent. The Modi Doctrine must double down on issue areas like these, where India is unbeatable while China is hollow. The current Indian prime minister's official profile claims that 'Narendra Modi's foreign policy initiatives have realised the true potential and role of the

[102] Sidiropoulos, Elizabeth & Chris Alden. 2015. 'Bringing Geo-Economics Back in: The India-Africa Forum Summit, Modi's New Foreign Policy Agenda and the Implications for Africa', *South African Institute of International Affairs*, p.22

world's largest democracy, India on the world stage.'[103] In Africa, this claim should translate into India donning new avatars over and above the routine livelihoods-based 'development cooperation' that it has carried out for decades.

African elites have always seen value in India in terms of its skilled service exports. Jakaya Kikwete, the President of Tanzania had remarked in 2011 that, 'the Chinese might build hospital buildings, but we need Indian doctors and nurses to serve there.'[104] The Modi Doctrine can capitalise on the human resource aspect by implementing the current Indian prime minister's vision of 'teacher export of high calibre' from India to developing countries to spread India's soft power.[105] To increase India's attraction in the minds of ordinary Africans, the Modi government could deploy young qualified Indian teachers to work in schools and colleges in selected countries to impart learning in subjects like English, mathematics, varied sciences, social studies, computers, healthcare, Indian civilisation and ethos, the Indian value system and its contributions to the world, Gandhian philosophy, *Vasudhaiva Kutumbakam*, pluralism, peace and conflict resolution and other locally relevant subjects, which are of high priority for governments of partner countries in Africa. A volunteer force of Indians akin to the American Peace Corps can represent India in Africa as the country's cultural ambassadors and brand-builders who can have a lasting impact on African society and make India stand above China in touching ordinary lives on the continent.

As I have demonstrated throughout this book, the Modi Doctrine has stretched India's zone of attention to encompass regions of the world where it had in the past a lacklustre presence. From a bit player in Latin America, India has now become a force to reckon with due to Modi's vision of a 360-degree foreign policy. Just two months after assuming the prime ministership, Modi was in Brazil and met twelve Latin American heads of state and pledged to 'work closely with South America than ever before at the bilateral level, as a BRICS member,

---

[103] PMO. 2016. 'Know the PM', Prime Minister's Office, March. URL: http://pmindia.gov.in/en/pmsprofile/ Last accessed on March 11th, 2016

[104] Jacob, Jayanth. 2015. 'In New Delhi's View, it's This Time for Africa', *Hindustan Times*, October 14th

[105] IANS. 2014. 'Make India a Hub for Exporting Teachers: Modi', *Business Standard*, September 5th

in the G-77, as well as other international forums.'[106] Modi knows the potential of Latin America better than anyone in India because his home state of Gujarat accounted for sixty percent of India's total trade of $46 billion with Latin America as of 2014. Shortly after he took over as India's prime minister, he had launched the MEA's first ever Spanish language web portal to make a point that India is not deterred by linguistic or geographical distance from the Western hemisphere.

Ronak Desai of Harvard University has argued that Modi can also engender a strategic dimension to India's approach to Latin America, which had been confined largely to economics owing to the geographical distance between the two. 'Many Latin Americans resent the deluge of Chinese imports flooding their markets and harming local businesses, while many Latin American governments are wary of becoming too dependent on Beijing's largesse. By contrast, India's modest trade and investment are welcomed with virtually no opposition. This confers New Delhi with an unexpected, long-term competitive advantage over China.'[107] Indeed, China's 'pivot to the Americas' is facing headwinds in the region. The Modi Doctrine must take advantage of India's smaller size and softer image to make inroads into the Latin American market, which is like Africa, on the expansion mode with a collective GDP of over $12 trillion and a consumer base of six-hundred million people. Modi's Commerce Minister Nirmala Sitharaman has issued a 'clarion call' to Latin American and Indian businesses 'to double the volume of two-way trade from the present US$ 42 billion in the next five years.'[108] The Modi government's facilitation of Indian businesses in Latin America is commendable, but as I have explained in Chapter 3, India needs to sign and activate new free trade agreements to convert its Latin dreams into reality. Modi's belief that 'possibilities of cooperation are limited not by distance but only by our imagination and efforts', and his emphasis on using internet and satellite-based means to bring India into the Western

---

106 Singh, Mahim. 2014. 'Modi for Closer Ties with Latin America', *The Hindu*, July 18th

107 Desai, Ronak. 2015. 'A New Era for India-Latin America Relations', *Forbes*, June 25th

108 CM. 2014. 'Potential to Double India-Latin America & Caribbean Trade Volume from US$ 42 Billion in Next Five Years: Nirmala Sitharaman', *Business Standard*, October 17th

hemisphere in fields like tele-medicine, tele-education, e-Governance and weather forecasting[109], are meant to harness India's comparative advantages. The digital approach is certain to distinguish India from the Chinese natural resource-predicated strategy in Latin America.

Deepak Bhojwani, a former Indian diplomat and Latin American hand, has observed that India had for ages failed to match China in coordinating trade, aid and investment strategies in that region, and that Indian political leaders had not invested enough in advancing India's footprint there.[110] The former Chilean ambassador to India, Jorge Heine, described how anaemic the diplomacy prior to the Modi Doctrine was in this context,

'In his 10 years in office, Prime Minister Manmohan Singh visited Latin America only a couple of times. Indian foreign ministers have also been sparing in their attention to the region. This has not helped the fluid exchange of perspectives and points of view among national leaders required to sign trade and investment agreements, and otherwise propel bilateral and inter-regional flows.'[111]

Indian lethargy stood in sharp contrast to China, which deliberately emphasised summit diplomacy 'to cultivate local support for expanding economic relations with the Latin American nations.'[112] The *Samvaad* pillar of the BJP's foreign policy and Modi's retail diplomacy skills are direly needed for India to finally make a mark in Latin America.

The hunger and the passion to make India a great power was missing before the Modi Doctrine's advent, and India has lost precious time as a result in Latin America. Today, there is a noticeable vacuum in defence diplomacy owing to the physical distance between India and Latin America. A leading power must forge strategic bonds in every

---

[109] IANS. 2014. 'Modi Seeks Stronger Economic Ties with Latin America', *Business Standard*, July 17th

[110] Bhojwani, Deepak. 2015. *Latin America, The Caribbean and India-Promise and Challenge*, New Delhi: Indian Council of World Affairs

[111] Heine, Jorge. 2014. 'Time for a New Impetus', *Gateway House*, June 19th. URL: http://www.gatewayhouse.in/la-nueva-india-time-for-a-new-impetus/ Last accessed on March 10th, 2016

[112] Chung-Chian, Teng. 2007. 'Hegemony or Partnership: China's Strategy and Diplomacy Toward Latin America', in Eisenman, Joshua et al (Eds.) *China and the Developing World: Beijing's Strategy for the Twenty-First Century*, London: M.E.Sharpe, p.93

corner of the globe. The International Fleet Review hosted by the Modi government in February 2016 witnessed the welcome participation for the first time of navies from Colombia, Peru, Chile and Brazil along India's east coast. The Indian navy's involvement in the USA-organised Rim of the Pacific (RIMPAC) exercises also generates contact with Latin American counterparts. Yet, at the level of sharing common threats and countering them on land and sea, India and Latin America have a hiatus to fill. The Modi Doctrine has to be alert to the intensifying naval rivalry between the USA and China in the Western hemisphere and initiate its own naval missions in support of the will of Latin American nations, which wish to avoid being dragged into yet another Cold War. There is room for India in this far-flung part of the planet if it cottons on to the rich harvest that lies in store.

North by Northwest

Apart from the USA, the Modi Doctrine has devoted due attention to a number of European nations and Canada as part of a multipurpose diplomacy to further India's economic interests. It has fashioned a 'Link West' agenda to complement the 'Act East' policy and presented India as a balanced player that is strategically attentive in all geographic directions. Industrialised Western middle powers have capacities to assist India's rising economic graph. Modi has tugged at the hearts and minds of corporate titans sitting over investible capital in France, Germany, the United Kingdom and Canada because he is perceived to be walking the talk on overhauling the Indian economy. His 'Make in India' campaign has garnered European and Canadian fascination, thanks to the accelerating pace of Indian GDP growth and the deep economic crisis many of these rich countries have been facing since 2008.

High-profile CEO forums with visiting Indian prime ministers are not Modi's inventions. They were held even by his predecessors during foreign visits. But now, these interactive sessions are laced with greater hope and belief among foreign investors in the Global North because Modi is hitting the right notes and running India like a CEO. As he struts the stage in Western Europe and North America, the proverbial wind is at his back, with the Indian economy entering a sweet spot after six years of listlessness from 2008 to 2014. Modi's message that India is fit for investment in infrastructure, defence and energy is not hot air, but is backed by the informed opinion of rating agencies and international financial institutions. With India overtaking China in GDP growth from 2015 onward, no one in Europe or Canada has been yawning when Modi turns up the charm offensive. Modi speaks to Western audiences from an innate sense of momentum and confidence that Western countries have lost since the global economic crisis, and which they could regain by partaking in the India growth story. India as the fastest growing major economy in the world is the substance behind the Modi Doctrine's commercial pizzazz. Although private investors are not bound by state guidance in Western capitalist systems, Modi is pushing his foreign governmental counterparts to advise, coax and guarantee their respective corporations as they eye a slice of India's second innings of rapid GDP growth in the twenty-first century. It is a lesson in economic diplomacy and a sharp improvement over previous Indian governments that were pussyfooted about wholeheartedly seconding Indian business and economic interests abroad.

Readers would recall from Chapter 1 of this book that Modi is in equal measure a teacher and a learner from other countries. There is much in the realm of cutting-edge ideas that he seeks to import from innovative leaders like Germany. His visit to the Siemens Technical Academy in Berlin in April 2015 was meant to get insights into the famed German vocational training structure, which is an inspiration for India's ambitious skill development plans. The German analyst Marc Saxer believes that Modi may be looking to Germany's social democratic capitalism as 'an alternative development model to American market radicalism and east Asian developmental authoritarianism.'[113] Meric Gertler, a Canadian urban planning expert, has termed Modi's '100 smart cities' blueprint for Indian urban planning 'breathtaking and inspiring', and has offered know-how to realise this dream.[114] The technology transfer India seeks

---

113 DW. 2015. 'Business as Usual? India's Modi in Europe and Canada', *Deutsche Welle*, April 7th. URL: http://www.dw.com/en/business-as-usual-indias-modi-in-europe-and-canada/a-18364495 Last accessed on March 10th, 2016

114 Jain, Ajit. 2015. 'Modi's 100 Smart Cities Idea is Breath-Taking, Inspiring', *The Indian Diaspora*, March 7th. URL: http://theindiandiaspora.com/news-details/conversations/primary_news/%E2%80%98modis-100-smart-cities-idea-is-breath-taking-inspiring%E2%80%99.htm Last accessed on March 10th, 2016

in the West is, thus, not limited to defence manufacturing. When a developing country is on the cusp of a historic economic modernisation, there are many intangible ideas and best practices in governance and public policy that it would be wise to borrow from successful exponents overseas. Like Deng Xiaoping's maxim that it does not matter whether the cat is black or white as long as it caught mice, the Modi Doctrine has relentlessly sought to import proven best practices from both East and West for India's domestic overhaul.

The rise of ISIS terrorism in Europe and the long shadow of jihadist attacks on India have also lent a new strategic content to the Modi Doctrine's engagements with the Western world. Modi's decision to invite French President Francois Hollande to be the chief guest of India's Republic Day parade in 2016 was made 'on the day when Paris was hit by terror attacks' by ISIS gunmen in November 2015.[115] The counter-terrorism cooperation that Modi has cemented with European countries is significant in the backdrop of disappointment that the 'EU-India Strategic Partnership has lost momentum' and in light of recommendations that the two sides could work together to reify the stalled Convention on International Terrorism at the UN, as well as improve defence coordination where European navies have a presence in the IOR to check piracy and seaborne terror.[116] Getting German Chancellor Angela Merkel and her country's business community to endorse 'Make in India' by means of fast-track clearances and single windows for FDI is no mean achievement, but the Modi Doctrine has to also plug into strategic cooperation to broaden its 'Link West' policies.

Although the USA is the bull's eye of Modi's diplomacy in North America, Canada has not been bypassed. In April 2015, Modi overcame a four-decades-long ban on Canadian export of uranium to India, and signed a $280 million civilian atomic energy deal to supply India's fuel-starved nuclear power reactors. It was nothing short of a coup for India, which had been blacklisted by Canada since it first tested an atomic

---

[115] ANI. 2016. 'Decided to Invite President Hollande the Day Paris was Attacked, says Modi', *Deccan Chronicle*, January 24th

[116] Sachdeva, Gulshan. 2015. 'Evaluation of the EU-India Strategic Partnership and the Potential for its Revitalisation', *European Union Directorate-General for External Policies*, June, p.1

bomb in 1974. I have shown at various junctures in this book that Modi is a clearer of obstacles like no other in the recent history of Indian foreign policy. The breakthrough with Canada on uranium occurred as a byproduct of Modi's earlier energy diplomacy with Obama that mitigated concerns about India's nuclear liability laws. It was enabled by Modi's trademark personal diplomacy with the then Canadian conservative Prime Minister Stephen Harper. The Canadian scholar John Stackhouse argued at that time that 'Mr. Modi and Mr. Harper may be the most closely aligned leaders of their two countries since the elder Gandhi and Trudeau.'[117] But true to form, Modi has also made overtures to the liberal successor of Harper, Prime Minister Justin Trudeau. Yet, the challenge posed by the TPP trade deal, which I have explained in Chapter 3 of this book, and the long-stymied Canada-India Comprehensive Economic Partnership Agreement (CEPA) mean that the task for the Modi Doctrine is cut out for optimising the presently underachieving trade volumes with Canada.

In conclusion, the kaleidoscopic engagement that Modi has effected with Western nations has already yielded numerous commercial and strategic benefits to India. Like the USA, many of these advanced industrialised democracies have differences with India on issues relating to religious freedom, the alleged persecution of minorities, intellectual property rights protection, returns on investment, and treatment of foreign-funded NGOs. Still, to call Modi the darling of Western establishments would not be inaccurate because he has wilfully engineered India's engagement with them with a panoramic sweep. He is the West's best friend by virtue of presenting India as a democratic alternative to China and a partner for checking the jihadist menace, and by giving Western corporate houses hope that they could revive from their shambolic economic conditions by clutching onto the Indian economic miracle.

The perceptive analysis of the Chinese state-owned media best summarises what the Modi Doctrine has done to attract the Western world and what remains to be achieved. According to Zhao Gancheng, Director of South Asia Studies at the Shanghai Institute for International Studies,

---

117 Stackhouse, John. 2015. 'Modi in Canada: More than a Diplomatic Leap Forward', *The Globe and Mail*, April 10th

'The roaring labour costs and stricter environment regulations in China have pushed enthusiastic (Western) investors to look away and eye India as a more desirable destination, particularly those from small- and medium-sized businesses. However, although there have been many meetings and visits between India and the EU such as regular business summits over the past decade, their talks have hardly translated into actual outcomes and no considerable European investment has been made in India. One reason is India's slow moving on infrastructure improvement. A dramatic improvement in India's relationship with Europe and remarkable progress in their economic cooperation is unlikely to happen. There won't be big strides forward in India and changes have to take place slowly and gradually.'[118]

The Modi Doctrine is on the job and it would be itching to prove the Chinese jealousy right and the scepticism wrong.

[118] Xiaobo, Sun. 2015. 'Modi's Warm Reception in Europe Marks Slow Steps Toward India's Emergence', *Global Times*, April 8th

Epilogue

> *Indians should take pride and inspiration from their great heritage. If they are excessively self-critical, if they damn each and every aspect of our own country, then why would the world look up to us?*[1]

Toward the Indian Century

I have demonstrated in this book that the Modi Doctrine is more than a grand strategy for India to conduct its foreign relations. It is also a manifesto for transforming Indian national identity and outlook towards the world. Modi's spiels that the twenty-first century would be an Indian century and his reiterations that, 'no one can hold India back now because it has the power of a youthful population',[2] are meant to brace Indians for a marathon journey to great power status. The positive vibes and delirious optimism in Modi's overseas outreach activities, which have been honed since his days as an RSS *prachaarak*, are necessary to lift a cloud of pessimistic attitudes that have limited India's foreign policymaking for decades.

Cynicism that the Indian century is easier declared than achieved, and that there are far too many structural hurdles and deficiencies

---

1 NM. 2016. 'PM Modi at the Inauguration of 2016 World Culture Festival by Art of Living in New Delhi', *Narendra Modi*, March 11th. URL: http://www.narendramodi.in/pm-modi-at-the-inauguration-of-2016-world-culture-festival-by-art-of-living-in-new-delhi-428085 Last accessed on March 12th, 2016

2 DC. 2015. 'No One Can Hold India Back Now, says Narendra Modi at Wembley', *Deccan Chronicle*, November 14th

for India to ever become the defining power in the world, are mental barriers that Indian society still needs to cross. Modi's chutzpah and confidence in India's destiny are departures from diffident political leadership of the past and a riposte to the self-flagellation and excessive problematisation in sections of the Indian intelligentsia. They are also retorts to myopia that India must sequentially first fix its cornucopia of domestic problems before dreaming of becoming a leading power in the international system. Economic historian Alexander Gerschenkron has argued that ideology separates backward nations from advanced ones. A less developed country could progress only if 'mountains of routine and prejudice'[3] were scaled by entrepreneurial instinct and hope. His prescription to overcome 'negative social attitudes' regarding innovation, and change through 'faith that the golden age lies not behind but ahead'[4] is being enacted by the Modi Doctrine.

By raising the bar of expectations to the level of an Indian century, Modi is trying to engineer a Gerschenkron-style mindset transformation. Only if Indians believe, can they realise their dreams. And this self-belief can only come through motivational leadership from the top. Modi exemplifies the theory that determined leadership and vision hold the keys to altering a nation's fate in world affairs. In foreign policy, military modernisation and energy security, his distinct personal imprint and intervention are writ large. The media entrepreneur Mike Bloomberg's tweet that, 'Modi's leadership is changing India and the world'[5] is an acknowledgement of this effect, and one out of myriad verdicts that India is headed upwards under the Modi Doctrine.

American scholar Charles Kegley has analysed the impact of individual leaders on transforming their countries' foreign policy as,

'Leaders react differently to the positions they occupy. Most people submissively act in accordance with the customary rules that define the positions they hold, behaving as their predecessors tended to behave

---

3 Gerschenkron, Alexander. 1962. *Economic Backwardness in Historical Perspective: A Book of Essays*, New York: Praeger, p.24

4 Ibid

5 NDTV. 2015. 'PM Modi's Leadership is Changing India, says Mike Bloomberg', NDTV, September 25th. URL: http://www.ndtv.com/who-said-what/pm-modis-leadership-is-changing-india-says-mike-bloomberg-1222803 Last accessed on March 12th, 2016

when they held the same position. Others, however, are by personality or preference more bold and ambitious, and they seek to decisively escape the confines of their narrow role by redefining how it will be performed.'[6]

Modi falls in the latter category of leaders who has, by dint of his own iron will, pushed the envelope and shifted the goalposts of Indian foreign policy to be substantively and geographically proactive and transformative.

Yet, India's image makeover and foreign policy reincarnation have to be institutionalised to last throughout the long twenty-first century. A new cadre of change agents has to be nurtured at different levels of Indian society to take forward Modi's notion that Indians have it in them to make it big in the world. India's demographic bulge needs not only a sustained dose of practical skills for employability and productivity, but also training to drive the global agenda. Modi's 'Team India' in the foreign policy sphere has to, therefore, expand and include more think tanks, educational institutions and youth organisations in actively debating, interpreting and formulating strategies on multiple issue areas and regions of the world. Without gainsaying the fact that the Indian Prime Minister has phenomenal political insight and instinct to innovate on his own in foreign policy, he will be doing a national service by broadening the policymaking space beyond the career diplomatic corps and his own brains trust in the BJP and the MEA.

What Gerschenkron termed as the 'spirit' or 'intellectual climate' to prosper and lead in the world has to be sustained if the Modi Doctrine is to play a long innings. In this book, I have shown how Modi has broken free of the traditional trappings of diplomacy by taking it out of the hands of bureaucrats, out of the chokehold of a New Delhi-centric mindset, and out of the straitjacket of a continental, land-based national security gaze. Yet, much remains to be done. The degree of acceptance of outside experts on foreign economic policy, commercial diplomacy and public diplomacy within the career bureaucracy remains undesirably low in spite of Modi's openness to fresh ideas and willingness to experiment. How far the

6 Kegley, Charles. 2009. *World Politics: Trend and Transformation*, Belmont: Cengage Learning, p.70

Modi Doctrine can deliver in the long-run depends not just on Modi's political fortunes in elections at home in the years to come, but also on his ability to reform and refurbish the foreign policy hardware and software.

As India's first CEO Prime Minister, Modi often issues business executive-style five or ten-point formulas for countering terrorism, reviving economic growth, pursuing good governance etc. Owing to the esoteric nature of foreign affairs and the resounding success of his external policies, there has been no corresponding bullet point list for foreign policy. Let me hazard a five-point plan to conclude this book.

1. Keep doing what the Modi Doctrine has already accomplished, i.e. avoid a let up in the intensity of what the BJP calls *Samvaad* or regional and global engagement. Naysayers who taunt Modi for overdoing foreign policy and neglecting domestic issues must be ignored because they are the negative energies that have no ken for the intrinsic linkage of global and local, and they had crippled India's march to great power status in the past.
2. Encourage new mediums, especially digital, through which India's public diplomacy can penetrate the hearts and minds of audiences worldwide, especially in developing countries, so that they will be receptive to India's activities and initiatives in their respective regions. Find pathways like an Indian world news TV channel or an online electronic army to present the face of India on a planetary scale and convey the mind of India on international current affairs and various global problems. Foreign policy doctrines imply clarity, not a muddleheaded hodgepodge that leaves the world perplexed as to what India does and wants.
3. Nurture non-bureaucratic talent in the field of foreign relations and implement breakthrough ideas that come from outside the stultifying corridors of power. The Modi Doctrine must evolve as a genuine public-private partnership (PPP) that is conducted like an open system of feedback, course correction and calibration. Modi has already democratised foreign policy consciousness and freed it from elite monopoly. He now needs to train future world leaders from among young Indians who can rise to the pinnacle in regional and multilateral intergovernmental and non-governmental institutions.

4. Prioritise speedy implementation of promises to the world, especially in infrastructure, connectivity and economic corridors. India's reputation as a slowcoach that has time and cost overruns in almost all transnational connectivity projects has been embarrassing and damaging to its image vis-à-vis agile China. Modi is aware of these lacunae, and has once acknowledged before African heads of state that 'there are commitments we have not fulfilled as quickly as we should have.'[7] The Modi Doctrine has already put India on course for what it calls 'fast-track diplomacy', but the world wants more of it and in larger scale. The record pace at which the Modi government is constructing domestic highways and modernising railways and ports needs to have a foreign counterpart in concretising and delivering on Project *Mausam*, the Cotton Route and other international connectivity linkages to position India as a power centre.
5. Do not permit Indian domestic politics from destroying the hard work and accumulated gains of the Modi Doctrine since 2014. The difference between a successful politician and a world statesman lies in a leader's ability to define national interests in consonance with global interests rather than in contradiction with them. I have shown in this book that the Modi Doctrine has been outstanding in unleashing the energies of India's cooperative federalism for commercial diplomacy and resolving intractable territorial disputes with neighbouring countries. India needs much more of that and much less of the dissuading cacophony from opposition politicians who want Modi to cut down on foreign policy as a priority or succumb to their vested interests, demands and allegations which are inimical to national interests.

In his iconic September 2014 speech to the Indian diaspora at the Madison Square Garden, New York, Modi had referred to condescending taunts from his political opponents about his humble origins as a tea-seller and responded, 'I am a small person and that is why I do big work for the

[7] TNN. 2015. 'India-Africa Summit: Full Text of PM Narendra Modi's Speech', *The Times of India*, October 29th

small people of India.'[8] I have illustrated through this book that he is also doing big work for the small countries of the world and rendering India an equal of the big hitters in the international system. The Modi Doctrine has years left to go and boundless reserves of diplomatic energy still to expend. By parking India on the international highway to greatness, what Modi is achieving in foreign affairs is monumental. If he gets a full tenure of one decade in power, I have little doubt that India would by then have entered the league of great powers. The 'Mother India' that he worships could not have asked for a worthier child and steward.

[8] NM. 2014. 'PM Modi's Speech at Madison Square Garden', *Narendra Modi*, September 28th. URL: https://www.youtube.com/watch?v=P34MFTKZjSk Last accessed on March 12th, 2016

Index

H

I

J

K

R

S

T

U

V

W

X

Y

Z